DEUTERONOMY

Text copyright © Philip Johnston 2005

The author asserts the moral right to be
identified as the author of this work

Published by
The Bible Reading Fellowship
First Floor, Elsfield Hall
15–17 Elsfield Way
Oxford OX4 5HG
ISBN 1 84101 318 8

10 9 8 7 6 5 4 3 2 1 0

Acknowledgments
Unless otherwise stated, scripture quotations are taken from The New
Revised Standard Version of the Bible, Anglicized edition, copyright ©
1989, 1995 by the Division of Christian Education of the National
Council of the Churches of Christ in the United States of America, and
are used by permission. All rights reserved.

Scripture quotations taken from the *Holy Bible, New International
Version*, copyright © 1973, 1978, 1984 by International Bible Society.
Used by permission of Hodder & Stoughton Limited. All rights
reserved. 'NIV' is a registered trademark of International Bible Society.
UK trademark number 1448790.

Scripture quotations are taken from The Revised Standard Version of
the Bible, Anglicized edition, copyright © 1946, 1952, 1971 by the
Division of Christian Education of the National Council of the
Churches of Christ in the United States of America, and are used by
permission. All rights reserved.

Extracts from the Authorized Version of the Bible (The King James
Bible), the rights in which are vested in the Crown, are reproduced by
permission of the Crown's Patentee, Cambridge University Press.

A catalogue record for this book is available from the British Library

Printed in Singapore by Craft Print International Limited

DEUTERONOMY

THE PEOPLE'S
BIBLE COMMENTARY

PHILIP
JOHNSTON

A BIBLE COMMENTARY FOR EVERY DAY

I dedicate this book to those who encouraged me
over many years to love and serve the Lord,
notably my parents, Alfie and May Johnston,
who devoted their lives to his service.

INTRODUCING THE
PEOPLE'S BIBLE COMMENTARY
SERIES

Congratulations! You are embarking on a voyage of discovery—or rediscovery. You may feel you know the Bible very well; you may never have turned its pages before. You may be looking for a fresh way of approaching daily Bible study; you may be searching for useful insights to share in a study group or from a pulpit.

The People's Bible Commentary (PBC) series is designed for all those who want to study the scriptures in a way that will warm the heart as well as instructing the mind. To help you, the series distils the best of scholarly insights into the straightforward language and devotional emphasis of Bible reading notes. Explanation of background material, and discussion of the original Greek and Hebrew, will always aim to be brief.

- If you have never really studied the Bible before, the series offers a serious yet accessible way in.

- If you help to lead a church study group, or are otherwise involved in regular preaching and teaching, you can find invaluable 'snapshots' of a Bible passage through the PBC approach.

- If you are a church worker or minister, burned out on the Bible, this series could help you recover the wonder of scripture.

Using a People's Bible Commentary

The series is designed for use alongside any version of the Bible. You may have your own favourite translation, but you might like to consider trying a different one in order to gain fresh perspectives on familiar passages.

Many Bible translations come in a range of editions, including study and reference editions that have concordances, various kinds of special index, maps and marginal notes. These can all prove helpful in studying the relevant passage. The Notes section at the back of each PBC volume provides space for you to write personal reflections, points to follow up, questions and comments.

Each People's Bible Commentary can be used on a daily basis, instead of Bible reading notes. Alternatively, it can be read straight through, or used as a resource book for insight into particular verses of the biblical book.

If you have enjoyed using this commentary and would like to progress further in Bible study, you will find details of other volumes in the series listed at the back, together with information about a special offer from BRF.

While it is important to deepen understanding of a given passage, this series always aims to engage both heart and mind in the study of the Bible. The scriptures point to our Lord himself and our task is to use them to build our relationship with him. When we read, let us do so prayerfully, slowly, reverently, expecting him to speak to our hearts.

Contents

PBC DEUTERONOMY: INTRODUCTION

Where should you start in reading and studying the Old Testament? Genesis, at the very beginning? Exodus, at the birth of the nation? Psalms, the much-loved book of prayers? Isaiah, sometimes dubbed 'the fifth Gospel'? All these are great books, and worthy places to start. In Jewish tradition, however, the first book taught to children is none of the above, but Deuteronomy.

Why Deuteronomy, you might ask? For three related reasons:

- Judaism is founded on the Mosaic law, and the bulk of Deuteronomy is a presentation of this law. Chapters 5—11 present general issues, including the Ten Commandments, and chapters 12—26 give the detailed law.

- Deuteronomy is a reasonably complete compendium of Israelite laws. Many of them are also found scattered throughout Exodus, Leviticus and Numbers, but Deuteronomy gathers up most of these laws into a coherent presentation. Sometimes there are interesting variations from the previous books, as we shall see.

- Deuteronomy is as much about encouragement as about rules. The English word 'law' is actually an incomplete translation of the Hebrew word *torah*, which really means 'teaching' or 'instruction'. In other words, it is not just rules and regulations. It is also guidance, help, exhortation, encouragement—in other words, all the positives that any good teacher will use along with rules and warnings. Deuteronomy stresses this repeatedly, with phrases more appropriate to the pulpit than the law court: hear, observe, obey, love, fear. And all this so that 'it may go well with you'.

No wonder Jewish children start their biblical study with Deuteronomy.

But why should Christians study Deuteronomy? This is actually a double question, relating to the Old Testament in general and Deuteronomy in particular. Christians see their main guide as the New Testament, the book of the new covenant established by Jesus Christ and explained by his apostles. But the new covenant builds on the old, and much of the theological basis of the Christian faith comes from the Old Testament. Of course our theology has changed in several crucial areas, and Christians must always read the Old Testament in the light of the New. But reading the Old Testament gives us a firm basis for understanding the Gospels and epistles, and for discerning the elements of continuity and discontinuity between Jewish and Christian faiths.

And if we read the Old Testament, then the reasons given above for focusing on Deuteronomy apply to us too. Besides, Deuteronomy is one of the Old Testament three books most quoted by the New Testament writers, along with Psalms and Isaiah. It is one of the 'big three' for them, so well worth studying by us.

Deuteronomy in outline

A very good way to get to know any book is to work through it yourself and draw up your own outline before consulting any commentaries. Most of us would find that rather daunting for Deuteronomy, but do try it with a shorter biblical book some time! Actually, like a large, rich and mouth-watering cake, Deuteronomy can be divided in many different ways. The most helpful ways initially is by contents:

- Chs. 1—4   Historical review and introduction
- Chs. 5—11   General law
- Chs. 12—26 Detailed law
- Chs. 27—30 Blessings, curses and conclusion
- Chs. 31—34 Epilogue with Moses' last acts and words

This division partly reflects the text itself, which presents the book as three speeches of Moses, beginning in 1:1, 4:44 and 29:1, and a final section 'when Moses had finished speaking' (31:1).

This is very similar to the concentric literary pattern discerned by the American scholar Duane Christensen in his *Word Biblical Commentary*. His outline differs only by placing chapter 4 in the second part:

- Chs. 1—3   A: Outer Frame: A look backward
- Chs. 4—11   B: Inner Frame: The great peroration
- Chs. 12—26 C: Central Core: Covenant stipulations
- Chs. 27—30 B': Inner Frame: The covenant ceremony
- Chs. 31—34 A': Outer Frame: A look forward

This gives something of the literary movement of the book.

Christensen's structure highlights covenant. There is a noteworthy similarity in structure between Deuteronomy and international treaties of the time made by the dominant Hittites. These treaties (or covenants) followed a set pattern, much like international treaties today, and this pattern is more or less followed in Deuteronomy.

- 1:1–5   Preamble
- 1:6—4:49   Historical prologue
- 5—11   General stipulations
- 12—26   Detailed stipulations
- 31:9–13, 24–26   Deposit and regular public reading
- 30:19; 31:26; 32:1 Supernatural witnesses
- 27—28   Blessings and curses

In other words, God's covenant with Israel followed much the same format as the Hittites' covenants (see p. 15) with their neighbours and with Egypt. The fit is not exact, but is close enough to suggest that a widespread model for political relationships was used to convey God's relationship with his people. God always reveals himself through recognizable customs and forms—as he did supremely in human form in Jesus.

Another approach notices that the detailed laws in chapters 12 to 26 follow to some extent the order of the Ten Commandments, as proposed by the German scholar Georg Braulik:

- 12—13   1st, 2nd, 3rd, about God: exclusive worship
- 14:28—16:17   4th, about sabbath: rhythms of life and care for poor
- 16:18—18:22   5th, about parents: human authorities
- 19:1—21:9   6th, about murder (opens and closes the section)
- 22:13–20   7th, about adultery: sexual offences
- 23—26   8th, 9th, 10th: compassion for the vulnerable (in this disparate section)

This is not an exact fit, but it does suggest that the Ten Commandments were foundational to Hebrew law, not only as a summary, but also as a general framework. Their influence was pervasive.

Deuteronomy in the ancient world

We are all children of our time and culture. The wider world has a huge effect on our language and customs, almost as much in church and religious settings as elsewhere. If you're unsure about this, note the illustrations and idioms used in the next sermon you hear, or consider church architecture and liturgy in different parts of the world.

Most of the time we don't recognize this effect because we live in our own culture, but any cross-cultural exposure makes us immediately aware of it.

It was the same in ancient times. However, the problem for most of us is that we know so little of ancient cultures. Hence we tend to assume that anything unusual or odd, or just different from today, was unique to ancient Israel. But the truth is quite different. Much of what we read in the Old Testament reflects an ancient Semitic culture encompassing the whole fertile crescent, from Israel in the west to Mesopotamia in the east. Many Israelite laws have parallels in Mesopotamian law, and many Israelite customs are seen among neighbouring peoples.

These parallels will often be noted as we proceed through Deuteronomy. Where possible, a reference will be given in the most widely available collection of texts in English translation: J.B. Pritchard, *Ancient Near Eastern Texts Relating to the Old Testament* (3rd edn, Princeton University Press, 1969), commonly abbreviated as *ANET* (and with a, b, c or d added to indicate the quarter-page). This large volume can be found in all theological libraries, possibly also in some large public libraries. If you have the opportunity, do look up some of the texts and read them for yourself. It will open up a whole new world.

A few words of introduction to the relevant people groups may help:

- **Egypt:** While Egypt was geographically the closest large country, and was the land that Israel left in the exodus, it was never very influential culturally. Throughout its long history, the Egypt of the Pharaohs was notoriously xenophobic, and didn't seek cultural interaction with its neighbours. On the other hand, Israel was a Semitic people with a Semitic language, so looked more to the north and east.

- **Local peoples:** We know very little about the Canaanites, since there are no surviving texts and little other archaeological data. We know a little more about the immediate neighbours: Philistines to the south-west; Ammonites, Moabites and Edomites to the east; Phoenicians and Arameans (Syrians) to the north.

- **Ugarit:** This was a coastal trading city about 200 miles north of Palestine. Hundreds of tablets reveal its economic, social and religious life, by far the largest set of texts from any people of the ancient Levant (eastern Mediterranean coastlands), and these texts are often used to illustrate beliefs of the wider area.

- **Hittites:** This empire was based in what is now central Turkey, and flourished in the 14th to 12th centuries BC, with many Hittites spreading to neighbouring lands including Palestine. Many Hittite texts testify to their laws and culture.

- **Mesopotamia:** This vast area, now Iraq, was ruled at different times by Assyrians (more northerly) and Babylonians (more southerly) and a few other groups. Many law collections have survived from different periods. Their famous law codes, like that of Hammurabi (Babylonian king, c.1750BC), were studied in Egypt, so a trainee Egyptian official like the young Moses could have been familiar with them.

Deuteronomy in Israelite history

When did the events of Deuteronomy take place? Dating ancient history is a difficult exercise, and becomes increasingly hazardous the further back we go. There is one great help, however. The Assyrians and Babylonians were keen astronomers, and cross-referenced their historical records to eclipses, comets, and so on. Modern science can now give us exact dates for these events, and hence for much of Mesopotamian history in the first millennium BC. Their records occasionally mention battles fought in the Levant, and the names of various kings of Israel and Judah, so we can derive reasonably clear dates for the Hebrew monarchies back to David.

As we work back to the second millennium BC, however, dating is less easy. 1 Kings 6:1 says that Solomon started building the temple 480 years after the exodus, which puts the events of Deuteronomy and Joshua in the 15th century. But many scholars think that archaeology puts these events in the late 13th century. In this case, the figure of 480 years is figurative for twelve generations, which in reality would have spanned much less time. The arguments for and against these two views are too complex to enter here, and in any case don't really affect our study of Deuteronomy.

Century BC	Events or people
15th (1400s)	Events of Deuteronomy, taking 1 Kings 6:1 literally.
13th (1200s)	Events of Deuteronomy, according to many scholars.
10th (900s)	David and Solomon.
	931: Solomon's death and division of kingdom.
9th (800s)	Elijah and Elisha (in Israel).
8th (700s)	Amos and Hosea (in Israel);
	Micah and Isaiah (in Judah).
	722: fall of Samaria, capital of northern Israel.
	729–686: Hezekiah king of Judah.
7th (600s)	640–609: Josiah king of Judah.
6th (500s)	587: fall of Jerusalem, and exile of many Judeans to Babylon.
	539: Persians conquer Babylon, and allow Jews to return.

Deuteronomy in modern scholarship

When was Deuteronomy written? The traditional view is that Moses wrote it himself, including the account of his own death! Some early rabbis attributed the ending to Joshua, and other Jewish scholars gradually noticed occasional verses and phrases that reflected a later historical period. A few early and medieval writers also suggested that Deuteronomy was 'the book of the law' which was found during Josiah's temple repairs and prompted his reform (2 Kings 22:8).

The development of critical scholarship from the early 18th century AD gave great impetus to the study of Deuteronomy. There is now substantial agreement that the book was largely responsible for Josiah's reform in 622BC, but there remain significant disagreements as to when and through what process the book achieved its present form. Many weighty articles and volumes have been written on this, and again the arguments are very complex. Nevertheless, they can be summarized into three views.

- **Radical:** Some scholars argue that the core of Deuteronomy was written up shortly before 622BC as a reform document. Many features of Josiah's reform reflect its laws, particularly the central-ization of all worship in Jerusalem, which comes at the start of the detailed laws (Deuteronomy 12).

- **Moderate:** Some laws, however, seem to reflect earlier times, when local leaders were more important than the king (for example, see comments on chapters 16—18). So some scholars posit a gradual process by which a collection of laws from the early monarchy was gradually expanded, and that this collection (or at least the faith it expressed) lay behind earlier reforms, including the one instigated by Hezekiah a century before Josiah.

- **Conservative:** The book itself is set in the Mosaic period, and consistently reflects this perspective. In particular, it tells Israel to build an altar on Mount Ebal (see ch. 28), which would be strange in a document written after the temple had been built. Also, as shown above, the book follows the Hittite treaty form, which disappeared after the twelfth century. (Suggested parallels with later treaties are less clear.) For all these reasons, conservative scholars still argue that the book accurately records the time in which it is set. Nevertheless, it records a developing legal tradition, and the material was updated, probably several times. Even in modern times, reference works can be significantly updated while still carrying the name of their first writer, for example, *Gray's Anatomy* in medicine (now in its 39th edition).

There is one further question to address: did the events of Deuteronomy actually take place? If we limit this question to the book itself, set after the exodus and before the conquest, the answer by everyone is that we simply do not know. Travel through a wilderness leaves few traces for later archaeology to find, and no other ancient text clearly supports or contradicts the story. So we simply accept it in faith, or reject it in scepticism. Obviously, the later the book is thought to have been written, the less likely it is to be accurate.

If we expand the question to the events that precede and follow the wilderness journey, there is more external evidence, but it is again complex and largely inconclusive. As before, there is a range of scholarly views, with radicals arguing for no historicity, moderates for some, and conservatives for the biblical account being substantially accurate when read appropriately.

Deuteronomy and this commentary

My own view on these issues is that Deuteronomy and its adjacent books authentically record the story of early Israel. However, like many books even today, they have been augmented and edited over the years, expanding on but remaining faithful to the original traditions. Whether specific laws reached their final form in the thirteenth, tenth or seventh centuries is mostly impossible to determine, so I do not discuss it. Instead I offer comments on the book in the form we have it, as Moses' final speeches. The material was relevant to Israelites, whether of his day or later, and we need to ponder that relevance and ask how it applies to our own time.

In preparing these comments, I owe much to many others, and in particular to two books:

- The large *Torah Commentary* (Jewish Publication Society, 1996) by Jeffrey Tigay, a moderate Jewish scholar who furnishes a wealth of detail on the ancient world and on later Jewish interpretations.

- The shorter and more applied *New International Biblical Commentary* (Hendreickson and Paternoster, 1996) by Chris Wright, an evangelical Christian scholar who combines extensive knowledge of ancient Israel with a keen interest in mission.

These have been my constant companions, and I have benefited far more from their insights than the occasional acknowledgment implies.

Any version of the Bible can be used with these notes. I have always consulted the NRSV and the NIV, probably the two most popular, and I quote from the former. But there are very few places where translation affects interpretation. A Bible Dictionary would also be helpful. I've given brief explanations of key terms and concepts, but it would be well to supplement these from other sources.

One key term that needs brief explanation is the name of God himself. Most English versions follow Jewish tradition and give this as LORD (in small caps). However, the Hebrew word is not the title 'Lord' but rather the name *yhwh*, which is usually pronounced as Yahweh. By New Testament times, religious Jews avoided pronouncing the name at all, in order not to break the third commandment, and used instead a word meaning 'Lord'. Christian tradition has followed this practice. Reverting to 'Yahweh', as I have done, emphasizes that Israel's God is personal and has his own name.

The only other requirement for you to benefit from these notes is a willingness to engage with the text, in order to understand it in its context and to apply it to our own. Deuteronomy looks backwards and forwards. It addresses many great issues on all levels: personal relationships, village life, justice, authority, war and peace. Above all, it encourages an ancient people to love and serve the God who redeemed them and offered them new life. With study and prayer, it can continue to encourage us whom God has redeemed in Jesus Christ to love and serve him.

WORDS *in the* WILDERNESS

We often remember significant moments in history by great speeches associated with them. And we remember those speeches by distinctive phrases. Churchill's 'we will fight them on the beaches' encapsulated his radio broadcasts, which both expressed and strengthened British resistance to invasion in World War II. Kennedy's 'Ich bin ein Berliner' epitomized Western resolve to face up to Soviet power in the Cold War. And Martin Luther King's 'I have a dream!' symbolized the hopes and aspirations of the American Civil Rights movement.

Similarly at this turning point in Israel's story, when the people are poised to enter the promised land after decades of aimless wandering, Deuteronomy is essentially a speech by Moses. Actually, there are several speeches through the book (compare the new headings at 4:44; 5:1; 27:1; 31:1), but the effect of bringing them together is to make a single 'super-speech', a sort of last will and testament by Moses to Israel. The Hebrew title of the book, 'Words' (the first noun in verse 1), aptly summarizes it. These are great words of challenge, warning and encouragement.

The speaker

Moses is, of course, the towering figure behind Deuteronomy. He had been Israel's leader in the tumultuous confrontation with Pharaoh and the exodus from Egypt, and then in the foundational events of receiving the law and instituting the tabernacle and the priesthood. Just as important, he had also been their leader during the 40 long years of waiting. The lengths of office of today's political leaders—a decade at most—pale in comparison. It's much harder to maintain a vigorous and active faith during apparent inactivity and stagnation than during bustling activity, and Psalm 90 captures the wistfulness and sense of futility of this period. Yet Moses maintained his faith and strength (see 34:7), and could still ask God to 'prosper the work of our hands' (Psalm 90:17).

The setting

Here in Deuteronomy the people are still in the wilderness. They are still outside the promised land. There is still all to play for. They have come round the south of the Dead Sea, and at this point are encamped east of the Jordan, more or less opposite Jericho. The term 'Arabah' (v. 1, NIV), meaning 'dry', can refer to the whole rift valley stretching from the Sea of Galilee to the Red Sea. Here it indicates that the Israelites were in the wide river valley, rather than up on the higher ground further east. The location of Suph and the other places listed in verse 1 is unknown, so we don't know the exact position of their camp. Some of these names also occur in the journey accounts in Numbers, but probably refer to different places there.

The background

While setting the scene, these opening verses already hint at both the negative and the positive in Israel's travels. On the one hand, verse 2 starkly reminds them that it could all have been so much shorter: eleven days rather than 40 years! It only took eleven days to travel from Mount Horeb (another name for Sinai), where they received their 'national constitution', to Kadesh Barnea, on the southern edge of Canaan. But instead it had taken them 40 years, and they had now travelled round to Canaan's east. Such has been the huge cost of their disobedience.

On the other hand, verse 4 reminds them that God has certainly not abandoned them. He had just defeated Sihon and Og, the two kings who had blocked their recent progress (see 2:24—3:11). Here, as in the later passage, it is not so much the people as God who wins the victory. So he could certainly be trusted for the future battles against the inhabitants of Canaan, the very people whose earlier intimidation of the spies (see 1:28) had led to the futile years of wandering.

Thus the opening of the book sets the scene as a decisive moment, the opportunity to move forward with God. The chance was missed in the past, but God continues to work through and for his people, and now gives them another chance. All is indeed still to play for.

PRAYER

Pray for leaders of churches and nations, for perseverance
in times of little change, and for courage to seize opportunities
when they arise.

2

TIME *to* MOVE ON

Leave Horeb

Horeb (Sinai) was the location of all the foundational elements of Israel's newly explained faith. Here God had shown his presence in thunder, lightning and fire, and called Israel his 'treasured possession... a priestly kingdom and a holy nation' (Exodus 19:5–6). Here they had received the Ten Commandments and a first set of laws, and had confirmed their covenant with him in a solemn ceremony (Exodus 20—24). This covenant was almost immediately broken in the worship of the golden calf, but God graciously re-established it (Exodus 32—34). Then the tabernacle was built (Exodus 35—40), sacrifices, priesthood, festivals and other laws established (Leviticus), and a census taken (Numbers 1—4). Finally, eleven very full months after they arrived (see Exodus 19:1; Numbers 10:11), they left that memorable mountain campsite.

Much had been experienced, both good and bad. Much had been learnt. But there came a time to move on. The book of Deuteronomy retells most of the story and repeats most of the laws of that period, as we shall see, but it starts with God's command to move on. Indeed, Deuteronomy presents it more forcefully and more urgently than in the original account (Numbers 10:13). It highlights the command, because the Israelites are now in a similar position. They have been in the desert 'long enough' (the same phrase is used in 2:3). So, just as 40 years earlier, it is now time to move on.

Sometimes God tells us it is time to move on. We may have experienced a time of great activity and much learning, as Israel did at Horeb. Or we may have been through a time of uncertainty, doubt and aimlessness, as Israel did in the desert. But there comes a time to move on. God grant that we may be sensitive to his voice, and obedient to his prompting.

Take possession of the land

God's original plan was for Israel to go directly from Sinai to Canaan. (Their failure to do so is explained later in the chapter.) Here the land is described in three different ways, all of which occur frequently elsewhere and with various levels of detail.

First, ethnically: it is the land of the Amorites and their neighbours, collectively called Canaanites. There are several lists of these peoples in the Old Testament, variously naming ten, seven, six, five or three groups, or simply calling them all 'Canaanites'. Extra-biblical evidence also testifies to many different people groups in the area—for example, the Amarna Letters written by Canaanite kings to Egyptian pharaohs in the 14th century BC. The ethnic designation emphasizes that other people were already living there. We will look at the ethical implications of this later (see comment on 7:1–11, pp. 80–81).

Second, geographically: the land of Canaan is described by its main features running north to south—the central hills, the rift valley to their east, the foothills to their west, and the coastal plain. To these are added the Negev in the south and the Lebanon in the north, right up to the Euphrates. We will examine later the extent to which Israel ever actually possessed all this territory (see comment on 11:24, p. 98).

Third and most important, theologically: it is the land promised to them, from their forefather Abraham onwards. God's very first call to Abraham (or Abram, as he was then) included the promise of land (Genesis 12:1, 7). This promise was often repeated, but wasn't to be fulfilled until 'the sin of the Amorites [had] reached its full measure' (Genesis 15:16). In God's assessment, now was the time to fulfil the promise. Now was the time to take the gift.

Obedience would of course involve effort, risks, battles and even death for some. For the nation as a whole, however, it would be the culmination of the process started in the exodus but sadly aborted for a full generation. Now was the moment. *Carpe diem!*

PRAYER

*Pray for vision and courage for yourself, to move on
and face new challenges.*

PROBLEMS *of* GROWTH

Growth, however welcome, brings its own problems. A first child brings delight to its new parents, but also a lot of hard work, sleepless nights and unsettled routine. An expanding business brings greater profit and increased potential, but may require painful restructuring. A growing church brings more opportunities in worship and witness, but also the need for more leaders. Similarly with the people of Israel.

Devolved justice

The former slaves had to set up a society almost from scratch, and initially Moses tried to resolve each issue himself, however trifling it was. Very quickly, however, and prompted by his wise father-in-law Jethro (Exodus 18), he accepted that this was impossible. Here he realizes that he couldn't do everything himself (v. 9, literally: 'I am not able to carry you by myself'). Not that he complained about the number of people: he immediately alludes to God's promise to Abraham of uncountable descendants (v. 11; Genesis 15:5), and wishes another thousandfold increase. No grudging resentment here! Nevertheless, the responsibility had to be shared. This was achieved by installing a series of judges at different levels, with Moses consulted only on the hardest cases.

Moses gives three qualities for leaders: they had to be wise and discerning, respected by the community, and able to judge impartially (vv. 13, 16; see Exodus 18:21). It is hardly surprising that similar qualities are required of church leaders in the New Testament (see 1 Timothy 3). Three different terms are used here (unlike in Exodus 18): commanders, officials and judges. We don't know if the terms were used interchangeably, or whether the roles had become more distinct. In any case, they must have been to some degree complementary and interchangeable.

Fairness must be the guiding principle in the exercise of justice, whether between fellow Israelites, or between Israelites and resident foreigners. The latter were particularly vulnerable, as they had no property as security, and no extended family to support them. Corruption is possible in every society, as much in a traditional rural one as in modern capitalism. But all should be treated alike, however small or great. The same principle holds for church life (James 2:1–9), and is the legal basis, at least in theory, for Western democracies. Is it working, in practice as well as in theory?

Crafted narrative

There are two interesting points to note about this story. First, Exodus 18 insists that it was Jethro who instigated the devolution of responsibility, but he isn't even mentioned here. Does this mean, as some commentators suggest, that Deuteronomy airbrushes him out of the picture, in good propagandist style, to give Moses the credit? No, not really. For one thing, as we shall see, Deuteronomy often retells the Exodus and Numbers stories in a shorter, more pithy way, concentrating on what it sees as essential. This doesn't contradict the earlier, longer accounts. (We can see similar issues in the different Gospel stories of Jesus.) More importantly, the text doesn't focus on Moses anyway. Rather, it highlights the structure of leadership and the principle of impartiality.

Secondly, this section obviously interrupts the story just begun, coming between the command to leave Horeb (1:6–8) and the people setting off (1:19). The vague opening phrase 'at that time' (v. 9) shows that it is not in exact chronological order—in Exodus it comes before all the events at Mount Sinai. And yet there are obvious links with the sections immediately before and after it. Moses' reference to Israel being as numerous as the stars (v. 10) shows that God's promise to Abraham just noted has indeed been fulfilled. And the different titles and levels of leaders imply that the nation was fully responsible for the rebellion about to be related, and so thoroughly deserved the punishment. While this section interrupts the story chronologically, it helps us to understand it theologically.

PRAYER

Pray for those who exercise justice in our land,
that they may show fairness to all.

GOD'S GOOD GIFT

Moses describes how, in obedience to the command of 1:7–8, Israel had set off *en route* to the promised land. The details of the journey are all omitted, though the laconic description of the 'vast and dreadful desert' (v. 19, NIV) hints at a difficult time. (Numbers 11—12 mentions three unsavoury incidents: an unspecified complaint, craving for meat, and opposition to Moses.) At the same time, the 'vast and fearful desert' contrasts markedly with Israel's intended destination, and this description highlights the folly of their subsequent rebellion.

At Kadesh Barnea, the extreme southern edge of Canaan, Moses sought to rouse the dispirited people, telling them not to be afraid or discouraged. God had given them the land, he reminded them twice (vv. 20, 21)—the land of the ancestral promise, he underlined (v. 21). The desert may have been fearful, but now they must fear no more. At another turning point not much later, when Joshua has to take over the leadership, he too is told not to be afraid or discouraged (Joshua 1:9). And many centuries later, Christ instructs his disciples, 'Peace I leave with you; my peace I give to you… Do not let your hearts be troubled, and do not let them be afraid' (John 14:27).

The spies' trip

Action was taken to reconnoitre the land, in particular the route to travel and the towns to conquer. Twelve representative men were chosen and sent out. In this abbreviated account, only three features of their trip are recorded, all positive. First, they explored the Valley of Eshcol, or 'Valley of Grape Clusters'; the geographical name evokes a land of plenty. Second, they brought back some fruit, to demonstrate the land's abundance. Third, and most noticeably, they reported, 'It is a good land that the Lord our God is giving us' (v. 25, NIV). No doubts, no equivocation. The picture presented here is entirely positive.

But we know, as the Israelites knew, that this isn't the whole story. It is only a truncated version, emphasizing one point very strongly. What is summarized here in a mere four verses (vv. 22–25) takes some 33 verses in Numbers 13. That account has two essential differences, as well as more detail on the men, their instructions and their route. First, it is God who takes the initiative for the spying enterprise, not the people. This is similar to the difference over who instigated devolution noted in the previous section, but is not really a problem. In practice Moses could easily have been prompted by both God and the people.

The spies' report

More importantly, in the fuller account the spies give a mixed report: yes, 'the land... does flow with milk and honey! Here is its fruit. But the people who live there are powerful, and the cities are fortified and very large' (Numbers 13:27–28, NIV). And they give mixed advice (Numbers 13:30–31): Caleb, supported by Joshua (Numbers 14:38), stresses the positive and urges them to go forward: 'we can certainly do it'. Despite this, the majority are afraid ('we can't attack'), and spread their fear, with disastrous consequences.

Why does Moses give a one-sided account in Deuteronomy? He could hardly have intended to fool the Israelites. They knew all too well this story of lost opportunity. In their years of aimless wandering, it must have been told and retold thousands of times, over many a campfire, as parents tried to explain to curious children why they were growing up in the desert. No, in the light of the ensuing miserable decades, Moses emphasizes the possibility that had been there, and was spurned. The people's representatives had confirmed God's promise: the land really was good. God had kept his word so far. He could have been trusted for the rest.

'Two men looked out through prison bars; the one saw mud, the other stars.' What would you see? Do you think of a glass—or your church—as half-full or half-empty? By temperament, some of us may be more optimistic, some more pessimistic. But by grace, all of us can take God at his word, remember his past goodness, and seize the opportunities presented to us.

REFLECTION

'It is a good inheritance that the Lord our God is giving us' (v. 25).
Make a list of God's gifts to you, and give thanks for them.

5

DEUTERONOMY 1:26–40

LOST OPPORTUNITY

'But you were unwilling…' (v. 26, NIV). These chilling words pour cold water on all the great plans God had for his people, and on all the high hopes Moses had for a triumphant second stage to his leadership. The Israelites were unwilling to seize the opportunity. Now we hear the other aspect of the spies' report, which focused on the physical size of the Canaanites and the strength of their cities. And we notice that it is presented, not as the report of a few men, but as the defeatist conclusion of the whole population grumbling in their tents. The blame is laid not so much on the individuals who reported their findings, but on the people who backed their conclusion. All were to blame, paralysed by fear rather than energized by faith. How ironic and tragic, when God had promised to make the Canaanites fear them instead (see 2:25).

God's fault?

But it was worse than that. The people were not only unwilling, they not only grumbled—they actually accused God of hating them (v. 27)! They immediately forgot God's deliverance of them in the plagues and the exodus, and his power and glory revealed at Mount Horeb and in the tabernacle. Instead, in a twisted travesty, they portrayed God as a spiteful despot. They were so faithless, so fickle, so immature! Perhaps they had naively expected that God would continue to do everything for them, and felt that their high hopes had been cruelly dashed. Perhaps they were early adherents of the 'Let go and let God' mentality, and when this seemed inadequate they accused God rather than reconsider their view. Whatever the reason, like immature children— and some adults—they swung violently from love to hate.

Moses pleaded poignantly with them (vv. 29–31). He reminded them of what God had already done at the exodus. He cited the tender and evocative image of God carrying his child. (Note that the father–son image occurs elsewhere in Deuteronomy with a variety of connotations, for example, at 8:5; 14:1; 32:5). He pointed to God's presence in the desert in the fiery cloud—but all to no avail. So God himself gave his verdict (vv. 34–36). He had sworn to give them the land, but now he swears (same expression) to delay this gift for a whole generation. Only Caleb, the man of vision and faith, would survive to enter the land.

Caleb, Moses and Joshua

Again the two accounts vary. In Numbers 14, Caleb seems to be the only person to propose entering the land, but obviously Moses would have supported him. Here only Moses' arguments are noted, since Deuteronomy focuses on him, but Caleb is then immediately praised. As before, we see different perspectives but no contradiction.

Moses then mentions his own exclusion from the promised land, blaming it squarely on the people (v. 37). We know from Numbers 20:7–12 that God was punishing him for his own lack of faith at Meribah, but Moses himself never mentions this in Deuteronomy. In his mind, the people's sin, which obviously caused the frustrating desert years, was the main cause of his own sin. In this he was largely right, though not completely. Even the great Moses, whose love for God and Israel could hardly be bettered (see Exodus 32:9–14, 31–32), had his faults.

Instead, it will be Joshua who leads the people. Joshua played a support role to Caleb in the spies' report, but had already come to prominence as a capable leader. Before Sinai he led the rout of the Amalekites (Exodus 17:8–13), and then became Moses' assistant (Exodus 24:13), learning from him in the long desert years. Moses is hugely disappointed at his own exclusion from the land. But he is too large a man to let this colour his judgment. Instead, he warmly commends his successor, both here and later (31:1–8) when he formally commissions Joshua.

Glimmers of hope

Lack of faith and turning against God meant a lost opportunity, and years of waiting. Nevertheless, in this tragic incident there are glimmers of hope. The people wouldn't enter Canaan, but Caleb would. Moses wouldn't lead them, but Joshua would. Despite unimaginable disappointment, both national and personal, there were some who remained faithful. But how much better if the opportunity hadn't been lost in the first place!

PRAYER

Pray for faith to seize opportunities, and patience and faithfulness when the church doesn't.

DISASTROUS REMEDY

Hardy or foolhardy?

The Israelites' immediate response sounds so right. Yes, the Lord had commanded them to go up and fight. Yes, they had sinned by refusing to go. But now that they had realized this, they wanted to put things right and go up after all. Surely, better late than never! So they 'strapped on their battle gear' (v. 41) and were all ready to set off.

There was only one small problem. God said 'No'. He would not be with them, and they would be defeated. God had responded to their earlier lack of faith by changing his plan and postponing his promise. His offer to be in their midst and fight for them was no longer on the table. The last time God had threatened to absent himself was after their idolatry around the golden calf. Moses then realized the enormity of the implication, and refused to proceed unless God relented (Exodus 33:3, 14–17). This time the people showed no such discernment, and proceeded anyway.

Spiritual or stupid?

Of course, the result was disaster. The very defeat which they had gloomily imagined when they heard the spies' report now occurred, and they fled as if chased by a swarm of angry bees (v. 44). We aren't told how far they advanced into the land, but they were certainly chased back out: Hormah was probably near Beer-Sheba. What's more, the name Hormah comes from the same stem as *herem*, the word used for total destruction in war (see comment on 7:1–11, pp. 80–81). Fittingly, therefore, they were defeated all the way to 'Destruction-ville'. No wonder they came back to the camp and wept. Such bravery, and such loss of life—all in vain. And their reaction seems very spiritual: they wept 'before the Lord' (v. 45). But God would have none of it. They had first distrusted him, then disobeyed him, and their tears now were not going to change this. God was not going to be trifled with.

Again, we note that Deuteronomy highlights the people's role. Numbers 14:36–37 records the death by plague of the ten faithless spies before this incident—so the people's response might possibly be understood as a desire to make amends. But Deuteronomy removes even this lame excuse. They were to blame, fairly and squarely, for the humiliating debacle that followed.

Regret or repentance?

Why had it all gone so horribly wrong? Surely they had recognized the error of their ways, and tried to put things right. One could hardly expect more! But had they properly realized what had gone wrong, and were they really sorry?

The Israelites saw their earlier refusal to trust God as a temporary glitch, a small hiccup in their progress to the promised land. They regretted it, and would soon make amends. However, God saw things very differently. Their refusal to exercise faith was a fundamental denial of his presence with them. They needed to realize this in genuine repentance and return to him for guidance. After the golden calf idolatry, the covenant needed to be completely renewed. Now the relationship similarly needed to be restored, and God's new instructions accepted.

Regret is a good start, and the desire to make amends is commendable, but neither constitute real repentance. As many people sadly know, a broken relationship leaves its scars, often deep and sometimes indelible. Any attempt to restore the relationship must first acknowledge the seriousness of the breakdown We cannot pretend it never happened. Whatever the relationship afterwards, it will be different because of the earlier failure. Israel never acknowledged this, and only compounded their disaster. They got as far as regret, both before attacking the Amorites and after their humiliating defeat, but not as far as repentance. And God wasn't really interested.

REFLECTION

Where do I stand between regret and repentance,
towards God and towards others?

7

GOD'S WAY *for* ISRAEL & ESAU

New people, new start

With hardly a pause for breath in Moses' account, it seems that the Israelites are on the move again, *en route* to the promised land. The lengthy penalty for disobedience quickly fades out of the picture. They're off again on their adventurous pilgrimage, and everything is rosy.

However, this initial impression is quite wrong, as soon becomes clear. There are two initial references to 'many days', in 1:46 and 2:1. (The NRSV links 1:46 with the following section. This is certainly possible, since chapter and paragraph divisions were not part of the original Hebrew text.) The phrase 'many days' simply means 'a long time', and its repetition underlines that it really was long. Then a few verses later we read that the Israelites have been in the wilderness for 'forty years' (v. 7). This is clearly a round figure: 2:14 gives it more precisely as 38 years. But the round figure makes a strong point. Four decades of wandering in a hostile wilderness! Forty wasted years of doing nothing. Half a lifetime of simply sitting around, waiting until all who had left Egypt had died off (also noted in 2:14). They learnt the hard way that God keeps his word, in punishment as well as in blessing.

Nevertheless, that was all behind now. There is an emphasis throughout Deuteronomy on looking forwards, and here on moving forwards. This was the time to get going. Now they had to face again the dangers of travelling through unwelcoming territories, and of by-passing or defeating their hostile inhabitants. During all the 40 years of marking time, God had 'blessed' them, and they had 'lacked nothing' (v. 7). How much more, now that they were on the move, would he continue to look after them. Surely they could trust him and obey his precise instructions.

Don't mess with Edom!

God took the Israelites on a different route this time, across to the east of the rift valley, and up the east side of the Dead Sea and Jordan river. This meant that the first group they met were the Edomites.

These were the descendants of Jacob's brother Esau, who had settled to the south-east of the Dead Sea. The Edomites were the Israelites' own kin, children of Abraham and Isaac, and on no account to be attacked. Instead Israel must make their peaceful intentions clear, and pay for any provisions they needed.

What's more, the text makes clear that God himself had specifically given Edom their territory around Mount Seir (v. 5). Israel were not the only people God looked after—his purposes were wider than including just them. What exactly these purposes were in respect of Edom was never spelt out, and wasn't to concern Israel. Israel simply had to accept it, and act accordingly.

As it happened, the Edomites refused the Israelites free passage, and brought their army out to enforce this refusal (Numbers 20:14–21). In their later history, relationships between Israelites and Edomites were often uneasy, with sporadic warfare throughout the period of the monarchy. They eventually broke down completely, as Edomites sided with the Babylonians in the destruction of Jerusalem, and betrayed those who escaped. For this they were severely condemned by the prophet Obadiah (see Obadiah 10–14).

But Deuteronomy ignores Edom's reaction here. This is not a blow-by-blow account of all that happened, but a selective survey, emphasizing key features. As the Israelites stand on the plains of Moab, about to enter the promised land, they are reminded that God had provided for them both in the wilderness and as they set out on their journey to Moab. They had obeyed him and travelled past Edom unharmed. The lesson for them was clear: faith and obedience bring blessing.

PRAYER

Thank God for the wideness of his mercy,
and pray for obedience in your immediate tasks.

MOABITES, AMMONITES & OTHERS

At first reading, this section looks both disjointed and quaint. It switches without warning from historical narrative to antiquarian note and back again, and the asides are full of long-gone people with weird and wonderful names. But there is more pattern and purpose here than meets the eye.

Ungrateful cousins

As they progressed northwards, Israel was told to march peacefully past Moab. The Moabites lived between two river wadis, the Zered, just south-east of the Dead Sea (v. 13), and the Arnon, roughly halfway up the Sea's eastern coast (v. 24). They must then also pass peacefully by the Ammonites, who lived north-east of the Arnon. God had already allotted this territory to Moab and Ammon, not to Israel. The Israelites again accepted this order, obeyed the instructions, and marched past without incident. Numbers 21:10–20 gives further details, with the names of campsites *en route* and the joy of finding vital well-water, but in Deuteronomy the story moves rapidly on.

According to Genesis 19:30–38, Moabites and Ammonites were descended from Abraham's nephew Lot. The story is truly pathetic: Lot only just escaped Sodom, lived as an outcast, failed to provide for his daughters, and was tricked by them into fathering their children. Centuries later there was no love lost between their descendants and Abraham's. Here they apparently failed to reciprocate Israel's gestures of peace, and refused to provision them. The king of Moab even hired the well-known local prophet Balaam to curse them (Numbers 22—24). These two factors explain the severe restriction on Moabites and Ammonites assimilating into Israel, harsher than for Edomites or even Egyptians (23:3–8). We will consider later how to interpret these restrictions. For now we simply make a basic observation with profound consequences: present actions affect future generations.

Fearsome legends

This passage also has parenthetical asides concerning the area's former inhabitants (vv. 10–12, 20–23). These legendary ancient peoples were collectively known as Rephaim, though they were given local names as Emim and Zamzummim. They had a fearsome reputation: strong, numerous, and tall as the Anakim, another group whose very name conjured up fear. Both these notes also refer to the Horim, who previously inhabited the region of Edom, and the second further mentions the Avvim around Gaza in the west, who had been destroyed by the Caphtorim (another name for the Philistines, whose roots in Caphtor/Crete are known from Amos 9:7).

Are these notes factual, or are they simply later embellishments of folk-history, rather like the tales of King Arthur or of Robin Hood? On the one hand, there is no external corroboration of all these ancient peoples living in these places, and these notes were probably compiled later, since the Philistines did not settle in Canaan before the Israelites did. On the other hand, the notes seem authentic, since the details are specific and presented without embellishment. Further, there is at least some external support. An Egyptian papyrus from the 13th century BC mentions exceptionally tall Canaanites (*ANET*, 477d), and Ugaritic texts of the same period mention the Rephaim as an ancient people. So while we can't prove that these notes are accurate, we have no good reason to doubt them.

More importantly, why are they included here? The answer is clear, and breathtaking for the Israelites. Two of Deuteronomy's major themes are God's care for his people and his gift to them of a land. But in this, Israel is not unique. God has also given land to Edomites, Moabites and Ammonites, and has enabled them to capture it from its previous inhabitants.

There is encouragement here: as God enabled these people to conquer fearsome foes, so he will enable Israel. But there is also a warning. Israel's uniqueness lies not in receiving land from God. It is rather in their covenant relationship with him. Their land would be a gift, and a very important one, but it was not of ultimate importance. And these apparently arcane notes about lost peoples convey that there is more to faith than the gifts God gives his people.

REFLECTION

Am I trusting in the gifts more than the giver?

DEFEAT *of* BOASTING SIHON

Amorites and Sihon

Next up were the Amorites, who lived along the north-east edge of the Dead Sea, from the Arnon wadi northwards to the town of Gilead —that is, north of the Moabites and west of the Ammonites. They were probably a branch of the Amurru peoples well-known in the fertile crescent in the third and second millennia, though no extra-biblical source mentions this group or King Sihon.

These Amorites were only one of several people groups clustered round the Jordan, and yet they had such a reputation that they were often cited as the leading group of Canaanites. In the previous chapter, Israel had refused to follow the advice of the two optimistic spies, and grumbled that God wanted to hand them over to 'the Amorites' (1:27). Long before, God promised land to Abraham but put this promise on hold, because, as the text explains, 'the iniquity of the Amorites is not yet complete' (Genesis 15:16). Much later, Amos refers to Israel's land as that of the Amorites (Amos 2:9–10). There was good reason for this reputation: the Amorites had recently defeated the Moabites and captured some of their land, and had even written a song to boast about it (Numbers 21:27–30).

As before, Moses made a peaceful approach requesting safe passage, with several reassurances: they would stick to the main road; they would buy provisions, which of course would benefit local people; they had already passed others peacefully; and they were *en route* elsewhere, across the Jordan. This wasn't the full story, since the Edomites hadn't let them go through their territory. But at least their peaceful intentions towards Edom and Moab had been demonstrated.

Sihon rebuffed this approach, however, and refused passage (v. 30). Perhaps the Amorites' recent victory over Moab had further enhanced their sense of superiority, and made them feel invincible. In any case, Sihon turned down the chance for peace, engaged battle, and was soundly defeated.

Divine and human will

This apparently straightforward passage about military confrontation actually poses several theological problems. Why did Israel promise to pass peacefully if this was land promised to them by God (see Genesis 15:18–20)? There is no clear answer to this. Possibly the Israelites wanted to press on and take the heartland of Palestine first.

More importantly, wasn't it grossly unfair of God to harden Sihon's heart? In the dramatic confrontation before the exodus, we read several times that God hardened Pharaoh's heart (Exodus 7:3; 9:12; 10:1), but we also read that Pharaoh hardened his own heart (Exodus 8:15, 32; 9:34). Divine and human responsibility are inseparably intertwined, and the ancient Israelites saw no need to untangle them, especially in their early writings. The same probably applies here. God was responsible, but so too was Sihon. (For another interesting example, compare the attribution of responsibility in 2 Samuel 24:1 with that in the later account of the same incident in 1 Chronicles 21:1.)

War and victory

So Sihon led out his troops, but the Israelites defeated them, captured their towns, wiped out all the inhabitants, and took the animals as spoil. All war is dreadful, but this annihilation of men, women and children, apparently divinely inspired, poses the biggest problem of all. We will consider it more closely when we have got further into the book, and when its reasons are spelt out in chapter 7. For the moment, we note three factors. First, such massacre only occurred in the conquest, not throughout Israel's history; second, its primary reason was punishment for sin (cf. Genesis 15:16 again); and, third, the same fate awaited any Israelites who became apostate (Deuteronomy 13:12–15). We may take sin lightly, but God certainly doesn't.

There are several other important features of the story. The Israelites attributed their victory to God. They were obedient in not attacking Ammonite land. And they saw their worst fears evaporate: where they had quailed before the 'large, fortified cities' (1:28), they now found that 'no citadel was too high' (2:36). God had given them a first victory against feared opponents. He could be relied on for the battles ahead.

REFLECTION

What do 'the fear of God' and 'trust in God' mean to me today?

DEFEAT *of* GIANT OG

Prime grazing land

Israel continued to march north and attacked the other main Amorite group of the region. They lived in Bashan, which lies to the east of the northern Jordan and the Sea of Galilee. The latter is called Chinnereth or Kinnereth in the Old Testament (v. 17: note that *ch* in a Hebrew name is always pronounced as *k*). Bashan was fertile pastureland, excellent for cattle, which is why some tribes wanted to settle there (v. 13), and why Amos later describes pampered rich women as 'cows of Bashan' (Amos 4:1).

Bashan was well populated and defended, having some 60 walled fortress towns and many more villages (vv. 4–5). That meant many armed men, and a potentially difficult campaign. But again victory was complete, and attributed directly to God. He handed the people of Bashan over to Israel, and they were completely annihilated. It seems that they all came out for one decisive battle near the large town of Edrei, and were decisively routed. As before with the southern Amorites, Israel kept their livestock and goods as booty (v. 7).

The story then breaks off for a geographical summary of the land taken. The text itself contains a sense of wonder—'all the towns... the whole of... all of...'—and this is reinforced by a glance at a map. Mount Hermon was in the far north, nearly as far as Damascus, though in fact Israelite settlements may have stopped some way to the south of it, since two other groups continued to live between Lake Chinnereth and Mount Hermon (v. 14). After two quick battles, Israel had possession of a large swathe of land over 100 miles in length, narrow at the southern end (bounded by the Ammonites to the east), but wider further north in the tableland of Bashan. This was not much smaller than the area of land which they eventually conquered west of the Jordan, after more numerous and more difficult battles. No wonder the writer is amazed.

An old iron bed

As before, there are some interesting historical asides, especially concerning the legendary Og. For one thing, he was reputedly the last of the Rephaim. (The Ugaritic texts also link the Rephaim to the towns of Edrei and nearby Ashtaroth, giving external support to this identification.) Then he had an amazing bed (v. 11), large enough for a whole family: around 4 by 1.8 metres). Presumably the huge size indicated his inflated sense of status: even Goliath wouldn't have needed a bed that big!

Further, this bed was made of iron, or possibly made of bronze and decorated with iron. For many of us, iron bedsteads are distinctly old-fashioned. But at the very end of the Bronze Age, when these events are situated, an iron bed would have ranked as the last word in technology, something only kings could afford. No wonder the bed had been carried off as booty, and was still preserved many years later by the Ammonites. This reference to an iron bed is so unusual that some scholars think a mistake was made, and the text originally referred to a sarcophagus. However, the terms are never confused elsewhere. More likely, this is a genuine historical reminiscence, an odd detail which has been accurately passed down and later recorded.

A great start

While the defeat of Sihon gave Israel their first victory, the defeat of Og gave them a much greater area of good pastureland. These initial victories provided both spiritual encouragement and a territorial base for the coming campaign into the heartland of Palestine. Thus they constitute not just a historical introduction to the following laws and exhortations, but a theological prologue: God has already started to fulfil his promises. He can surely be trusted for the rest.

PRAYER

Lord, you have already given me so much…
I trust you for the future.

FIRST ISRAELITE LAND

The first land taken by the Israelites was allotted to several tribes: the furthest south to Gad, the next section to Reuben, and the northern part to Machir, an important clan which constituted about half of Manasseh. Verses 12–13a give the initial summary, then 13b–17 give more detail, with some repetition.

The eastern tribes

The account here omits the heated exchange recorded in Numbers 32. There we read that these tribes noted the good grazing land and asked Moses directly if they could settle in it. Haunted by the spectre of Israel's previous failure to enter the promised land, Moses immediately sensed a similar lack of enthusiasm, a breakdown in tribal solidarity and resultant defeat, with a further generation dying in the wilderness as punishment. No wonder he called them a 'brood of sinners' (Numbers 32:14).

The would-be easterners replied that their men would indeed cross the Jordan with the main party and fight with their comrades, a proposal that Moses accepted. The text could be read as if they planned this all along, but hadn't been able to say it before Moses blew his top. But that is probably to misread the direct style of the storyteller. More likely it was Moses' strong reaction that prompted their reply and maintained the vital sense of 'one for all and all for one' so necessary in warfare. As we have already seen, Deuteronomy omits detail given elsewhere, since these early chapters are simply a summary of the events between leaving Sinai and arriving at the Jordan.

Gifts and responsibilities

Gift features prominently in these verses. We read four times that Moses 'gave' territory, and then see that he was only acting on behalf of the real benefactor, Yahweh himself (v. 18). This was the first gift of land to any of the Israelites, the first indication that all those promises were beginning to come true. But with gift came responsibility, as the agreement reached in Numbers 32 made clear: the men of these eastern tribes would cross the Jordan to risk their lives and fight alongside the other tribes. Further, they would actually function as a vanguard unit, easier to do when travelling without their families, but also more dangerous. Only when all the tribes had captured all their territory would they return home. Thus they were the first to receive their land, but would be among the last to settle in it.

In practice, the conquest of the land was patchy, as the books of Joshua (13:1) and Judges (1:27–36) both make clear. But the easterners fulfilled their promise, and were eventually dismissed by Joshua with full honours (Joshua 22:1–6). An incident soon after their return almost provoked civil war, but they successfully argued that they had been misunderstood (Joshua 22:10–34). Certainly in later history, as far as the biblical record testifies, these eastern tribes remained loyal to the rest of Israel. When schism eventually came, it was between north and south, not east and west. The lessons of solidarity and responsibility had apparently been well learned.

Cometh the hour, cometh the man!

Moses knew that Joshua, not he, would lead Israel in their future conflicts. He probably sensed that Joshua, capable though he was, felt overawed at the task. So Joshua too must take note that God would continue to give Israel victory: as here in Transjordan, so there in Palestine; as now against Sihon and Og, so then against the many other boastful and seemingly powerful kings.

'Do not fear them, for it is the Lord your God who fights for you' (v. 22). The exhortation not to fear is frequently repeated in the formal commissioning of Joshua by Moses (Deuteronomy 31:1–8) and by God himself (Joshua 1). This suggests that Joshua was a natural worrier, one of the world's more timid people who often needed reassurance. Yet in due course he responded to Moses' charge, rose to the task, and fulfilled it very ably. Indeed, his eventual legacy almost put Moses in the shadow (Joshua 24:31). Not only did he overcome his fear and serve God wholeheartedly, but he helped Israel do likewise. Moses threw out the challenge to the eastern tribes and to Joshua, and both rose to it.

PRAYER

Thank you, Lord, for the resources you give to all your people.
Please equip me to meet the challenges I face in my life.

VIEW *from* AFAR

No!

All his life Moses had had one great wish: to lead his people from slavery to freedom. As a young man he took matters into his own hands, killed an Egyptian, and spent decades in exile as a result. Then God met him at the burning bush, renewed his vision, and sent him back to Egypt to lead the Israelites out. But that was only the first half of the wish. They still needed to find freedom. Their initial attempt to enter the promised land had failed disastrously (1:19–45), and Moses spent several more decades in the wilderness. Now he desperately longed to enter Canaan, and repeatedly pleaded with God to be able to do so. What he had started, he wanted to finish.

En route, Moses had discovered much about God: at the burning bush, during the plagues in Egypt, at the crossing of the Red (or Reed) Sea, and above all at Sinai. He had come to know a God of 'greatness and might', whose 'deeds and mighty acts' were incomparable (v. 23). He had no doubt that God would fulfil his promise and enable Israel to conquer the promised land. And he wanted to be there, to experience it himself, to complete the task God had given him.

But God said, 'No, you can't.' Moses' dream would not happen; the goal of his life would never be realized; he would not cross the Jordan. Actually, God's reaction was even stronger: he literally 'burned with anger' (v. 26). Moses had been asking persistently, and God now said, 'Enough, never speak of this again.' This was final. He was to ascend Mount Pisgah just east of the Jordan to see into Canaan, but would not set foot there. He was to commission Joshua to lead the people across, but he wouldn't go himself. That was it.

Forgive and forget?

The reason for God's refusal was, of course, Moses' sin at Meribah, recounted in Numbers 20, when in anger he struck the rock rather than simply speaking to it. But here and elsewhere (1:37; 4:21), Moses seems to blame the Israelites: 'It was your fault!' Why?

It could be that Moses had become an embittered old man, frustrated that his greatest wish had been denied, and looking round for someone else to blame. After all, he wasn't perfect. But there is much more to it than this, as the book's generally positive tone and the later, fuller explanation make clear (see comments on 32:48–51, pp. 212–213). In some ways it *was* the people's fault. It was their refusal to enter Canaan at the beginning that led to the wilderness years, and it was their grumbling against God and quarrelling with Moses that provoked the incident at Meribah. So they were partly to blame.

But there is still more to it. After the dreadful incident of the golden calf, Moses had magnanimously offered to be punished in place of the people (Exodus 32:32). God declined the offer then—but maybe there is an element of that punishment here. The generation born in the wilderness seemed as rebellious as their parents. They didn't deserve to enter the land either, and perhaps Moses was being punished partly on behalf of the people as a whole. He was being punished for his sin, but also for theirs.

The Meribah incident in particular and the wilderness years in general raise the issue of forgiveness. In some circles today the phrase 'forgive and forget' is bandied around, as if one automatically includes the other. And it is partly biblical: a psalmist describes forgiven sin as 'covered' (Psalm 32:1); a prophet describes it as 'remembered no more' (Jeremiah 31:34). The Christian gospel is founded on forgiveness and new life. But sin has other consequences, which are not necessarily removed by forgiveness. Thank God, we can be forgiven for injuring or killing others, breaking up families, and the countless little hurts and grievances we cause. Nevertheless, there are still consequences that have to be faced and lived through, as many of us know only too well.

Moses seems to have chafed at his punishment but then accepted it. The rest of the book bears eloquent testimony to his rising above his own massive disappointment and doing all he could to prepare everyone else to receive what he was denied.

REFLECTION

In what spirit do I accept disappointment?

'SO NOW, GIVE HEED!'

At last, the introduction seems over and the main part of the book is about to start. Chapters 1—3 have given a brief historical background, like the opening chapter of many a novel, and have introduced some of the main themes to be developed, like the overture of many an opera. Now, verse 1 seems to say, let the real business commence!

With chapter 4 we have reached the inner frame of the book (see Introduction). In many ways, chapters 4—11 are the most memorable, as they deal in broad brush strokes with God's commitment to his people and their expected response. The historical survey just given and the detailed laws to come illustrate the main themes in practice, but these intervening chapters state them vigorously and eloquently.

Hold fast and live

The first paragraph is almost Deuteronomy in a nutshell. In the space of a few verses, it includes promise, command and warning. Israel must heed God's law (often summarized as 'statutes and ordinances'), firstly, in order to live. And this means not just simple existence, but life in all its fullness, life that provokes worldwide envy (v. 6), life that is happy, fruitful and peaceful (28:1–14). This theme, which opens the inner frame, is developed throughout and repeated at its very end: 'Choose life so that you and your descendants may live, loving the Lord your God, obeying him, and holding fast to him... so that you may live in the land that the Lord swore to give to your ancestors' (30:19–20). This reminds us of a later son of Israel who offered to all people 'life to the full' (John 10:10, NIV).

With the promise there comes a command, not to add or subtract from God's law (v. 2). It is not an à la carte menu from which one can choose what one likes and politely decline the rest. No, it is a set menu, all or nothing. The same warning is repeated at the very end of the Bible in a passage that echoes these verses (Revelation 22:18–19). God really does know best, and following him means accepting all his revelation, not a pick-and-mix version.

There also comes a warning (vv. 3–4). The last chapter ended with a simple geographical reference to Beth-peor, and these next verses include a brief reference to the same incident. This was Israel's most recent failure, and it had tragic consequences. The full story is given in Numbers 25 (see also Numbers 31:16; Psalm 106:28–31). They had been beguiled into false worship, sacrifices to the dead, and sexual immorality. As a result, God had sent a devastating plague, halted only by the prompt action of Aaron's grandson, Phinehas. This terrible event was still very recent, and Israel needed to heed the warning, and 'hold fast' to the Lord.

Witness to the nations

Verses 5–8 are amazing. Israelite obedience will not only benefit themselves; it is part of God's purpose of witness to the whole world. Back in Genesis, God had promised to Abraham that in him all the nations of the earth would be blessed (Genesis 12:3; 18:18). Here we see one of the first signs of that promise being fulfilled. The wisdom of obeying Yahweh would be transparent to all, and would point outside observers to two things. They would note how Israel's God was close to his people, caring for them and answering their need— in significant contrast to their own gods. And they would note the justice or righteousness of Israel's laws—again presumably in contrast to their own. Most Mesopotamian law codes boasted of their divine origin and just measures (for example, *ANET*, 151d, 164b, 523c). Deuteronomy is consciously setting Yahweh's law code over against them, and inviting comparison.

The text does not say that the nations will immediately flock to worship Yahweh alone and obey his laws. That vision is glimpsed later by the prophets (see Isaiah 2:2–4; 19:19–25), and opened up fully by the ministry of Jesus and the preaching of his apostles (John 10:16; Galatians 3:26–29). But the nations' acknowledgment of Israel's wisdom and their envy of her God would be an important first step. Personal obedience has social repercussions; community obedience has international repercussions.

PRAYER

Lord, may the people around me, and the community around my church, glimpse you through our obedience, and be amazed.

DISTINCTIVE GOD, DISTINCTIVE PEOPLE

Lest the dizzying heights of the previous few verses make Israel proud, this next section opens with a typical and forceful Deuteronomic expression. The recent scholarly Jewish translation (NJPS) captures the original sense well: 'take utmost care and watch yourselves scrupulously' (v. 9). For good measure, the same command is repeated later with slight variation (v. 15). This is immediately backed up by further commands: don't forget, don't let them fade from memory, teach your children, and then your grandchildren (v. 9). This is the ancient equivalent of bold, italic, underline, and a bright fluorescent highlighter all at once, just to make sure you don't miss it!

An invisible God

What exactly is being highlighted? What should they remember at all costs? Ostensibly it is 'the things that your eyes have seen' (v. 9). But this phrase really means 'what you have experienced'. And as we read on, it becomes clear that it's actually a matter of 'what your eyes *haven't* seen'. The next verses recall the momentous events that their parents had witnessed: Yahweh's awesome presence and voice at Mount Horeb (Sinai); his declaration of the covenant; its summary in the Ten Commandments; and its further crystallization into one single all-encompassing concept.

Yet throughout this section one feature keeps returning in every paragraph, as a leitmotif through the whole section: no images and no idols. You didn't see any visible form of God, Moses says (vv. 12, 15), so don't make any image of any sort (vv. 16–18); don't worship the sun, moon and stars (v. 19); don't make an idol (v. 23); idolatry will bring punishment and exile (vv. 25–26); even in exile you will serve lifeless idols (v. 28); only when you turn from them to Yahweh your God will he rescue you (v. 30). Verse 23 puts it in a nutshell: making an idol is as good as abandoning the covenant.

This leitmotif has a double focus, which is taken up in the first two commandments (5:7–10): don't worship other gods or aspects of creation, and don't make images of Yahweh your God. We'll reflect more on these later, but focus for now on two related features highlighted here.

An audible God

God was not visible, but he was certainly audible. This contrast is made explicit in verse 12: 'You heard the sound of words but saw no form; there was only a voice.' And there are many other references to God speaking: 'the Lord said... hear my words' (v. 10); 'the Lord spoke' (v. 12); 'he declared' (v. 13); 'the Lord spoke' (v. 15). Wright draws out the significance of this emphasis very well (p. 51, emphasis added):

> *Idols are visible but dumb. Yahweh is invisible but eloquent, addressing his people in words of promise and demand, gift and claim. This introduces a fundamentally moral distinction into the contrast between the faith of Israel and surrounding visual polytheism. What sets Yahweh apart is not that he looks different, but that he calls for a people who will look different, with a different way of life, a different social order, and a different dynamic of worship.*

A distinctive people

So Israel's God was very different from everyone else's, and Israel itself should be very different from everyone else. Their God was invisible but present in every aspect of their lives, as spelt out in great detail in the following chapters. Others might worship the sun, moon and stars, though verse 19 states simply that they have been given to everyone, not that they should be worshipped. (See the similar 32:8 and the discussion there, p. 208.) But Israel must not.

Our distinctiveness as Christians is not the same, in that we are less tempted to make idols or worship other gods. But it should be equally marked. We worship a God who has now made himself visible in Jesus, and audible in new ways through the New Testament and by his Spirit living in us. And he wants us, like Israel, to be distinctive in our faith and obedience.

PRAYER

Lord, help me to be distinctively Christian in the way I live.

WHAT *a* GOD!

With this section we come to the climactic end of the first 'speech of Moses', the first movement of the magnificent symphony of Deuteronomy. Like many a great composer, the writer takes a familiar theme and gives it a new dimension, a distinctive element, building up to a memorable finale. Where Tchaikovsky would brighten the tone, pump up the brass and throw in the percussion, Moses reprises a basic motif and projects it into a universal dimension. It's not just a matter of God's provision for Israel over the last 40 years and recently in their victories over Sihon and Og—nor even just the distinctive feature of God as never to be represented by an image, something that was unique in the ancient world. No, it's something of cosmic and eternal dimensions.

He begins (v. 32): enquire throughout human history, from the very beginning of creation. Enquire throughout the whole earth, from one end to the other. Has anything like it ever happened before? Have you not witnessed something completely and utterly distinct, truly unique, totally *sui generis*? The sweeping rhetorical questions are eloquent and grandiose. What is he referring to?

A magnificent God

Moses has two unanswerable points. Has any other god ever spoken audibly to a whole people, with them surviving to tell the tale (v. 33)? And has any other god ever rescued a set of slaves from oppression to make them a new nation, with such obvious signs of supernatural power (v. 34)? Well, has any? The logic is inescapable. Israel's God is not just different, he is on a completely different plane from any other deity. The ancient world acknowledged many gods, but the major or high gods were remote, unknowable, inscrutable, and their ways seemed capricious. Ordinary mortals spent their time trying to please the lower personal gods, in the hope that they would then intercede on their behalf towards the high gods. For a high god like Yahweh to speak directly to his people was absolutely extraordinary. And for him to free them with such awesome power was breathtaking.

Then for good measure Moses repeats his double summary of God's work (vv. 36–38), this time in fuller description and with further elaboration. He made you hear his voice to discipline you (v. 36). God brought you out of Egypt because he loves you (v. 37), and consequently he will drive out other nations to give you their land (v. 38). This was still in the future (literally: 'in order to bring you in'), and we will consider its moral dimensions later. But for now we notice the dual reasons of love and discipline, similar to those two human responses of love and reverence that characterize the book, indeed the whole of scripture. And interestingly we note that God's self-revelation at Horeb is mentioned first, even if the exodus preceded it. This seems to underline that God's primary purpose was relationship, and deliverance was simply a means to that end. Being free must lead to knowing God.

An obedient people

So this first movement comes to an end. And the conclusion returns to the leitmotifs of the chapter with a statement, a command and a result: Yahweh your God is all-powerful and unique; you must obey his laws; and you will prosper in your new land.

Christians today face a similar challenge as ancient Israel, but in a very different situation. We have the same magnificent God, though we know him far better now through Jesus. We have the same command to obey, though the 'law of Christ' is both more straightforward and more searching. We know that obedience leads to blessing, though this may well not be the material blessing promised to Israel. We are involved in conflict, though we do not have to capture and defend a geographical land. Above all, we know that God has rescued us, revealed himself, and provided for our welfare.

REFLECTION

Lord, you delivered Israel from Egypt and slavery, and in Christ you delivered us from sin and death. Help me to live in grateful obedience and loving service.

SMALL FOOTNOTES, BIG MESSAGE

Ancient footnotes

Today's reading covers two disparate sections. The first seems to be an appendix or coda to Moses' first speech. Having reached the heights of lyrical rhetoric and the heart of Israelite theology in the previous verses, the speech seems to end in anticlimax, with this footnote on practical matters concerning three small towns in Transjordan (vv. 41–43). The role of these towns is not unimportant, as we shall see, but their mention here does seem a little strange—until, that is, we remember that ancient writing was unlike modern publishing, and didn't have the convenience of chapter headings, appendices, footnotes and editor's notes. All these elements were simply included in a running text.

We can see this illustrated elsewhere. Leviticus comes to a rousing theological climax in chapter 26 with the consequences of obedience and disobedience, and a concluding verse, 'These are the statutes…' which seems to signify 'the end'. But it then has a supplementary chapter on votive offerings, which concludes with a similar 'These are the commandments…'. The book of Judges has a clear narrative structure for chapters 1—16, but then two stories in chapters 17—21 unattached to this structure. And 2 Samuel tells the story of David's reign more or less in chronological sequence until chapters 20—24; these final chapters constitute an appendix of various incidents, lists and poetry in chiastic structure. So a coda like Deuteronomy 4:41–43 is not unusual in ancient writings. The book's opening speech has concentrated on incidents prior to reaching the Jordan, and this provision for the eastern tribes is mentioned here before moving on.

Cities of refuge: a coda

The cities of refuge are first mentioned in Numbers 35:9–34, which explains their rationale and notes that there should be six, three on each side of the Jordan. Deuteronomy 19:1–13 further summarizes their function (which we will consider in a later study) and notes the three western cities. Our present passage simply notes the three eastern ones. These are all about 20–25 miles east of the Jordan:

Bezer opposite the northern end of the Dead Sea, and the other two close together near the Sea of Galilee. Bezer was in the heart of what was later Ammonite country, and soon disappears from Israelite history. This suggests that we have a genuine historical record here, not a later invention. Ramoth-Gilead became something of a frontier town and features in accounts of war with the Arameans (also called Syrians), for example, in 1 Kings 22:3. Golan, inland from the present Golan Heights, is otherwise unmentioned. The uneven geographical spread probably represents an uneven population density of the eastern tribes.

Why bother noting these cities here? Why would a writer or compiler feel compelled to include them at this point? Why not simply omit them, or add them into the fuller account in chapter 19? We'll never know for sure, but it may well be the urge for completeness. Not just historical completeness, reflecting when these cities were apportioned; nor even a literary completeness, dealing with all matters relating to Transjordan in this first speech; but a theological completeness—the eastern tribes were very much part of Israel, with the same provisions as those in the heartland to the west, and therefore the same obligations. All the magnificent exhortation just delivered, and all the encouragement and warnings to come, apply as much to them as to the others. Geography is no bar to solidarity.

This is the law: *prolegomena*

The other section of today's reading is the introduction to Moses' second speech, which stretches from here to 26:19 and covers the bulk of the book. It summarizes material already covered at greater length in chapters 2—3, and provides a temporal and geographical context for the second speech. In some ways it is redundant, since the first speech has already given the detail. Again, we are reminded that ancient writers did not follow modern conventions of editing. But we are also reminded of the clear rooting of this material in a specific place and time.

REFLECTION

Geography was no bar to solidarity for Israel. It should be even less for Christians, united in Christ!

The TEN COMMANDMENTS

We now come to the best-known passage of the Old Testament, often seen as the very foundation of Judeo-Christian civilization: the Ten Commandments or 'decalogue'. Most Jewish synagogues display them prominently on a wall. Many Christian churches present them alongside the Lord's Prayer or the Beatitudes. And many people who don't attend worship regularly anywhere still know, or at least know of, the Ten Commandments.

A ten-point covenant summary

Let's consider a few interesting facts in general, before we look at the commandments in detail. Firstly, they divide neatly into two groups, with the first four directed to honouring God and the other six to respecting fellow humans. Older commentators thought that the two tablets (see 9:9) contained one group each. It is more likely, however, that both tablets contained the full set, with one copy for each party to the agreement. With any ancient human treaty, each nation had a copy to keep in its main temple. With Israel, the two copies were kept together, inside the ark of the covenant (10:2), in the holiest part of the tabernacle and later the temple.

Secondly, the Hebrew text gives them a special name, not quite 'ten commandments' as we refer to them, but 'ten words' (hence the name 'deca-logue', 4:13). This term shows their special place at the head of and as a summary of Israelite law. Thirdly, they also come in Exodus 20, with one main difference. Check the two passages and think about possible reasons for this—we'll come to it in due course.

Fourthly, they're numbered differently—we'll follow the main Protestant numbering system in these comments. Mainstream Jewish tradition takes verse 6 ('I am Yahweh your God') as the first 'word', and then combines verse 7 ('no other gods') with verses 8–10 ('no images') as the second 'word'. This fits the idea of ten words, but makes the first into a simple statement, very different from the other nine, which are all direct commands. By contrast, Roman Catholic tradition takes verses 7–10 as all part of the first commandment, re-numbers commandments 3 to 9, and subdivides the prohibition against coveting into two commands. This is less helpful, both in combining two distinct ideas and in subdividing a single concept. Whatever system of numbering is used, though, the content remains the same.

A covenant with us

Moses begins with a brief but telling introduction. First, he summons Israel to hear, as frequently in this sermonic book: see 4:1, also 6:3, and most famously 6:4. Listening is an essential prerequisite to obeying. Then he asserts that the covenant was 'not with our ancestors [literally, fathers]... but with us' (v. 3). The following phrase, 'who are all of us here alive today', might suggest a contrast with the precious generation who died in the wilderness. But the term '(y)our ancestors' elsewhere in Deuteronomy always means the patriarchs Abraham, Isaac and Jacob. Moses is more probably making a contrast with them: God promised them the land, but he's made a covenant at Sinai with us. As we've already seen, in Deuteronomy Moses frequently includes the present generation in that event, even though they weren't physically there. He is more concerned with the present than with the past, even the immediate past. It is in the here and now that Israel must respond.

Based on God's deliverance

Verse 6 gives a one-sentence introduction to the whole decalogue, setting out the basis for Israel's obedience. Such pithy introductions often precede important statements, as when God appeared to Abraham (Genesis 15:7; 17:1). Here God identifies himself as Yahweh, the one made known to Moses in the burning bush, whose very name ('I am' / 'the one who is') indicates that he is present with his people. And he is the one 'who brought you out of the land of Egypt', a simple phrase which understates the incredible act of their deliverance. God has revealed himself, rescued his people, and established a unique relationship with them. He deserves to be obeyed.

REFLECTION

Christian faith, like the Ten Commandments, rests on what God has done. Meditate on the following two verses: 'Though he was rich, yet for your sakes he became poor' (2 Corinthians 8:9); and 'We love him because he first loved us' (1 John 4:19).

WORSHIP YAHWEH ONLY

The commandment

The very first commandment proclaims that Yahweh alone is to be worshipped. This is categorical, with no room for debate: Israel is to have one god only. Admittedly, this doesn't deny the existence of other gods. But it is not a statement in a philosophical debate about the supernatural world. It is a command to people living in a polytheistic world, where all their neighbours had several different gods. The Old Testament often accepts the starting point of polytheism. It occurs here in Deuteronomy (see 3:24) as well as elsewhere (see Psalm 82:1). However, Yahweh is so far superior to other gods that they are all insignificant. This may not be monotheism in theory, but it certainly is in practice. A few texts do affirm that there are no other actual gods (see 4:35, 39), but there will still be the temptation to worship other apparent gods, and this is expressly forbidden.

The final two words seem slightly ambiguous. The traditional translation, 'before me', might seem to allow other gods as long as they are not placed ahead of Yahweh, but this would be to misunderstand it. While the Hebrew expression is unusual and perhaps idiomatic, there is a partial parallel in Genesis 31:50 where Laban warns Jacob not to take any wives '*besides* my daughters'. Laban doesn't want Jacob to have any other wives at all. Similarly, Yahweh doesn't want Israel to have any other gods at all.

The command focuses on Yahweh. It's not a question of worshipping just one god, and leaving open their exact nature and the appropriate style of worshipping them. It certainly gives no basis for pluralism today, of the 'all views of God are more or less the same' variety. No, this is expressly Yahweh, who redeemed Israel from slavery, as just stated in verse 6. He alone is God.

The practice

Sadly, Israel often forgot this. The historical books from Judges onwards reveal how often they forgot it, and with what disastrous consequences (2 Kings 17 gives a tragic summary), and the pre-exilic prophets show how deep-seated this apostasy was in Israelite and

Judean society. Recent archaeological discoveries underline the point: several eighth-century inscriptions pair Yahweh with the goddess Asherah as his consort, and little goddess figurines, probably of Asherah, abound in Judah in the seventh and sixth centuries, just before the exile.

Some scholars suggest that Israel developed from early polytheism to later monotheism, and that much of the Old Testament writes back the later view into the earlier period. But even if we leave aside the trustworthiness of the biblical text (which many Christians accept), there is good evidence that Yahweh's supremacy in practice was an ancient belief. It is reflected in a great variety of references, including poetic texts which are often accepted as the oldest, for example, 'Who is like you, Yahweh, among the gods?' (Exodus 15:11). Incidentally, this verse is still part of Jewish liturgy today, used by devout Jews who obviously deny the existence of other gods. This illustrates how ancient language can still be used even when it reflects obsolete concepts.

God's people frequently ignored his first commandment, and paid a heavy price. The northern state of Israel was conquered by Assyria, exiled and dispersed, never to reassemble or return. The southern kingdom of Judah was conquered by Babylon with much death and destruction, and only a small remnant ever made it back.

The cure

The remnant did return, however, and the small Jewish community in Judah did revive. Sheshbazzar and Zerubbabel led the return, and Haggai and Zechariah encouraged them to rebuild the temple (Ezra 1—6). A generation later, Ezra and Nehemiah travelled to Jerusalem, and at some unknown stage Malachi critiqued religious laxity. But in all these post-exilic texts, there is virtually no mention of serving other gods. (There are a few references in Isaiah 56—66, but these chapters are notoriously hard to date.) For all its tragedy, trauma and upheaval, the exile at least seems to have cured Yahweh's people of worshipping other gods. It was extremely harsh medicine, but it worked.

PRAYER

Lord, help me to worship you alone,
in practice as well as in theory.

19 DEUTERONOMY 5:8–10

WHAT'S WRONG *with a* PICTURE?

Visualizing life

We live in a highly visual age. Television is all-pervasive, films are widely discussed, photographs sell newspapers, posters are everywhere. From school to business seminar to church, multi-media presentations proliferate. No wonder—psychologists tell us that we retain far more of what we see than what we hear or read.

We're certainly not the first society to like images. From time immemorial, humans have drawn pictures in caves and tombs, or on scrolls and parchments. Great civilizations from the Egyptians and Sumerians onwards have left their mark in sculpture and monument. Medieval cathedrals throughout Europe used stained-glass pictures to teach the biblical story. In fact, everywhere you look, however primitive or literate the society, pictures are popular.

It's no wonder, then, that beliefs are translated into the visual, and images are made of gods. Open any illustrated encyclopedia or visit any museum of antiquities, anywhere in the world (or via the web), and you'll find dozens of images of gods of all types, shapes and sizes. Ancient societies all had images of their deities, which were accorded great care and attention. Ancient Near Eastern temples all had special niches for the deity's statue, and often had special ceremonies when the statues were taken on parade. All, that is, except Israel's.

Unique among ancient peoples, the Israelites were expressly forbidden to make any pictorial representation of God, in any form whatsoever. In their temple stood no image, but rather a gilded box. On its walls were no pictures of God, but only of his creation. Indeed, when the great empires of the Old Testament period were eventually superseded by the Romans, and the conquering Pompey entered the Jerusalem temple in 63BC, he found nothing but a table, a candelabra and various utensils. Unlike in any other temple he had ever entered, there was no divine image.

Visualizing God?

Why, what's wrong with a picture? We're not told directly here, but there are several clues, which we've already seen (4:15–18). Even in his fullest self-revelation at Horeb, God chose to remain invisible. No image could do him anywhere near justice. Any image would approximate to one of his creatures (or any aspect of creation), an insult to the creator himself. God must never be limited by our imagination, however fertile or spiritual that may be. Images can be controlled. Priests and people can decide what to do with them, when, and how often. The biblical God would never be tamed by his worshippers. And perhaps most importantly, an image is lifeless. This is the very antithesis of God—living, speaking, judging, forgiving, in sum relating to people.

The first commandment protects the uniqueness of God. The second safeguards his character. As soon as we make an image, we imagine him with the characteristics of that image. And those characteristics tend to exclude other aspects. The best-known 'Christian' painting of God is that by Michelangelo on the Sistine Chapel ceiling in the Vatican. There, God is an old bearded man reaching out to touch Adam. Michelangelo tried to convey something of the authority of God, but his painting has given popular culture its caricature of God as an old man with a white beard sitting on a cloud. His many other important characteristics are simply ignored: majesty, holiness, love. Images of God, however well intended, hinder more than they help.

A passionate God

Then comes an incentive for obedience, concluding the second or perhaps the first two commands (vv. 9–10). God is zealous or jealous —we think of these qualities as positive and negative respectively, but actually they come from the same Greek word (*zelos*). Translators struggle over which to use, because they are both partly right. Both words conveyed impassioned emotion. God is passionately concerned that we get this command right. He will punish those who ignore it, and the three or four generations who live together in the same household will suffer together. But he desperately wants the reverse, and promises to bless, virtually for ever (work it out, at roughly four generations per century). This isn't just an academic issue about a few images. It is vital to how Israel would relate to God—and equally vital for us.

REFLECTION

'If God made us in his image, we've certainly returned the compliment' (Voltaire). How do you visualize God?

WHAT'S *in a* NAME?

'O God!' or 'O my God!' How often have you heard these expressions in the last week? For many people, these words are an instinctive response to anything remotely interesting or unusual. They trip off the lips of colleagues and friends, and even small children, without a moment's hesitation. The names of God in general and of Christ in particular litter many a conversation. Blasphemy has become a way of life. Is this what the third commandment prohibits?

Yahweh's name in ancient Israel

Yahweh's name symbolized his powerful presence with his people. It was often used properly in worship—the Hebrew word Hallelujah (*hallelu-yah*) means simply 'praise Yahweh'. It was also used in blessing, both formally, as in the solemn priestly blessing ('Yahweh bless you and keep you...', Numbers 6:24–26), and informally, as in the delightful morning greetings by Boaz and his workers ('Yahweh be with you', 'Yahweh bless you', Ruth 2:4).

Swearing an oath in the name of one's gods was common in the ancient world. The gods were both witnesses and guarantors of the oath, and were entitled to enact punishment if the oath wasn't kept. The Old Testament has many references to swearing oaths 'in the name of Yahweh' or 'as Yahweh lives' or simply 'by Yahweh'. For various examples, see Judges 21:7; 1 Samuel 14:39; 20:42. Another more elaborate form was the self-curse, that is, promising to harm oneself, and illustrating this graphically, if the oath was broken: 'May God/Yahweh do this to me, and also this, if I...' (see 2 Samuel 3:35). We are left to imagine the gestures! Some versions, like the NIV, make the intent clear by paraphrasing the oath as 'May God/Yahweh deal with me, be it ever so severely, if I...'

However, Yahweh's name could also be used 'in vain' or 'wrongly'. The Hebrew word (*shav*) conveys both emptiness and sinfulness, and both these ideas apply to misuse of God's name. Worship could be addressed nominally to Yahweh and yet become a mere formality, divorced from any sense of real devotion or righteous living. Prophets repeatedly condemned this, from one of the first (Isaiah 1:10–17) to the last (Malachi 1:6, 13). And worship could also become corrupt, with Baal and others joining or replacing Yahweh in Israel's worship (Hosea 2:13). One could use Yahweh's name very fervently in sacrifice and worship, yet all the time be misusing it.

Similarly, oaths taken in God's name could be rash and foolish, for example, those of the Israelites (in Judges 21:1) and of Saul (in 1 Samuel 14:44–45). They could also be deceitful and malicious, as is often noted and condemned (see Psalm 24:4; Jeremiah 5:2). God's name was not simply a lucky charm, to be used regardless of intent or, worse still, as a cover for evil purposes.

Yahweh's name in later Judaism

During the intertestamental period, pious Jews came to believe that it was better not even to pronounce the name 'Yahweh', for fear of breaking the third commandment. Instead, whenever they saw it in their sacred scriptures, they would say the word 'Lord' (*adonay*). At first, Hebrew was written with consonants only. Later, when vowels were added, the name *yhwh* was written in a peculiar way, with the vowels of *adonay*, to remind them to say the latter rather than the former. This hybrid term was then written as *yehowah* (the first *a* changing to *e* for technical reasons). Medieval Christian scholars didn't fully understand what had happened, and translated the hybrid word as 'Jehovah', which then entered the Authorized (King James) Version and some traditional Christian hymns.

God's name today

How does all this apply to Christians today? Well, for a start, we can avoid blasphemy by not using God's name in casual conversation. When surrounded by others who constantly swear, this itself is often a telling witness to faith. But there is much more. Jews in Jesus' time avoided God's name, yet Jesus criticized them for splitting hairs in the way they swore oaths, and he committed his followers to plain speaking and transparent truthfulness: 'Let your "Yes" be "Yes"...' (Matthew 5:33–37). That too should characterize our lives. Further, worship can be full of God's name and yet misuse it terribly. So in both religious and secular life, in church and community, this commandment is ever relevant.

REFLECTION

'Hallowed be your name.'

SATURDAYS & SUNDAYS

The seven-day week is so embedded in Western culture that it is hard to imagine life without it. Large-scale experiments to change it, like one Russian attempt to impose a ten-day week, have failed miserably. And small-scale work patterns that ignore it leave many people completely disorientated. From its beginnings in a small, politically insignificant corner of the Middle East several millennia ago, the seven-day week has become a worldwide institution.

Holy rest

There are several fascinating aspects to this fourth commandment. Everyone must work for six days—and subsistence on small primitive farms was certainly hard work—but the seventh day is a Sabbath, literally a 'rest' day. And the day is made holy simply by resting! Almost everywhere else in the Old Testament, holiness involves purification, sacrifice, priests, and ritual—in other words, elaborate ceremony and significant expense. Yet here the day is made holy without any procedure, indeed without any activity at all. Holiness through doing nothing. Why?

The reason given in verse 15 is that God rescued them from slavery in Egypt. (This is the main difference between the two versions of the Ten Commandments: see Exodus 20:11). Slaves have no rest, no day off, no chance to recuperate, no opportunity to enjoy life. God had rescued Israel from this. They should never return to such conditions themselves, or oblige others to do so. A frequent, regular day off would constantly remind them of their deliverance. Any personal experience of work without respite or a moment's thought will immediately make us realize how important this is.

There was also the aspect of discipline. After days of rain, farmers in Israel, as anywhere else, would desperately want to get out to the fields. If the first good day fell on the Sabbath, however, they would have to show their faith in God and wait another day. Resting was truly honouring God, making the day special, or holy.

The Sabbath day wasn't marked by religious gatherings. Most Israelites lived far too far from the temple, and there were no other legitimate places of worship. Sabbath-keeping was a family affair, and synagogue services only developed much later. Even today, the Jewish Sabbath is mostly a family custom, revolving round a meal with special Sabbath candles and prayers. You don't need to go to a meeting or a service to be holy.

Rest for all

The Sabbath had a very important social dimension. In most societies, those at the top of the pile have plenty of leisure and those at the bottom have none. Not so in Israel: everyone had the seventh day off—children, slaves, animals, foreigners, but especially slaves, who are mentioned twice (another small difference in comparison with Exodus 20:10). 'Slaves' in Israel were more like bonded servants than slaves as we think of the term (see comments on Deuteronomy 15:12–18, pp. 118–119). The Israelites had been real slaves once, under a repressive regime. They should never impose the same helplessness and hopelessness on others. Whatever their precise status, slaves/servants in Israel were entitled to dignity and respect, and a weekly day off.

A Christian Sabbath?

The early Christians met instead on the first day of the week, the day of Christ's resurrection (Acts 20:7). But this wasn't simply a 'Christian Sabbath'. Paul writes explicitly to mixed congregations of Jewish and Gentile Christians that those who want to observe special days may do so, but no one is obliged to (Colossians 2:16). For Christians, all days are alike. Nowhere does the New Testament apply the Sabbath to Christians, so we keep Sunday more for celebration than for rest.

Nevertheless, one day's rest each week for everyone is still an important social principle. Everyone, from the managing director to the floor sweeper, should have a day off. The time when almost everyone could have it on the same day of the week is probably now gone for ever, despite the many advantages for family life, but the principle of a day off needs to be maintained for the good of everyone. God knows how we function best—and deserves the credit for it.

REFLECTION

As a voter, and as an employer or employee,
how can I encourage fair rest for everyone?

RESPECT!

We are rightly shocked when we hear stories of 'granny-dumping'—elderly, often senile parents abandoned at the doors of nursing homes with no means of identifying them or their callous offspring. We are also shocked when we hear of estates where many live in fear of youth gangs, and where those who dare to stand up to them are terrorized, driven out, sometimes even killed. Today's text directly addresses these situations—and more.

Honouring parents in Israel

In ancient Israel, as often in pre-modern societies, people lived in extended families of three or sometimes four generations. The 'father's house', as it was called, was the basic unit of society. It owned the land, raised the children and provided for all the family. The father of the house was one of the village elders who together regulated life in the community, settled its affairs and judged any disputes. After all, there were no social services, no schools and no police. Everything was provided literally 'in-house'.

In this context, honouring parents was vital in many ways. Children growing up learned a healthy respect for adults, who provided for them and taught them all about life and faith. Proverbs (see 1:8) has much about both mother and father teaching their children, and Deuteronomy (see 4:9) has much about passing on to them the great truths of faith. As children became adults and increasingly took over the hard agricultural work, they in turn were to provide for their parents and grandparents. This is beautifully illustrated in the way Naomi's first grandchild (Ruth's son) is described to her: 'He shall be to you... a nourisher of your old age' (Ruth 4:15). By contrast, any who neglected this provision condemned their parents to poverty and perhaps even starvation.

Further, honouring parents was more than a private, family matter. It affected all of social and community life. Since parents were also educators, and fathers were local elders and judges, they fulfilled an important role in society. Disrespect for them amounted to cocking a snook at all authority and therefore, since such authority was divinely ordained, at God himself. This helps to explain the seemingly harsh death sentence on a rebellious son (21:18–21). His own parents describe him as 'stubborn and rebellious… a glutton and a drunkard' and God condemns his activity as 'evil'. Whatever we think of capital punishment today, we must acknowledge the effect of disrespect in Israel, both in its immediate material effect on the impoverished parents and its wider corrosive effect on society.

The fourth and fifth commandments stand out as the two which are expressed positively. (The others would, of course, have a positive effect, but they are framed negatively: 'Do not…') These two appear together elsewhere (Leviticus 19:3), showing that they were seen as a pair. Honouring God week in week out by keeping the Sabbath, and honouring parents day in day out, would lead to a happy, healthy and prosperous society.

Honouring parents today

Society now is very different. We live mostly in nuclear families, at least until children leave home. The nuclear family has many variations, with same-sex parents, single-parent families and two-home children. And we have social services, schools and police, which we pay for through substantial taxes.

This commandment transfers to today in different ways. We should certainly give our parents respect, and care for them as they have cared for us. How that care is provided may differ, but it is still primarily our duty, not that of society at large. And we should encourage the state through its tax laws and benefit provisions actively to support those who look after elderly parents at home. It makes sense economically as well as socially.

We should also do all we can to foster respect for authority at different levels, and to ensure that this authority is worthy of respect. This, of course, is a huge order, and in today's climate is often counter-cultural. But we can each start where we are. An important feature of the commandments is that they put the onus on individuals, each in their own home and village. We too, in our own homes and communities, can foster respect and harmony.

REFLECTION
Jesus condemned those who used religion as an excuse
for not providing for parents (Mark 7:11–13).
What excuses do we use today?

MURDER MOST FOUL!

Before the 2003 American and British invasion of Iraq, huge anti-war rallies occurred in cities across the world. Among the many placards, there often featured the words 'Thou shalt not kill', the sixth commandment in its traditional rendering. Similarly, protests staged before the execution of murderers in the USA often feature banners with the same blunt message. God forbids the taking of life. And yet other laws in the Old Testament prescribe capital punishment, and Israel's history is full of wars, often apparently instigated by God himself. Surely God should practise what he preaches!

Do not *murder*

The English language has many terms for taking human life: kill, murder, slay, slaughter, execute, put to death, not to mention the many euphemisms and slang words. Hebrew also has several terms. There are two common words for 'kill' (*harag, hemit*), which cover the whole range of meanings. Then there's a third term (*ratsach*), the one used here, which covers all *unlawful* or unauthorized killing. It includes both intentional killing, which we call murder, and unintentional, which we call manslaughter and often describe as 'without malice aforethought'. For the latter, ancient Israel had the special arrangement of cities of refuge, which recognized both that a crime had been committed and that it was unintentional (see 4:41–43; 19:1–13). The sixth commandment refers to unlawful killing, but by its very nature a command can only address what is intended. Therefore it specifically envisages *intended, unlawful killing*, that is, murder, and should be translated: 'Do not murder.'

So the first point to note is that this commandment does not address the issues of war and capital punishment. Whatever we as Christians think of these difficult and thorny issues—and both are addressed elsewhere in Deuteronomy—we have to acknowledge that both are seen as lawful and legitimate in the Old Testament. We cannot use the sixth commandment as an argument against them.

Do *not* murder

Most societies prohibit murder—indeed, we see this as one mark of a civilized society. However, much depends on what is defined as 'unlawful'. Primitive tribes, urban gangs and terrorist groups see only their own people as protected. Everyone else is a legitimate target. The Old Testament has a much broader and deeper perspective: men and women are created in the image of God (Genesis 1:26–27), and God himself will 'require a reckoning' from everyone who takes human life (Genesis 9:5–6). Human life is God-given and God-protected. God gives life but he can also take it away again, as he did momentously in the flood. The Bible never talks of the 'sanctity' of life, as if life in and of itself is sacred and must never be taken. No, life is a gift from God, and respect for it is part of our respect for him.

The texts just cited come from Genesis and deal with Israel's basic understanding of humanity long before its division into different nations. Therefore they apply to all humanity, both within the nation and beyond. Foreigners who come to reside in Israel should be treated equally, since they come under Israel's legal protection. And the rich cannot escape punishment for murder by paying off the victim's family (with the single exception of wilful negligence with a goring ox: Exodus 21:29–30). This could happen elsewhere—for example, among the Hittites (*ANET*, 188–97)—but not in Israel. 'Murder most foul' is a phrase we connect with Victorian melodramas or modern board games. But in God's eyes, murder is always 'most foul'.

Do not even *think* of murder

The Old Testament presents life at its best and its worst, including, sadly, many murders. From Cain's murder of Abel to David's of Uriah, to the psalmists' pleas for deliverance, to the prophets' condemnation of anarchy, we see the results of human sinfulness all too clearly. But we also see the motives: Cain's jealousy (Genesis 4), David's lust (2 Samuel 12), general greed (Proverbs 1:10–19) and personal hatred (Leviticus 19:17–18). As Samuel was reminded in a different but equally important context, 'Yahweh looks on the heart' (1 Samuel 16:7).

REFLECTION

'You have heard… "You shall not murder"… But I say to you that if you are angry with a brother or sister, you will be liable to judgment… First be reconciled…' (Matthew 5:21–26).

JUST *a* BIT *of* FUN?

Just a fling, an affair, a one-night stand, a harmless bit of fun—our many off-hand terms for sex outside marriage reveal how common it is in today's culture. Casual sex, sex without commitment, is widely accepted in our society. Sexual attraction is used to sell anything: cars, furniture, holidays, double glazing—you name it, sex sells it. Sexual innuendos and blatant references are plastered every day across newspaper stands. Sex invades TV, from Saturday morning teenager shows to midday talk shows to evening soaps to late-night soft porn films. Sex is great, sex is fun—what's the problem?

Sex has always been a hugely powerful human drive. Evolutionists see this as necessary for the survival of the species. The Bible goes much further: it is one of God's great gifts, cementing and maintaining a lifelong relationship of companionship (Genesis 2:23). The Song of Solomon revels in sexual attraction and fulfilment. Sex in this context is good and wholesome, indeed vital, but sex elsewhere is tainted and destructive.

Adultery then

Daily life in Israel three thousand years ago was very different from life in the developed world today. Yet men and women then were just like us now. They had the same physical urge for sex, the same psychological desire for happiness and security. Their social context may have been very different, but we must be careful not to ignore the essential similarities, and therefore the essential relevance of their God-given sexual boundaries.

The importance of these boundaries is seen in the number and the extent of Old Testament passages dealing with them. Leviticus (18:6–18) contains the famous list of 'forbidden degrees' of marriage, stating who may not be married, traditionally accepted by Christendom and printed in old editions of the Church of England's Book of Common Prayer. Deuteronomy (22:13–30) legislates for various cases of adultery and premarital sex, whether suspected or proven, and we will consider these in due course. Fundamental to all this legislation was the belief that sex outside marriage was wrong, and merited serious punishment. Whatever its short-term attraction, adultery challenged the stability of the extended family by diluting its coherence, it undermined its economic viability by questioning the paternity of children, and it led to further human misery. In God's eyes, it was simply wrong.

The historical books give one notable example of the tragedy that adultery can breed. David's lust for Bathsheba led not just to the murder of her husband and of other troops (2 Samuel 11:17), terrible in itself. It was the backdrop to the following sorry chapters (2 Samuel 13—20): one son rapes his half-sister; Absalom kills him, flees, returns, foments a rebellion which nearly succeeds; another rebellion follows. The story of David, so positive until then, becomes a sad tale of one disaster after another, and it all hinges on an uncontrolled desire for sexual gratification. We may think it will not have such serious consequences for us and our families, but this story remains a stark warning.

Adultery now

There are many undeniable differences in today's society. The extended family is not central to our economy; we have much more leisure time and much higher expectations of personal fulfilment. Most notably, contraception enables sex without conception, and abortion provides a 'safety-net'. So sex without commitment, whether we're single or married, is very tempting.

But it remains wrong. God's original purpose of sex within lifelong commitments is upheld by Jesus and his apostles, however their comments on divorce are interpreted. Sexual sin has sometimes been singled out in Christian tradition and stigmatized as the worst of crimes, which distorts the biblical picture of all sin as insidious and harmful. But we can be tempted to react by going to the other extreme and downplaying its importance, ignoring Paul's comment that there is one crucial difference (see 1 Corinthians 6:18–20). As Christians, our attitude to adulterers needs the same mixture of compassion and firmness as that of Jesus (John 8:11)—never easy in the complicated web of emotions and relationships. But our text reminds us forcibly that adultery remains wrong in God's eyes.

REFLECTION

'I say to you that everyone who looks… with lust has already committed adultery in their heart' (Matthew 5:28).

WHAT'S YOURS IS MINE?

Looting in Baghdad in the aftermath of the invasion of Iraq—one day
the TV news was full of it. Desks, computers, food—people were
carrying away anything they could get their hands on. Even medical
equipment and dentists' chairs were swept off in the frenzy of looting.
That very evening there was a programme on theft in central London,
with gangs of thieves preying on unsuspecting tourists, and in turn
being tailed and caught by police. At the same time, the news was full
of the trio who tried to cheat their way to a million pounds in a
famous quiz show. We may have some sympathy with the Iraqi
people, denied so much for so long. We have none at all for cheats
and criminal gangs. And yet, in different ways, they are all stealing.

Is it serious?

Stealing was strongly condemned in Israel's law—but not just there.
Other writers give us many glimpses of its insidious effects. Hosea
lists it in his catalogue of the broken commandments and the breakdown of Israelite society summarized as 'no knowledge of God in
the land' (Hosea 4:1–2). His contemporary, Isaiah, describes thieving
Judah as no better than the proverbially iniquitous Sodom and
Gomorrah (Isaiah 1:10, 23). A century later, Jeremiah echoes Hosea
in his condemnation of Judah as breaking all the commandments and
turning the temple into a house of robbers (Jeremiah 7:9–11). The
Psalms are full of protests against enemies who steal and oppress.
And Proverbs, with its kaleidoscope of faith in action, equates stealing with profaning God's name (Proverbs 30:9).

Many societies have had differing penalties against theft according
to social status. Thus among Israel's neighbours in Mesopotamia,
penalties differed significantly according to whether you were noble-
man, commoner or slave. In medieval Britain and Europe, serfs and
peasants were put to death for killing animals for food or felling trees
for fuel just to survive—what we would consider minor, even justifi-
able, offences.

The Old Testament has none of this. Theft of property in Israel
was never punished by death. Life mattered far more. Further, if you
caught a robber in action and killed him, you yourself were guilty

of manslaughter, if not murder—unless it happened in the dark, when you could plead self-defence (Exodus 22:2–3). Property was important and must not be stolen, but people were always more important, and the two could not be interchanged.

We have already seen some ways in which Deuteronomy stresses generosity. Various passages later on allow strangers to eat grapes or crops as they walk through fields. It's not stealing, as long as they don't take the produce with them. So goods and property are never given special sanctity, but they are still personally owned, and not to be stolen.

Is it kidnapping?

The Ten Commandments do not themselves prescribe punishment. However, we know from elsewhere that breaking any of the commandments discussed so far merited the death penalty. Some scholars therefore suggest that all ten originally carried the death penalty, and that the eighth actually referred to stealing people, kidnapping them to sell them as slaves. This dastardly act, well-known in the ancient world, and sadly still in parts of ours, certainly did merit the death penalty (Exodus 21:16). According to Amos, God would punish even a non-Israelite nation for it (Amos 1:6). However, it is not necessary to read 'steal' here as meaning 'kidnap'. The Ten Commandments don't just deal with the so-called worst crimes. They deal with all types of activity that undermine godly, just society. Stealing is not a capital offence (except for kidnap)—but it is still serious.

Do not steal!

This commandment is simple, straightforward, categorical. There are many ways we can justify taking what is not rightfully ours, and there are some grey areas. But most of us are far too keen to exploit the grey areas and to fudge the clear ones. Today's text doesn't really need explanation—it needs obedience!

PRAYER

Lord, in our materialist and self-centred culture,
help me to resist all temptation to steal.

The TRUTH, the WHOLE TRUTH & NOTHING but the TRUTH

What is the basis of a good society? Philosophers, political analysts, thoughtful people from all walks of life have often reflected on this fundamental issue. Of course there are many aspects to it, and much depends on the definition of 'good'. But two things are crucial: good laws, and their fair enactment. It's no good having one without the other. Even the best legal framework can become ineffective, for many reasons: imbalance of priorities, over-complication, neglect, corruption or sheer expense. Yet one of the most basic reasons is deceit. The fairest system in the world depends on human truthfulness to be effective. God had given his people a complete set of laws and instructions, but they would not work without truthfulness.

No false witness

The ninth commandment addresses this, by insisting on honesty. The phrase 'bear false witness' implies legal proceedings. They normally took place in the open space just inside the town gate, where the elders would gather and conduct the local affairs. This gathering may have been less formal than a modern courtroom, but it was no less important. Whether accusing someone else or defending yourself against such accusation, the requirement of honesty was fundamental. To break it would in many cases involve also breaking the third commandment, since many a declaration would have been sworn in Yahweh's name. Just as importantly, it could have dire consequences on others.

Ancient Israel had no police. Every community had to govern itself from its own resources. There was no independent force to check things out, take fingerprints, send for DNA analysis or whatever. It was often simply your word against that of others. Obviously in such cases character and general trustworthiness would be taken into account. But utter truthfulness remained paramount.

There were several safeguards built into Old Testament law, spelled out later in Deuteronomy. First, there must be more than one witness. This applied not just to capital crimes (17:6) but also to 'any offence' (19:15). Second, if someone was convicted of a capital offence, the accusers had to be the first to throw the stones. In other words, they had to be so sure that they were prepared to inflict the punishment. And third, false accusation was so serious that those convicted of it had to pay the same penalty that they tried to inflict by their false accusation (19:16–21).

A dastardly example of false witness is that concerning Naboth's vineyard, in 1 Kings 21. Ahab wanted it, Naboth said no, and Ahab went home and sulked. Incidentally, this shows that, for all his faults, Ahab accepted that the Israelite king did not have absolute power. Then his wife Jezebel, who came from Phoenicia where there was no concept of covenant law, took over. She accused Ahab of being a wimp, set up false witnesses, had Naboth and his sons executed, and presented his vineyard to Ahab. No wonder Elijah was incensed!

Like king, like people. By the following century, the prophets were roundly condemning that unholy trio of injustice, callousness and religious arrogance. Micah (6:8) phrased it memorably: 'What does Yahweh require of you but to do justice, and to love kindness, and to walk humbly with your God?' His contemporaries Amos, Hosea and Isaiah equally castigated Israel and Judah for frequent abuses of justice. False witness abounded, and the very basis of society was under severe threat.

Little white lies

Today, lying is increasingly part of society. From pretending a colleague is absent to doctoring the company's accounts, to vast corporate scandals, what matters to most people is not what you say but whether you're found out. How many legal cases would never come to court if people told the truth to begin with, or would be settled speedily if they told the truth in court? We excuse all these untruths with euphemisms like 'little white lies', but in reality, they are all big black lies.

However, there is an alternative. Jesus is the truth, who declares that the truth sets us free, and whose Spirit of truth will guide us in all truth (John 8:32; 14:6; 16:13). No wonder we are commanded to speak the truth (see Ephesians 4:25).

PRAYER

Lord, help me to be truthful, even when it hurts.

I WANT IT!

If you want it, you can have it. Just sign on the dotted line, have it now and pay later. Or simply take it: no one will stop you, you're not hurting anyone. To keep progressing, our capitalist society needs us to consume more and more products, not just the basics of food, clothing and housing, but all the many other things we think we need. And just in case we don't realize that we need them, we are constantly bombarded by subtle and pervasive advertising. Every time we read a newspaper or magazine or watch commercial TV, we are confronted by what we 'need'. The more we think we need, the more we desire. And the more we desire, the more we covet.

But we can't just blame pushy manufacturers and clever advertising agencies, which simply play to a basic human force. Desire in and of itself can be positive, motivating us to improve life for ourselves and others. The very words used in the tenth commandment occur elsewhere of legitimate desire: for example, God 'covets' his holy mountain (Psalm 68:16, literally), and the king 'desires' his bride's beauty (Psalm 45:11). But desiring what is not ours is clearly wrong.

Don't covet

This tenth commandment is significantly different from the others. The first nine commands prohibit specific actions, and whether you follow or break them is clear to everyone. But you can covet without anyone else knowing. It's a secret sin, a sin of the heart. And it can lead to breaking any of the others, as a moment's thought demonstrates. This shows again that the Ten Commandments are not a legal code which can easily be implemented. Rather, they summarize the most fundamental aspect of Israel's life and faith. Like the great commandment to love one's neighbour (Leviticus 19:18), and like many passages in Deuteronomy 4—11, they appeal to the heart and inner motivation as well as to outward acts.

The word 'covet' can also by extension mean 'take', as when God reassures Israelites that if they travel to the annual festivals, other people won't 'covet' their land (Exodus 34:24). Some interpreters from early Judaism onwards have argued that the tenth commandment therefore prohibits stealing in general (while the eighth prohibits kidnapping). However, this unusual meaning is unlikely in a fundamental section like the Ten Commandments, and this interpretation loses the deeper, more incisive character of the commandment.

This commandment has two slightly different forms. In Exodus it first mentions 'house' in the sense of 'household' (as often in Hebrew), and then spells out the meaning in terms of wife, servants, animals and anything else. In Deuteronomy it first mentions 'wife', and then lists house (home), fields, servants, and so on. This is another difference (as in v. 15) which shows that the commandments were a living tradition, acquiring slightly different forms as they were handed down.

More importantly, the command is even more extensive than it appears in our translations. Reference to one's neighbour sounds rather limiting, especially when many of us have minimal contact with our neighbours. Actually, the word 'neighbour' is idiomatic Hebrew for 'anyone else'. And to remove any doubt, Jesus' famous parable of the good Samaritan shows that there are no social, ethnic or religious barriers to neighbourliness (Luke 10:29–37).

Be grateful

The tenth commandment may seem the least serious in our estimation, but it is actually the hardest to keep. When the rich young ruler claimed to have kept all the commandments since his youth, Jesus didn't reject his claim. By telling him to sell his possessions, however, he highlighted the man's desire to own things, to acquire (Matthew 19:16–22). It's not exactly the same as coveting, but one so often leads to the other. Elsewhere, Jesus tells us bluntly that we cannot serve God and money (Matthew 6:24). Paul goes so far as to call greed 'idolatry' (Ephesians 5:5; Colossians 3:5).

How do we avoid coveting? The key is surely gratitude. Deuteronomy constantly exhorts Israelites to be grateful to Yahweh for all he has done for them. The New Testament reminds us of all God has done for us in Christ. And Christians down the centuries have learnt to be content with their lot, and use their energies for the benefit of others rather than themselves.

REFLECTION

'Godliness with contentment is great gain' (1 Timothy 6:6, NIV).
Am I content with what I have?

LEADERSHIP

We're fascinated by our leaders. We listen to their speeches, we read their biographies, we discuss their policies, we analyse their strategies, we tell them when we disagree. Leaders of the past are just as fascinating, and history programmes have never been so popular on TV. Even though school and university syllabi have broadened out from their previous concentration on kings and queens, it's still the leaders who capture the popular imagination.

The Bible contains many lessons on leadership, both explicit and implicit. From Moses onwards, we see Joshua, judges, kings, prophets and priests all exercising leadership in different ways and with mixed results. In the New Testament, we note Peter, Paul, other apostles, elders and deacons all as leaders. There have been, of course, many changes between Israel and the church, notably that the church is not a political entity, and all Christians now have God's Spirit in them, so some aspects of Old Testament leadership no longer apply today. Nevertheless, there is much we can still learn.

Opportunity knocks

After presenting the Ten Commandments, which we paused to consider in detail, Deuteronomy now resumes the narrative of those momentous events at Mount Horeb. The events were truly awesome: remember the summary in 4:11–12 (and the fuller description in Exodus 19). No wonder the people were afraid. They heard God speaking, though whether they could make out the words or whether they needed Moses to interpret them is not entirely clear. Moses certainly had a closer experience of God, as he had done previously at the burning bush (Exodus 3), and was his spokesman. But the people now realized that such an experience was survivable: 'Today we have seen that God may speak to someone and the person may still live' (v. 24). They may have been thinking initially of Moses here, but the Hebrew phrasing clearly indicates anybody. The old adage that to see God meant certain death was not absolute. God wanted close communion with his people, and even wanted to appear to them at special moments, as this incident illustrates.

God's desire is made clear in the second paragraph: 'If only they had such a mind as this...' (v. 29). If only, indeed—then it would really go well for them. All the promises of blessing so constantly repeated in Deuteronomy would come true. God really meant it. Before we criticize Israel for not seizing this opportunity, we need to ask ourselves how keen we are to get to know God better. Do we have 'such a mind as this'?

You go yourself!

The Israelites had a choice. They could be bold, adventurous, courageous. They could go on to get to know God and his ways better, or they could push Moses forward and step back themselves. True to form, they chose to play safe. It would be too risky, too uncertain: 'why should we die?' So despite affirming that it is possible to see God and live, they shrank back in fear, and told Moses to do the risky bit: 'Go near, you yourself' (vv. 25–27).

And that's where real leadership comes to the fore. Leaders may plead, argue, persuade, cajole all they wish, but at certain points their people may not agree. Then it's up to them. This is still true in the Christian church. As Christians, we know more of God than our Jewish forbears did, yet our knowledge is still very partial. Christian leaders do not have the same authoritative roles as Moses and other political leaders. In New Testament times, Paul was clearly a good team player, as the regular lists of colleagues and the affectionate greetings in his letters demonstrate. But at certain points he had to go it alone, to stand up for God's truth, such as in his showdown with Peter (Galatians 2:11) or his disciplining of some members at Corinth (2 Corinthians 7:8). Like Moses, he was prepared to exercise true leadership, however costly.

PRAYER

Pray for your church leaders, and give them your support.

FAITH *in a* NUTSHELL

Long sermons aren't fashionable any more. Two centuries ago, many Christians regularly sat through hour-long sermons, with numerous elaborate points and sub-points. How much they actually listened is another matter! Today few of us would have the patience to listen for so long. And of those who had patience, even fewer would have the ability, since we're so used to variety in communication, the multi-media presentation or constantly changing TV image. Moses gives a long and dense sermon in the next few chapters, beginning with phrases we've already met (6:1–3), and repeatedly exhorting his hearers and listeners to faith and obedience. So it's helpful that he starts with the most basic aspect of all—what we would call the bottom line.

Shema, yisra'el

Could you sum up your faith in ten words or less? Paul's phrase 'Jesus Christ is Lord' gives the essence of Christianity. The Muslim creed is often summed up as 'There is no God but Allah, and Mohammed is his prophet'. For Jews it is 'Hear, O Israel: the Lord is our God, the Lord alone' (v. 4). This is commonly called the 'Shema' (pronounced *sh'mah*, the Hebrew word for 'hear'). For several millennia, pious Jews have recited it every morning and evening. Children should learn these as their first words, and the dying should repeat them as their last. This is the bottom line of Jewish faith.

Interestingly, there are different views as to what exactly the Shema means. Of the six words in Hebrew, the first two are straightforward: 'Hear, Israel'. The remaining four words are 'Yahweh, our-God, Yahweh, one'—although, as we have seen, Jews never pronounce the name Yahweh and use 'the Lord' (or something else) instead. These four words do not include a verb, so can be fitted together differently. The phrase is sometimes translated as 'The Lord is our God, the Lord is one'—two brief statements about Yahweh. The first stresses his relationship to Israel, the second his nature. However, the second of these statements would only have been relevant after Christians started describing God as Trinity, thus affirming the different Jewish view of God. It would not have been particularly meaningful in the ancient world. Hence many people think that the original meaning of the phrase was 'Yahweh is God, Yahweh *alone*'. The word 'one' sometimes means 'one and only', 'alone'. What God commands in the very first commandment, his people now repeat in a credal statement. They have only one God, Yahweh, to whom they give sole allegiance.

To us this may seem inconsequential. In the ancient polytheistic world, it was revolutionary. Every nation had its major gods and a host of minor ones. In the 14th century BC, the Egyptian Pharaoh Akhenaten tried to replace the plethora of Egyptian deities with the single Sun-God, worshipped in an austere non-moral religion. As soon as he died, however, his more famous son Tutankhamun and the Egyptian officials put everything back to normal. In Israel, there was a constant temptation to worship other gods, as the prophets repeatedly condemn, and as some archaeological finds now confirm. For Israel, there should only ever be one God, their God Yahweh. This was the bottom line.

Love and devotion

But faith needs action. The Shema is followed by the equally famous command to love God with heart, soul and might (v. 5), a command cited in the New Testament as the first great commandment (Matthew 22:37). Love of God demands all our devotion, all our being, all our energy. We note that here, as so often, fear (v. 2) and love (v. 5) are brought together not as opposites but as complementary aspects of the same attitude to God.

How do you love God? The following chapters spell this out for Israel, but already here we note the other verbs used: observe diligently (v. 3), keep (v. 6), recite/talk (v. 7), bind/write (vv. 8–9). It should be a constant preoccupation, inculcated in children and constantly before their eyes. Verses 8–9 are still often taken literally, with these and other key verses kept in little boxes bound to the forehead (in *tefillin*), or attached to doorframes (in a *mezuzah*). We may not see the need to take this command literally, but we should take it equally seriously. After all, Jesus endorsed it, and enabled us to love God by demonstrating a similar love for us.

REFLECTION

What would I like my last words to be?

DON'T FORGET

There is a pattern which has been sadly repeated down through the Christian centuries. People are convicted of sin and cry out to God in repentance. He graciously responds, and brings them to faith. They start living new lives, working hard and wasting less. Their improved lifestyle gradually leads to self-sufficiency and complacency. And God gradually becomes less important to them and their families. The reformers were aware of this tension. Later, John Wesley expressed his fear that it would recur after the great 18th-century revival of faith in Britain. In the 20th-century West, a new dimension emerged: as people became better off, they moved up-market, leaving rundown communities with little or no Christian witness, no 'salt and light', and these areas simply deteriorated further.

How do we remain faithful when we experience God's blessing? Our passage gives three important guidelines, which are then spelled out at greater length in the following chapters.

Remember

God's gift of a promised land to Israel is a constant theme of Deuteronomy, and here for the first time some details of the gift are described. It will not just have fields for crops and land for homes. There will also be ready-built cities, houses, water cisterns, vineyards and olive groves. Israel would not have the back-breaking work of starting everything from scratch. We can easily imagine the advantage of ready-made cities and houses, but the other things mentioned are no less important. Water cisterns are vital when rain only falls half the year. New vineyards and olive groves, unlike crops, take years to produce fruit. So having these things already provided would be a huge advantage.

God is all too aware of the common human tendency to become complacent, yet he remains generous, and still gives Israel these good gifts. However, they come with a divine health warning: 'don't forget' (v. 12). He delivered them from slavery in Egypt for service (or 'slavery', the same word in Hebrew) of himself. They must fear him, swear allegiance to him only, ignore all potential rivals. If not, the warning is clear (v. 15).

For Israel, the constant temptation was to follow other gods, thus breaking the first commandment. For us, the constant temptation is to construct a different, less demanding picture of God, thus breaking the second commandment. To us, God equally says, 'Don't forget.' The New Testament epistles constantly remind us of what God has done for us in Christ, as a spur to renewed commitment.

Trust

No sooner had the Israelites left Egypt, following all God's 'signs and wonders' (v. 22), and before they even reached Mount Horeb, than they were quarrelling with Moses and testing God concerning water. The place where this happened became known as 'Testing and Quarrelling' (Massah and Meribah, Exodus 17:1–7), and the incident became proverbial for lack of trust. Many an Israelite later sang, from the Psalms, and many a Christian has since repeated in liturgy, 'Do not harden your hearts, as at Meribah, as on the day at Massah in the wilderness, when your ancestors tested me' (Psalm 95:8–9).

Here in Deuteronomy the lack of trust is spelt out as a consequence of immediately forgetting God and his deeds. By the time they had conquered Palestine with all its cities, they would have even more reason to trust God, and even less to test him. As Christians, knowing God in Christ and through his Spirit, we have all the more reason to trust him. Yet this is our temptation too.

Recite

A third exhortation (vv. 20–25) is to repeat constantly what God had done, to each successive generation. The wording is formulaic, with its pithy summary and sonorous phrases. It is interesting to note these 'mini-creeds' elsewhere as well—for example, 26:5–9. Indeed, some scholars see them as the kernel around which the book of Deuteronomy developed. Whether this is a valid deduction or not, they are certainly key summaries, doubtless often repeated.

Christians too have their pithy summaries of the faith, both in key scripture texts and in the famous creeds. They too should be often repeated, and often pondered. This won't guarantee faithfulness, but it should help to promote it.

REFLECTION

'The lure of wealth chokes the word, and it yields nothing'
(Matthew 13:22).

GOD'S ETHNIC CLEANSING?

We have always known that war is terrible. But now, with increasingly realistic documentaries of past wars, and TV cameras everywhere in current conflicts, there is no escaping the fact. In some ways, we have become more 'civilized'. We have the Geneva Conventions, which try to reduce barbarity and protect non-combatants. We are appalled at the wholesale massacres in Rwanda, the Balkans and elsewhere. So when we turn to the Old Testament, and read that God himself ordered the massacre of complete peoples, we're aghast. How could God do it? Why? This issue, more than any other, has led many to reject the Old Testament, and some to reject the whole Bible. So how can we come to terms with this command?

The sacred ban

The first thing to notice is the terminology. This is not just any type of war. This is *herem*, variously translated as 'proscription', 'sacred ban' or 'devotion to destruction'. *Herem* was a well-known concept in the ancient world (see *ANET*, 320d). It involved a total, complete destruction of all life in devotion to one's god, and sometimes consecration of any precious metals to his temple. So it is a religious as well as military term. It is only used of Israel's early wars of conquest and consolidation, in Deuteronomy, Joshua and 1 Samuel. Once the land was firmly secure, warfare became simply defence.

Other passages seem to have a different emphasis. Exodus repeatedly notes that God will 'drive out' other peoples (Exodus 23:27–30; compare Deuteronomy 7:22), though whether by death or banishment is unspecified. Deuteronomy itself allows citizens of surrendering towns to live (20:10–11), and non-combatants of conquered towns to be spared (20:12–15), though this only applies to distant towns. Perhaps more importantly, the accounts of the actual conquest suggest only occasional application of the *herem*: at Jericho, Ai and some other resisting towns (Joshua 6:21; 8:25; 11:12). Other texts reveal that many Canaanites were spared, though admittedly this happened because of Israel's military weakness rather than any moral compunction (Judges 1:27–35). This attenuates the problem historically, but it doesn't resolve it theologically.

Why did God command it?

There are three key explanations. First, it was divine punishment on people for their sin, not their race: 'the iniquity of the Amorites' (Genesis 15:16) was now complete. Their abhorrent practices included sacrificing their very own children to appease the gods (12:31; 18:10). So they were to be punished for basic crimes against humanity, like the nations listed in Amos 1—2.

Several points show that *herem* was punishment for sin, not extermination of race. On the one hand, Canaanites who trusted in Israel's God were spared, like Rahab and her family (Joshua 2:11; 6:25). On the other, Israelites who fell into similar sin would meet equally severe punishment, like Achan and his family (Joshua 7:24–26), and any apostate Israelite town would also be subject to annihilation by *herem* (Deuteronomy 13:12–18). Of course, these texts reflect the group solidarity of ancient times, which we struggle to understand: all in a family or clan lived or died together.

Secondly, it was prevention for Israel from adopting pagan beliefs and practices (v. 3–4, see also 7:16). God knew how strong was the temptation to sin, and wanted to protect his people. Sadly, the incomplete conquest and the survival of many Canaanites led to exactly what God feared, as the book of Judges amply demonstrates. Even today, complete separation from temptation is sometimes the best way of avoiding sin.

Thirdly and most importantly, most of the Old Testament has no developed concept of life after death, so God's punishment of sin had to be seen in this life, if it was to be seen at all. The New Testament tells us more about judgment after death, both God's acquittal of those who believe and his punishment of those who do not. Here in Deuteronomy, divine judgment is equally certain and equally severe —it is just less visible to us. How God will ultimately judge those who have never had a chance to respond is for him to decide. But the Israelite experience of immediate judgment reminds us of the Christian doctrine of ultimate judgment.

PRAYER

Lord, have mercy on family, friends and neighbours who do not know you. Please lead them to acknowledge you in this life, before having to do so in the next.

DEMANDING LOVE

What is your picture of God? Sadly, many people see him as a harsh, autocratic, rather distant figure. This hardly does justice to all that we've seen of God's character so far in Deuteronomy, though admittedly the text up to now has focused more on his severe side. Now one word is striking: 'he will *love* you' (v. 13). God loves those he redeems.

This concept isn't new here—God's love for his people in the past has already been noted (4:37; 7:8). But here there is an ongoing, open-ended promise that God will continue to love them, as long as they remain faithful to him. He had bound himself by solemn oath to bring them into the promised land. Now he states that he will continue to keep his side of the covenant as long as they keep theirs. In fact, we know from later history that God frequently kept his side when Israel broke theirs, during the periods of the judges and kings. And God's love eventually led not just to temporary deliverers, like the judges, but to his Son as a once-for-all deliverer.

Prosperity gospel?

Verses 13–15 give a very physical picture of blessing, with abundant fertility of humans, animals and land. There would be no sterility, a constant problem in the patriarchal period, or illness. The 'dread diseases of Egypt' could refer either to the plagues they had recently experienced or to diseases in general: even in Roman times Egypt was associated with elephantiasis, ophthalmia and dysentery (Pliny, *Natural History*, 26:3, 4, 5, 8). Whatever their exact nature, God promised that these diseases wouldn't afflict the Israelites as long as they were obedient in the *herem* of the conquest and in life after that.

Some Christian groups use passages like this to preach that God will always bless his people, that we should expect blessing, and that if we're not experiencing it then something is wrong with our faith. But this is to assume that a provision under the old covenant necessarily applies in the new covenant, which is a major error in interpreting the Bible. In the Old Testament, God's blessing was generally shown in material ways, though even this could be withdrawn in special circumstances, as for Job. In the New Testament, God's blessing is shown by the gift of his Spirit, giving believers strength and joy whatever their circumstances, and by the promise of eternal life. The Israelites didn't know these forms of blessing, and we cannot assume that we will know theirs. They were promised prosperity for obedience, while we are given the gospel—the two are quite different.

Continuous faith

In Deuteronomy, however, that is all still in the future. In the meantime, there's the small matter of attacking well-defended towns with a motley army. So God anticipates and addresses Israelite concerns (vv. 17–24). First, there is a reminder of the past. God dealt resoundingly with the Egyptians, with 'signs and wonders' and with 'mighty hand and outstretched arm' (v. 19), two signature descriptions of the exodus. Accordingly, Israel can have confidence in their confrontation with future enemies. We too can learn, or relearn, this simple but vital lesson. As an old Christian chorus says, 'I'll praise him for all that is past, and trust him for all that's to come.'

Secondly, he will clear their path in stages, not all at once (v. 22). Israel would not have the resources to profit from immediate capture of all the land, and some of it would then revert to the wild. As amply illustrated by the conflicts in Afghanistan and Iraq, it is often easier to win the war than to win the peace.

Insidious idolatry

The chapter's main theme of rooting out Canaanites and their religion has also surfaced in this section, mentioned briefly but forcefully (v. 16), and then summarized even more powerfully at the end (vv. 25–26). The strong language used ('abhorrent… utterly detest… destruction') reminds us of the seriousness of idolatry and its threat to biblical faith. As Chris Wright comments (p. 119), it 'portrays a divine attitude towards idolatry that cannot be easily relativized or patronized with an allegedly more enlightened perspective'.

Israel's response was to destroy both the people and their idols. Ours today is to do neither, but we must never use this different response to conclude that unbelief or idolatry do not matter, or that God's attitude to those who worship images rather than the creator has changed (see Romans 1:23). God's love is not blind.

REFLECTION

What is your picture of God?

NO PAIN, NO GAIN

We all know the slogan, 'No pain, no gain', and the reality behind it. Whether it's pounding away in the gym to get fit, or forgoing our favourite nibbles to lose weight, or endlessly rehearsing a musical passage to get it right, we know that progress involves hard work and physical discomfort. But we still go through with it to achieve an end result. Sometimes we find that even unplanned and unwelcome hardship brings unexpected gain. In both cases, whether planned or not, we emerge the better for the experience.

Lessons from the past

Here in chapter 8, Moses continues addressing Israel on God's behalf, and draws lessons from the pain of the previous 40 years of wandering in the wilderness. Deuteronomy begins with an impatience to move on. It now pauses to reflect on this recent experience. God's purpose through it all was to humble his people, to teach them a vital lesson, to show their need to exercise faith. He tested their heart—and sadly they often failed the test, as the book of Numbers makes abundantly clear.

However, the emphasis here is not on their failure but on God's provision. Day by day he gave them manna, a completely new food, as a special sign of his care (v. 3). And they managed to survive with whatever clothes and footwear they had brought out of Egypt (v. 4). Later verses note protection from the many dangers of the 'great and terrible wilderness, an arid wasteland with poisonous snakes and scorpions', and also God's provision of food and water (v. 15–16). There has been much pain—but there has also been gain. They should now realize that God had been providing for their needs all along.

More than this, they should now see the need to live in dependence on 'every word that comes from the mouth of Yahweh' (v. 3). These words are well-known to us from Jesus' citing of them in his temptation, when he declares the need to see beyond the gift to the giver (Matthew 4:4). We too need to see beyond the pain of humbling experiences to the God who speaks to us through them.

Hope from failure

But wait a minute. Wasn't Israel's time in the wilderness a result of their own sin (1:34–35)? How, then, can God say that he did this to test them? Here we meet one of the rich paradoxes of biblical faith. Yes, Israel's faithlessness was the primary cause of their wilderness years. But God still used this period to teach them lessons. He could still work through the ongoing situation to bring about his purposes. And he could even transform it to give a better outcome.

A later example is the establishment of kingship. Israel wanted a monarchy because of their lack of faith, and Saul, the first king, was a tragic failure. But the institution was redeemed by David, who, despite many faults, retained his trust in God. What's more, David became the model for God's future work in the world through his own Son, Jesus. So a form of government which was requested for wrong reasons and which got off to a shaky start became transformed by God.

This has profound implications. Sometimes Christians think that if they make a decision with unhappy consequences—career, marriage, location—then they have sidelined themselves for ever. But the lesson from the wilderness, the monarchy, and many other passages, is quite the reverse. God can use such experiences to bring about his purposes, and to bring us closer to him.

Warning for the future

Israel was about to move on, to experience blessing in a new way, to have fine houses, food, land and cattle (vv. 12–13). Then what? From Moses to Amos, to Francis of Assisi, to John Wesley, and on to today, countless leaders have noted the danger of allowing God's material blessing to become a cause of pride and spiritual apathy. Here the danger is noted, and the response is clear. First there is a reminder of the source of prosperity: God's salvation, protection and ongoing covenant promises (vv. 14–18). Second, there is the solemn warning of the same dreadful fate as that meted out to the Canaanite nations: 'you shall surely perish' (v. 19). The warning is equally clear for us.

REFLECTION

Pain can bring gain, but gain can also bring pain.

DON'T BOAST!

Like any skilled communicator, Moses goes back over what he has just been saying, repeating and developing his points. In these next few verses he repeats both the promise of victory and the warning against pride, only this time the warning concerns pride in claiming that the victory would be due to their own virtue.

Fearsome foes

In an earlier chapter (7:1) the seven traditional inhabitants of Canaan were listed, 'mighty and more numerous than you'. Here a different group is mentioned, the legendary 'strong and tall' Anakim (v. 2), feared as the hardest foe that the Israelites might meet. But God's promise to cross over ahead of Israel as 'a devouring fire' (v. 3) and defeat their enemies is reasserted. Israel would even proceed quickly, as actually happened in the early stages of the conquest, according to Joshua 1—12. The consolidation would take much longer, and indeed it never fully occurred, as Judges records, but the early stage would be rapid. Fearsome foes were no problem to God.

Some have suggested that the tradition of tall Canaanites is a later embellishment of the story, rather like the size of the proverbial 'fish that got away'. However, several factors caution against assuming this. First, Deuteronomy only attributes great height to certain groups, not to all indigenous peoples indiscriminately. Thus the Anakim, Emim and Rephaim are described as tall (2:10, 20–21), whereas others are not (7:1). Similarly, later there were apparently giants among the Philistines, notably Goliath, but not among other local peoples. Second, the name 'Anakite' may well mean 'long-necked' or 'tall one'. Third, a 13th-century Egyptian papyrus mentions exceptionally tall Canaanites. The text reads, 'The narrow valley is dangerous with Bedouin, hidden under the bushes. Some of them are four or five cubits [7–8.5 ft] from their noses to the heel, and fierce of face. Their hearts are not mild, and they do not listen to wheedling' (*ANET*, 477d). So there are good grounds for accepting this description as accurate, and the Israelites' fear of these mighty warriors as genuine—but it still didn't show much faith.

Victory and virtue?

We have already noted the sinfulness of the Canaanites, and seen that the conquest was God's judgment on them. Now Moses warns Israel not to think of the conquest as due to their own righteousness. The rest of the chapter goes on to describe the most glaring incident of their unrighteousness, just to remind them of how fickle they have been in the recent past. But in the flush of rapid success, even if they knew it was God-given, it would be so easy to think of it as earned and deserved. So they are told bluntly, and twice (vv. 4–5), 'No way!'

In the last half-century, there have been many instances when powerful nations, not least Britain and America, have gone to war against what they saw as naked aggression or manifest evil. In many cases the description was accurate, as in Korea, the Falklands, Kuwait or Bosnia. In other places, the situation was less clear but there was certainly wickedness to confront, as in Somalia and Iraq. However, there is always the temptation in the propaganda war to assume a moral superiority and, especially when victorious, a triumphant jingoism. Even when the evil seems most obvious, the motives of the invading nations are inevitably mixed, and their own moral values less pure than they think. The warning here in Deuteronomy, not to assume that our victory implies our virtue, is as relevant now as then.

On a personal level, faith in God is such a tricky balance! We, like the Israelites, know that we have done nothing to earn God's mercy and grace. They had been liberated from Egypt without having to lift a finger, except in obedience to a few specific commands at the end. We have been given forgiveness, life and hope through Christ without doing more than confessing our sin and praying for mercy. Pride is insidious—watch it!

PRAYER

Lord, be merciful to me, a sinner.

An Appalling Outrage

Yesterday a friend recounted a terribly embarrassing incident that happened 40 years ago, the memory of which can still wake her up in a cold sweat. It has remained deeply etched in her mind. The incident that remained deeply etched in Moses' mind 40 years later, and must have woken him in many a cold sweat, was far more than embarrassing—it was the day Israel nearly self-destructed in an appalling outrage against God.

There are many ways to tell a story. A common one is to 'start at the very beginning', and proceed chronologically through to the end. The book of Exodus mostly does that in its account of events at Sinai. Another way is rearrange material thematically, recounting specific incidents as they illustrate each particular point you make. Deuteronomy takes the latter approach to the same events. Now, after lengthy exhortations to obedience, it comes to the outrageous disobedience shown in making the golden calf idol (see Exodus 32—34). Throughout, Deuteronomy retells Israel's recent history, sometimes out of chronological order, to illustrate its message.

Two extremes

It's hard to think of a greater contrast. On the one hand, Moses was having that most stupendous of all mountain-top experiences, communing directly with God and receiving his laws. No wonder he was oblivious to normal physical needs—and before we dismiss his 40 days without water as impossible, we should remember that it involved an exceptional man in extraordinary circumstances, and that certain mystics today undergo incredible endurance feats. As a climax to these momentous weeks, Moses received the two tablets of the law 'written with the finger of God' (v. 10), the very essence of his covenant law.

On the other hand, and at the same time, Israel was breaking the most fundamental aspect of this covenant law. They immediately questioned the very feature of their faith that made it distinct from all other ancient religions, and tried to make an image of God (v. 12). Exodus (32:17–25) notes further disturbing aspects, though the detail isn't absolutely clear—the calf idol may have represented gods other than Yahweh, and their idolatry led to revelry and perhaps immorality. But Deuteronomy concentrates on the religious apostasy.

Two reactions

There were two reactions to this crisis, and they were not what we might expect. We often focus on God's gracious forgiveness of sin, and might think that this would be immediately apparent. We know how easily we get frustrated with the failings of others, and might imagine Moses reacting similarly. Amazingly, both responded in quite opposite ways. God threatened to destroy his rebellious people, to 'blot out their name from under heaven' (v. 14)—exactly the same fate awaiting the Canaanites (7:24), and for the same reason. Further, he was so incensed that he threatened to abrogate not just the covenant with Israel, but the covenant with Abraham on which it was built, offering to start again with Moses.

Moses, by contrast, took immediate action: he broke the tablets, smashed the idol to smithereens, and then interceded at length for Israel. The last two elements are recounted in reverse order, clearly rearranged for dramatic effect. Again Moses spent 40 days in God's immediate presence, and again without food and water, though this time for very different reasons. He prayed constantly for the very survival of Israel, as recorded in the following verses (9:25–29). He also prayed for its high priest, his own brother, an aspect not recorded in Exodus. We'll look more closely at this intercession in the next section. Here we note and salute his incredible concern for others.

Two possible outcomes

Israel was on the very brink of catastrophe, and the outcome was uncertain. Knowing the end of the story, we perhaps fail to realize just how close they came to annihilation, under God's judgment. It is a sobering reminder of God's judgment, which still awaits those who refuse to turn to him in repentance and faith, a judgment affirmed repeatedly by Jesus. But it is also a reminder of God's grace extended to the undeserving.

REFLECTION

'Do not be deceived: God is not mocked…' (Galatians 6:7).

DON'T GIVE UP, GOD!

Increasingly we meet people who profess faith in God but have abandoned the church. They are happy to be followers of Jesus, but not part of a Christian community. They feel able to live out their faith as a personal matter, without sharing in the life and work of any congregation, whether traditional denomination or modern house church. Some of their reasons are cogent and perceptive. Often our churches are not the communities they should be, both in themselves and in relation to the wider world. It's not surprising, then, that many find it easier to give up formal church links and live out their faith by themselves.

If we are tempted to give up on God's people, how much more is God himself? Right from year one, his people were rebellious, as the golden calf incident tragically shows. And this rebelliousness was endemic, as shown by another four examples reeled off in quick succession (vv. 22–24; see Exodus 17; Numbers 11). God's New Testament people likewise had their failures and rows (see Acts 5:4; 15:39). Throughout history there have been notorious stains and constant blemishes on the church's reputation. As for today's Christians, it's not hard to list our many failings. So it's actually more surprising that God didn't give up long ago!

True, costly leadership

Leadership is relatively easy when things are going well. Whether in politics, business, sport or whatever, leading is straightforward when everyone is content, co-operating and succeeding. The mark of true leaders, however, is the way they act under pressure, when things begin to unravel and people become discontented. And the mark of great leaders is the instinct to put others before themselves.

Moses reacted instinctively here. He had no time to plot and plan. He dealt summarily with the idolatrous calf, burning it, grinding it to powder, and throwing the dust into the nearby stream (9:21). But just as important was the broken covenant, symbolized by the smashed tablets. Could this possibly be repaired? Could God ever restore relationships with such a sinful people? God was ready to wipe out people and priesthood (9:19–20). Could he be persuaded otherwise?

Moses didn't know, but he would try his utmost. Again he spent

40 days and nights without food and water (the least of his concerns, vv. 18, 25). This time it was less God speaking to him and more him pleading with God. Rather than accept God's tempting offer to start again (9:13), Moses focused all his attention and authority into interceding for Israel. Exodus 32:32 adds that he was even prepared to sacrifice himself for their sake. Moses certainly displayed true leadership.

Reasons for continuing

Moses gives three main reasons for God not to act as he had threatened. First (v. 26), God had already invested heavily in Israel. They were his very own people (literally, his 'inheritance'), whom he had redeemed (the word implies great cost), and had freed from Egypt with great power. This obviously appeals in human fashion to God's self-interest. But it also hints at the relationship he has begun to establish with the Israelites. Second (v. 27), God promised to his loyal 'servants' the patriarchs (on oath, see 9:5; 10:11) to give them an unlimited posterity, and Israel was the fulfilment of this promise (see conclusion of this section in 10:22). To wipe out Israel and to start again with Moses would go against it. Third (v. 28), God's own reputation was at stake. How the other nations would laugh at this God, who was either impotent to fulfil his often-trumpeted promise or too fickle to know what he wanted! Moses makes no attempt to minimize Israel's stubbornness, wickedness and sin (v. 27). Instead he stresses again that they are God's 'very own possession'.

And it worked. God changed his mind, at least as far as human perception and written record are concerned. It may have been caused as much by Moses' attitude as by his arguments, though the latter were repeated by later leaders, prophets and intercessors (for example, Joshua 7:9; Jeremiah 14:7), and are echoed in many post-biblical Jewish prayers. God changed his mind, because of one man's remarkable leadership. He didn't give up on Israel, because Moses didn't give up praying for them.

REFLECTION

Don't give up on God's people; pray for them instead!

37 DEUTERONOMY 10:1–11

PARDON

Advance hints

We often realize how a situation will turn out long before the outcome is formally announced or confirmed. Political initiatives are leaked in advance, miscarriages of justice become obvious before a final court ruling, state pardons are carefully negotiated in advance. And even if the general public is kept in the dark, relevant officials and inquisitive journalists realize what is happening.

Similarly, our passage implies what the outcome of Moses' intercession would be long before it is formally stated. Moses was to 'carve out two tablets' for the commandments, thus reinstating the covenant (v. 1). He was to make an ark to preserve them for the future, implying the covenant's permanence (v. 2). The Israelites in general and Aaron in particular survived the golden calf incident, and moved on in their travels (v. 6). High-priestly succession was secured, as was priestly service of the ark (vv. 6–8). Even successful entrance to the promised land is implied in the note that the Levites had no allotted territory (v. 9).

Formal announcement

But all the hints, leaks and preparation are of minor significance compared to the formal announcement. Reporters pore over the detail of the policy speech itself, TV cameras zoom in on the prisoners taking their first steps in freedom, experts interpret the unfolding detail to an enraptured audience.

The focal point of this passage remains verse 10: 'Yahweh listened to me [and] was unwilling to destroy you'. This is the word of pardon, of forgiveness, of complete absolution. It's not that the Israelites hadn't sinned, or that their sin was unimportant. They had, and it was extremely serious. But God was willing to forgive, and for life—and faith—to continue.

Many of us worship in churches that include confession of sin in weekly services. We repeat the words of liturgy or listen to a leader pray on our behalf, and we know that God promises forgiveness when we approach in true faith. But we still need formally to make our confession, and to receive his forgiveness.

Practical forgiveness

Divine forgiveness meant that Moses and Israel could start again. In verses 1–5, anticipating verse 10, Moses was to go ahead with setting up all the tangible signs of the covenant relationship: new tablets and the ark to contain them. Exodus gives full details of this gilded wooden box and its craftsman Bezalel (Exodus 25:10–22; 31:2), but Deuteronomy is simply concerned with its function and with Moses as its initiator. Other passages note that the ark symbolized God's presence (Exodus 25:22; Numbers 10:35), a fitting rebuff to the attempt to represent him with a golden calf, but Deuteronomy mentions the ark simply as the appropriate receptacle for the covenant tablets. The rich symbolism of these other passages is certainly important, but the point here is that God's covenant is re-established.

The next section, verses 6–9, jumps even further ahead, as recognized by the parentheses surrounding it in most modern versions. Aaron's death occurred at the end of the wilderness period, some 40 years after the renewal of the covenant (Numbers 33:38), and the place names reflect the final journey from the desert to the banks of the Jordan (see Numbers 33:31). Moses' audience would have known this well, so the reference here shows that Aaron did survive the near catastrophe. But it also hints that his death was an eventual punishment for his role in it, even if it is directly attributed to a later sin (Numbers 20:24; Deuteronomy 32:50). This section also notes succession and development in the priesthood, with Eleazar succeeding Aaron, and their tribe, the Levites, assuming wider responsibilities. Provision is made; continuity is assured. Forgiveness has been worked out in practice.

Many of us find forgiveness one of the hardest aspects of our faith to work out in practice. Whether at home or work, with family or neighbours, we often find it difficult. And we really struggle when someone hurts us or a loved one really deeply. Jesus exemplified forgiveness in his life and especially in his death. But already here God gives us a profound example.

PRAYER

'Forgive us our sins, as we forgive those who sin against us.'

38 DEUTERONOMY 10:12–22

The BOTTOM LINE

So what's the deal? What does it all boil down to? When all is said and done, what's the bottom line? Our text moves abruptly from narrating the golden calf incident back to its main theme of obedience, and straight into a summary. Indeed, the opening words seem to be an ancient equivalent of 'Conclusion'.

Fear and love

'So now, O Israel, what does Yahweh your God require of you?' (v. 12). Moses gives five quick-fire answers—fear, walk, love, serve and keep—which Wright likens to a harmonious five-note chord. We could summarize the answer even more briefly in two words: reverence and obedience. These are the hallmark of biblical faith throughout Old and New Testaments and beyond. Fear and love combine to form a healthy reverence. They are complementary attitudes, not opposites, in relating to the God who had revealed himself so awesomely at the exodus and at Horeb, including the golden calf incident just recalled. Walk, serve and keep are different ways of spelling out what obedience entails. Revere and obey, or to put it more succinctly, as long as the terms are properly understood, love and serve.

The prophet Micah famously asks almost the identical question, addressing Judah's social and religious malaise in the late eighth century BC. His immediate answer is justly memorable: 'to do justice, and to love kindness, and to walk humbly with your God' (Micah 6:8). Faced with a social corruption and religious complacency which he fearlessly exposes, as do his prophetic contemporaries (Amos and Hosea in Israel, Isaiah in Judah), he spells out the significance of the Deuteronomic programme for his day. The same three themes of justice, generosity and humility, applied radically, would go a long way to addressing the ills of our own times.

While the focus is on Israel's response, two reasons to love and serve God are given. First, it really is for their own good (v. 13). The historical books record that times of obedience were generally times of blessing. The correspondence wasn't exact, and of course there were many other factors involved—history is too complex for simplistic correspondence—but there is nevertheless a correlation. Second, out of all of heaven and earth which he controlled, God had specifically chosen them as the focus of his love (vv. 14–15). They didn't earn it and didn't deserve it, but they should respond to it. Divine election to God's people is also affirmed in the New Testament. As an abstract concept, it remains an intellectual puzzle, but as an invitation to relate personally to this awesome God, it frees us from notions of merit to respond in love and service.

Hard hearts and stiff necks

Male circumcision was practised by many of Israel's immediate neighbours as a rite of puberty, but in Israel it became a rite following birth as a sign of entering into God's covenant. So while the wording of verse 16 may seem strange to us, 'heart circumcision' became a suitable metaphor for a life of faith or a return to it. Interestingly, the modern Jewish version (NJPS) rephrases the metaphor as: 'Cut away the thickening about your hearts'. This conjures up more meaningful images of engulfing fat or hardening arteries, though it loses the allusion to the covenant. The next idiom is easier (v. 16b), since the idea of being stiff-necked is straightforward, and NRSV already interprets it as 'stubborn'. However we translate these idioms, their meaning, and the warning they convey, is absolutely clear.

He is your praise

The passage ends (vv. 17–22) with a paean about Yahweh: his greatness, impartiality, justice, love and redemption. (Was this Micah's cue?) The required response, noted above, is then repeated in slightly different terms. And God's honouring of the promise to the patriarchs is reiterated: only 70 entered Egypt, but an innumerable people left it. In the midst of this comes the curious but enormously expressive phrase, 'He is your praise' (v. 21). He is indeed.

PRAYER

Praise God today.

WHAT'S *a* TESTIMONY?

Testimonies have mostly gone out of fashion in the Christian world. A few decades ago, many churches, most Sundays, would have someone 'giving their testimony' in an evangelistic service. It was an inevitable prelude to the sermon and appeal, and added that essential element of personal experience. If it can happen to Joe or Susan, standing in front of you, it can happen to you too, was the clear message. But now such testimonies are rarely given.

This isn't necessarily a bad development. The old-style evangelistic service no longer works in many contexts, and other approaches are used: coffee mornings, 'seeker-friendly' services, Alpha courses and so on. Also, the evangelistic testimony became stereotyped, focusing on dramatic conversion and ignoring less dramatic Christian living. Nevertheless, testimony remains an essential part of Christian witness. The form may have changed, but the basic feature of witnessing to God's work in our lives remains the same.

Israel too had a testimony. Here it starts with that incredible prelude, the plagues in Egypt (v. 3) and deliverance at the Sea of Reeds (v. 4). It includes provision for their needs in the wilderness, and punishment of their rebellion (vv. 5–6). Interestingly, this version omits the 'conversion' experience at Sinai, focusing instead on God's activity before and after it. The elements of the testimony are selected with the specific purpose of encouragement and warning. Likewise, our testimonies can and should focus on different aspects of God's work in our lives, as appropriate to different contexts. Let's follow the biblical example of rich diversity.

A sober warning

Numbers 16 recounts the full story of the Levite Korah and the Reubenites Dathan and Abiram who led a rebellion of some 250 men. They chafed at the idea that only Eliezar's descendants would be priests, and argued that all Israel was holy. This principle was of course correct, but their conclusion that everyone should be able to perform priestly duties reflected their own pride rather than concern for God. Consequently they and their families suffered immediate punishment: the hard surface of the mud flat on which they were camped suddenly broke open, and they plunged to their deaths. God must be served in his way, not ours, and the sober lesson was important to Israel not just in the past but also for the future.

An enticing prospect

The land they were about to enter was, in the familiar phrase, a land of milk and honey (v. 9). In other words, it was a land of pastures for flocks and of fields for cultivation. It would produce all they needed to eat, in abundant variety. But it would be a new type of agriculture. Egypt had an irrigation system of cultivation, needing intensive work to construct and maintain irrigation channels, and no doubt some Israelite slaves had been employed in this work. By contrast, cultivation in Palestine was rain-fed, with the advantage of not needing so much work and the disadvantage of being at the mercy of the weather. Here the land, in a wonderfully evocative phrase, 'drinks' rain from heaven (v. 11, literally). God would look after it and send rain regularly—if they remained faithful (vv. 13–15). Then they would have grain, wine and oil, and eat their fill. This sounded idyllic, almost like the garden of Eden. There was just one basic condition.

An abiding command

The leitmotif of these introductory chapters becomes a dominant motif in this concluding section: love and obey. It's there at the start (v. 1), and resurfaces regularly (vv. 8, 13), culminating in a repetition of what Jesus called 'the greatest commandment' (v. 13; see 6:5; Matthew 22:37)—simple to state, yet profound in its implications and consequences. Here a further element is added, that of witness. This generation alone had witnessed in person the foundational events recounted, not their children (vv. 2, 5). The best way to witness to and provide for their children, to ensure that their own descendants would live long in the land (see v. 9), was to love and obey the one who had made it all possible. Testimony in word must become testimony in life.

REFLECTION

What is my testimony, in word and in life?

The TWO WAYS

Good preachers often repeat their material, but by the time we reach this final section of a lengthy introduction, we may feel we've had more than enough repetition! And we've certainly had plenty. Most of the material in chapter 11 has already appeared earlier, in very similar format. Perhaps, though, the very repetition gives us food for thought. Israel needed to be told many times, and still didn't manage to follow these instructions. We often hear the same message repeatedly: how do we respond?

Famine or faith

After the encouragement to obedience (11:13–15) comes the warning against disobedience (vv. 16–17), again with consequences for the land and its produce. A famous example of this occurred during Ahab's reign, when Elijah pronounced a drought as divine punishment (1 Kings 17:1). Another drought occurred later, and Amos interpreted it similarly (Amos 4:6–7). God's blessing was shown mainly in material terms in Old Testament times—that's why Job receives so much after his vindication (Job 42). But so too was God's judgment.

However, Deuteronomy always balances warning of punishment with instruction on how to avoid it. So it immediately reiterates the command to have God's law always in view, even literally on hand and forehead, and to teach it regularly to the next generation (vv. 18–21). That way they will not forget it, and God will give them success in their new land.

The dimensions of this land are then given in their ideal maximum (v. 24; see 1:7), south to the Negev wilderness and north to Lebanon, north-east to the Euphrates river and west to the Mediterranean Sea. In fact, according to the historical books, the Israelites only controlled territory as far as the Euphrates for a brief spell under David and Solomon's empire. Normally this area was governed by the independent states of Aram (Syria), Hamath, and others. This shows how difficult it is to use biblical texts for modern national boundaries. Not even the most committed Zionists claim all this territory.

Curse or blessing

Some of us think in terms of the bottom line as *what* we need to do. In this case, as we have seen, it is to obey or disobey. Others think more of what happens *when* we do it, or perhaps when we don't. In this case, it's blessing or curse (vv. 26–28); or, in a modern idiom, carrot or stick. But this wasn't left as an abstract promise. It was epitomized by two monuments, in fact, the largest monuments possible —two mountains (vv. 29–30).

Mount Ebal and Mount Gerizim rise some 300m above the narrow valley between them, and some 430m above the town of Shechem (near modern Nablus) in the central part of the new territory that Israel was about to occupy. Visible for miles around, these landmarks were to become a permanent reminder of God's promise. As soon as Israel crossed the Jordan and established a bridgehead, they were to set up an altar on the first mountain. Then six tribes would solemnly pronounce a series of curses from it, while the other six would similarly pronounce blessings from Mount Gerizim. The whole procedure is explained in detail in chapters 27—28, and its actual enactment then recounted in Joshua 8:30–35. It must have been a hugely impressive, dramatic ritual, a sort of liturgy in the wild! And it would have left a vivid impression on all those who were there.

There were only two mountains, only two options. Similarly the author of Psalm 1 presents just two ways, which he labels as wicked and righteous. At times our choices may seem less specific, and the results less clear cut. But at the end of the day, for us as for Israel, it boils down to whether we really want to love and obey the Lord our God, or not. Deuteronomy describes obedience as the way of life (30:19). And the psalmist describes those who choose it as happy (1:1).

REFLECTION

*'Put these words of mine in your heart and soul' (v. 18),
perhaps by resolving to learn one verse of scripture every week,
and reciting it every day.*

41 DEUTERONOMY 12:1–7, 29–31

WORSHIP ONE GOD, IN ONE PLACE

Now for the small print

With chapter 12 we turn from the grand oratory of chapters 4—11 to the nitty-gritty. After all the injunctions to obey Yahweh's statutes, ordinances, commands and laws, and all the many good reasons for doing so, here we get to them at last! Some readers will be sad to move on, preferring the big picture and the stirring sermons of previous chapters. Others will be happy to get to the detail at long last. And there's certainly enough small print to keep us going for 15 chapters! We are all different, and it is interesting to note how Deuteronomy (and scripture more widely) has enough variety to speak to us all, with our various temperaments and approaches.

However, it's one thing to wax eloquent in general terms about following God. It's quite another to see what it means in practice. From a Christian perspective, it's easy to apply general Old Testament exhortations to ourselves. It's quite another to see if there is any current relevance in the specific laws, so these chapters pose a real challenge. But that's no bad thing, since the more we have to wrestle with a topic, the more we will benefit in the long run.

Smash the shrines!

The very first instruction has to do with how Israel should worship God; and, as so often, it is both negative and positive. First (vv. 2–4), they must demolish completely all the pagan shrines. The language is unequivocal: break down, smash, burn, hew down, blot out. There is to be no prevarication, no doubt whatsoever. The reason is given at the end of the chapter (vv. 29–31): if they don't do this, Israel will be snared into imitating these people and their worship, involving 'every abhorrent thing', and even including child sacrifice. Phoenicia was renowned in the ancient world for child sacrifice, as seen in various texts and in archaeological evidence from her colony, Carthage. And there is also biblical witness to its occasional occurrence nearer home (2 Kings 3:27) and even in Israel, especially just before the exile (2 Kings 16:3; 23:10; Jeremiah 7:31; 19:5; 32:35).

Exactly the same instruction, and the same reason, has already been given in 7:3–5. Its repetition here at the start of the detailed laws shows its absolute primacy. Sadly, as the historical and prophetic books record, the Israelites failed to smash all the shrines, took over some of the gods and the practices associated with them, and were punished accordingly.

Our era of religious pluralism shies away from such exclusive fundamentalism. We much prefer the religious climate of the patri- archs in Genesis, where an 'ecumenical bonhomie' reigned and where the ancestors of Israel were quite happy to adopt other names for God, especially the common term *El* (for example, Genesis 14:19; 16:13). Israel could take over titles for God that did not compromise him, but they could not take over styles of worship that fundamentally contradicted his nature. All religions are definitely *not* the same, or of equal value. The New Testament certainly modifies the nature of our response to false beliefs and practices. For a start, there are no instruc- tions to smash shrines. But it still opposes all false notions of God and of our knowledge of him in Christ.

One place to worship

As an alternative, Deuteronomy quickly provides the positive response (vv. 5–14). Instead of worshipping many gods at many places, Israel must worship only one god, Yahweh, at only one place. The contrast with the many Canaanite shrines to their many gods is clearly intended. What's more, the chapter repeatedly stresses that God, not they, would choose the place (vv. 5, 11, 14, 18, 21, 26). In the immediate future, the place would be Shiloh (as in 1 Samuel 1; possibly also, at times, Shechem and Bethel), and then Jerusalem, but it remains anonymous here. From the book's pre-conquest perspec- tive, the sanctuary's location remains unknown. Equally important, though, is that this anonymity moves our attention away from the place itself and towards the chooser: it would be Yahweh's sanctuary, owned by him, a symbol of his ownership of the entire land. Thus there is an absolute contrast between Israel's God and the gods of the Canaanite nations. Her faith was unique.

REFLECTION

Reflect on Jesus' claim, 'I am the way, and the truth, and the life. No one comes to the Father except through me' (John 14:6).

42 DEUTERONOMY 12:8–28

WORSHIP CENTRALLY, FEAST LOCALLY

Two sets of related instructions are intertwined in this chapter. The repeated contrast between them has a good didactic effect, in constantly emphasizing the different elements of each. It may also perhaps reflect different layers in the editing of the material, which more detailed commentaries will discuss. For our purposes, it will be easier to take the chapter thematically than paragraph by paragraph.

Worship centrally

The instructions on how and where to worship God occur no less than four times in the chapter, with slight variation (vv. 4–7, 8–14, 17–19, 26–28). Each paragraph describes the sacrifices and offerings slightly differently, since each gives a representative rather than exhaustive list. Together they have a strong cumulative effect: whatever you offer to Yahweh, in any form of sacrifice or offering or tithe, must be brought to the one central sanctuary, 'the place which Yahweh your God will choose'.

Several notable features characterize this worship. First, it is laity orientated. In all the references to sacrifices and offerings, there is no mention anywhere of priests. There is a hint of proper ceremony in the sacrifices, in stating that the blood must be poured out beside the altar (v. 27), but not in terms of the officials who conduct the ceremony. The focus is entirely on the people themselves.

Secondly, it is family focused. It is for the whole household (v. 7), not just representatives, or males, or senior members. An illustration occurs in 1 Samuel 1, when Elkanah and his whole family go up in annual pilgrimage to Shiloh. Throughout its long history, Judaism has preserved this holistic family focus in a way that Christianity has not always emulated.

Thirdly, it is socially inclusive. It welcomes the whole household including children and 'slaves' (vv. 12, 18—perhaps better translated as 'servants'; see discussion on 15:12–18, pp. 118–119). There is no 'upstairs, downstairs' philosophy here. And it includes the Levites, who had no land of their own and therefore no fields or flocks from which to bring offerings.

And finally, it should be joyful, as is frequently noted (vv. 7, 12,

18). It is fascinating to see how joy is repeatedly mentioned in this book. No solemn, stultifying religion, this! Well might we learn from Israel's laws of worship.

Feast locally

There was a practical problem, however. What about those who lived far from the sanctuary, and wanted to eat meat more than once or twice a year? This seems an odd problem to us, many of whom eat meat in some form or another most days of the year. But in ancient times, as still in many impoverished communities today, meat was a luxury, and was only eaten on rare celebratory occasions. Because of this, killing an animal was often associated with sacrifice, so there was the temptation to perform a local sacrifice and have some meat, happily combining the two in one event. But this would immediately undermine the insistence on sacrifice at a central location.

God provides a solution that both maintains his unique place of worship and allows everyone to enjoy an occasional roast (vv. 15–16, 20–25). Israelites can certainly eat meat locally, wherever they live, whenever they want, but only on two conditions. First, it must never be confused with sacrifice—hence the reiterated instruction on central worship. It would be simply a family meal, which didn't require ritual purity (v. 15). They must not try to pass off a family feast as a sacrifice. And secondly, they must not eat blood, 'for the blood is the life' (v. 23; see v. 16). This reflects a deep-seated principle (see Leviticus 17:11, 14), which again has remained a central aspect of orthodox Judaism, and which later formed part of the instructions in the transitional period to the early Gentile church (Acts 15:20).

REFLECTION

*Is my church's worship laity orientated, family focused,
socially inclusive and joyful?*

WHO SAYS?

Who says what individuals may or may not do? How does this change from the private to the public sphere? Who says what businesses may or may not do? Are they really accountable? Who says what nation states may or may not do? And who polices them? These questions have vexed governments of all types from time immemorial. Now, in our highly integrated world, where decisions made in one boardroom or capital city may have repercussions for millions of people around the globe, these issues are as pertinent—and as perplexing—as ever.

And who says what we should believe? At the heart of every religious tradition lie issues of authority in matters of faith and practice. Of course the balance differs from one religion to another, but for 'religions of the book' (Judaism, Christianity and Islam), the issue is fundamental. In Christendom in particular, religious authority has been attributed variously to apostles, church fathers, bishops, the pope, the local prince, and the Bible. That authority has then been mediated to the ordinary Christian through priests, monks, nuns, pastors, writers and preachers. And at various times across the centuries it has been backed by claims of miracles. Does this authenticate the message? In the final analysis, who says?

Prophets

As we shall see in chapters 16—18, Israel had various levels of authority. Politically, local elders and judges had the regular responsibilities in a decentralized judicial system. A central monarchy could be added, with certain clear constraints, but was not required. Religiously, priests and Levites had the regular responsibilities of maintaining worship. Prophets could emerge at various times, but the nation could function without them and apparently sometimes did. There is an interesting symmetry here between political and religious life.

However, prophecy was open to severe abuse. Anyone could proclaim themselves a prophet and gain a following, and prophets who could predict the future were bound to be heeded. Were they, then, right in everything else? The question was not just theoretical. The prophet Balaam, hired to curse Israel, could only bless them at God's instruction (Numbers 22—24). He seemed authentic, but he then tried to subvert Israel by immorality at Baal-Peor (Numbers 25; see Deuteronomy 4:3 and commentary, pp. 44–45). Not so good! Later, the prophet Jeremiah had many tussles with 'false prophets' (see Jeremiah 23; 28). He kept saying that Jerusalem would fall to the Babylonians—they no doubt kept replying, correctly, that nothing had yet happened. So it looked as if he was the false prophet and they were true!

One difficulty was that there was no clear line of succession for prophets, as there was with the Davidic monarchy. Nor was there any central accreditation or membership of an official organization. How could one tell who was an authentic prophet?

Prophetic authority

Our text responds to the above dilemma. Prophets or dream interpreters (like Joseph) might be unrivalled experts in prediction, where everything came true, but even they did not have *carte blanche*. What they taught was to be tested according to a clear framework. Yahweh was the sole God; Israel should love and serve him, keep his commandments and 'hold fast' to him (v. 4). The first commandment echoed here was absolutely foundational, and absolutely nobody, however authoritative, could add to or subtract anything from it (see 12:32). Indeed, such people threatened the very core of Israel's faith by denying the power of her God, a power so amply demonstrated in the exodus (v. 5). They were truly evil, and had to be eliminated. Dire condemnation for such blatant refusal to acknowledge God at work is reinforced centuries later by Jesus himself (Matthew 12:22–32).

Christians are in a different place from this. We do not have a mandate to execute those who teach error. But we must be equally vigilant; and the principle of revealed truth to which our life, teaching and witness must conform is equally true. We have much insight from past Christian tradition and much wisdom for present godly leadership. But all must operate within the framework of scripture, particularly the New Testament, as God's word to us.

PRAYER

*Lord, help me so to absorb the truth of scripture
that I can discern error.*

FIFTH COLUMNISTS!

How can we enforce regulations? What sort of security and legal systems should a nation put in place? More urgently today, how can we oblige despotic leaders and rogue states to honour treaties or meet international obligations? Who knows which countries will become problematic in the next few years!

One response in the ancient Assyrian empire was to write very detailed instructions into treaty documents. For example, the enormously powerful Essarhadon (seventh century BC) imposed a treaty on all his subject peoples, to acknowledge and obey his son Ashurbanipal after his own death. This long document contains a series of blood-curdling curses on anyone and everyone who might threaten Ashurbanipal, including:

> *If any of you hears some wrong, evil, unseemly plan... whether they be spoken by his enemy or his ally, by his brothers, by his sons, by his daughters... or by your own brothers, sons, or daughters, or by a prophet, an ecstatic, a dream-interpreter, or by any human being whatsoever, and conceals it and does not come and report it...* (ANET, 535d)

This phrasing is very similar to that used in Deuteronomy 13, which also includes prophets, family members and other rebels. This reminds us that Deuteronomy is expressed in ways culturally relevant to the ancient world. Its wording fits as well to its context as references to Big Macs or organic farming fit ours.

Family members

After false prophets (13:1–5), the chapter next lists close family members (vv. 6–11), the very closest one can get: siblings, children, even your spouse, whose bed you share. Their invitation to deviant forms of religion would clearly have a strong emotional appeal—and their punishment would have an even stronger emotional and physical impact. Clearly such an invitation would represent a clash of loyalties. Even then, perhaps particularly then, Deuteronomy insists, the apostasy must be stopped in its tracks. It doesn't matter who the instigator is and how dear they are to you, or who the proposed deity is and how appealing it may be—no allowance can be made. Any other worship represents a rejection of Yahweh and must be ruthlessly eradicated.

The text here (vv. 8–10) seems to imply instant action by the recipient of the enticement, to expose the culprit and throw the first stone in execution. At first glance, this seems slightly different from the later section, where a thorough investigation is required first (vv. 12–18), and significantly different from a later law, which insists on at least two witnesses for the death penalty (17:6). These later provisions are simply omitted here, in order to keep the focus on personal responsibility. It is the recipient of such an approach who must expose the inciter, whatever the cost, and who must instigate the capital punishment. The drastic punishment pointed to a dreadful crime. No wonder all Israel would hear and be afraid (v. 11)!

Neighbouring towns

The chapter's third example is of an apostate town, led astray by 'wicked people' or 'scoundrels', literally 'sons of Belial'. Belial is a Hebrew term associated with chaos and destruction, and with those who commit heinous crimes. By New Testament times it had become a name for Satan himself (2 Corinthians 6:15). Here the whole apostate town would suffer the same penalty as individuals elsewhere. Indeed, it would be so contaminated that none of its goods or livestock could be taken as spoil, and it should remain a perpetual ruin. This is reminiscent of the *herem* (see 7:1–11), though the word is not used here. Again the seriousness of disloyalty to Yahweh is underlined: a desperate situation required desperate measures. There is one chilling account of this punishment being enacted. There the cause was moral degeneracy rather than religious apostasy, but the result was equally horrific (Judges 19—20; see especially 20:48).

Thankfully, we live in a different era, when our approach to unbelievers, even within our family, should be characterized by love rather than judgment. Yet we must remember that Jesus' call to discipleship takes precedence over family ties, and that Jesus' condemnation of those who reject him is no less severe (Matthew 10:33, 37–39).

PRAYER

Lord, help me to love you more than I love anyone else.

A HOLY WAY *to* MOURN

From death for apostates to haircuts in mourning may seem to us a strange jump, and the following sections on meat for dinner and money for spending may seem just as oddly placed. But these all illustrate crucial aspects of what it meant to honour Yahweh and him only. In some cases, the reasons are fairly clear; in some, less so. But the underlying rationale is presented in these opening verses.

Holy children

First, two images of intimacy and specialness are repeated. Back in 1:31, Moses reminded Israel that in the early wilderness period 'Yahweh your God carried you, just as one carries a child'. And in 8:5 he noted that God disciplined them 'as a parent disciplines a child'. Already intimate family imagery has been used for loving provision and loving discipline. Here (v. 1) it prefaces a specific law, giving a positive context for what might initially seem a petty prohibition.

Then, verse 2 (like 7:6) notes that Israel was holy—specially chosen and specially treasured. In chapter 7 the setting contrasts Israel's unique status and faith with those of the Canaanite peoples and their corrupting religious practices in general. Here (as there) the statement starts with 'for': that is, it explains the preceding command. So cutting one's hair and gashing one's body in mourning were in some way corrupting, and to be specially avoided.

Other texts give some more detail: 'You shall not round off the hair on your temples or mar the edges of your beard. You shall not make any gashes in your flesh for the dead or tattoo any marks upon you' (Leviticus 19:27–28). Similarly, priests in mourning 'shall not make bald spots upon their heads, or shave off the edges of their beards, or make any gashes in their flesh' (Leviticus 21:5). The first text immediately follows strictures against 'augury and witchcraft', so again it is in a 'top ten' list of practices to avoid.

Ordinary mourning

Various prophetic texts portray head-shaving as a widespread mourning practice: in Moab 'every head is baldness, every beard is shorn' (Isaiah 15:2); 'baldness has come upon Gaza' (Jeremiah 47:5); in

Tyre 'they make themselves bald' (Ezekiel 27:30–32). There is also ample evidence from other sources (*ANET*, 88, 139).

More surprisingly, this practice seems to have been common among Israelites, without being explicitly criticized. God predicts that the coming catastrophe will be so great that individuals will not be mourned: 'there shall be no gashing, no shaving of the head for them' (Jeremiah 16:6). When the catastrophe happened and Jerusalem was destroyed, 80 men travelled there to present their offerings, 'with their beards shaved... and their bodies gashed' (Jeremiah 41:5).

What's more, the prophets often tell Israel to adopt these signs of mourning for the coming exile: 'Make yourselves bald and cut off your hair' (Micah 1:16); 'Cut off your hair... raise a lamentation' (Jeremiah 7:29); 'Shame shall be on all faces, baldness on all their heads' (Ezekiel 7:18). And God himself enforces it: 'I will bring sackcloth on all loins, and baldness on every head' (Amos 8:10); 'On that day the Lord God of hosts called to weeping and mourning, to baldness and putting on sackcloth' (Isaiah 22:12).

Unholy mourning

How do we explain this discrepancy within the Old Testament? The clue must be the setting in Deuteronomy. Somehow, in a way obvious then but lost now, these gestures or the way they were enacted had clear pagan associations at an early period. As time went on, such associations were presumably lost, and the practices could then be adopted without problem.

A modern equivalent might be Hallowe'en. I remember celebrating it as a harmless folk tradition in my childhood, within an extended Christian family. But now, with the revival of paganism and the renewed association of Hallowe'en with witchcraft, I wouldn't think of celebrating it. All depends on what it means. This text reminds us that certain practices can be harmful in one period but acceptable in another. We need a discerning spirit.

REFLECTION

Are there practices I avoid which are now harmless,
or ones I accept which are now harmful?

To EAT *or* NOT *to* EAT?

Is it *kosher*? Many of us know this Jewish term, and have a vague idea that it applies to the complex Jewish dietary laws. But we probably know little about the origins or meanings of these laws, and we feel instinctively that they are irrelevant to Christians. In the next two sections we will explore this issue.

This section deals with animals, fish and birds which the Israelites could eat (the original reference of the term *kosher*), and those they could not. In the first two groups, there is a simple test. Permitted animals have cloven feet and chew the cud. Permitted fish have fins and scales. Everything else is forbidden. In the third group, a list of forbidden birds is given, with the inference that anything else is permitted. There may have been a simple test here too, which is not stated: those birds (and all insects) that eat dead animals are forbidden; those that don't are permitted.

Some of these animals and particularly birds are little known, and their exact translation uncertain, as a comparison of any two English translations will quickly reveal. In any case, it is hard to find modern English terms for the wildlife of a distant place in a distant time. More details—and a few more obscure names—are given in Leviticus 11. That seems to be the full list needed by the priests, who oversaw implementation of these laws. By contrast, Deuteronomy 13 looks more like a concise, practical list intended for laypeople.

What did these laws mean then?

These food laws have long puzzled scholars and laity alike. Why are they given? What do they mean? Perhaps the most common explanation is that of hygiene. Israelites would live more healthily by avoiding certain animals and birds, particularly pigs and scavenging birds, which often transmit parasites unless cooked very carefully. So they were given rules that excluded the most harmful foods. The rules may have excluded a few harmless animals, but that was a small price to pay for simplicity. This explanation certainly has some merit, but is inadequate. Some of the creatures forbidden here were eaten in neighbouring cultures, without harmful effect. And other harmful foods, such as poisonous plants, are omitted.

A second explanation notes that the forbidden food is described as 'abhorrent' or 'detestable' (v. 3). This is a very strong term. Elsewhere in Deuteronomy (in 7:25; 12:31; 13:14), it refers to Canaanite idolatry. It may be that some of these forbidden animals were used in Canaanite sacrifices, and this was another area where Israel was to be different. This explanation is uncertain, however, since we have very little evidence of such sacrifice.

A third and more likely explanation picks up on the principle of difference in general. Just as Israel was to be holy in its distinctive religion, so it would be holy in its distinctive diet. Certain animals and birds were ritually clean, suitable for eating and in some cases for sacrifice. Others simply were not. Interestingly, most peoples have their food taboos, as shown by historical and anthropological study. But in Israel, these taboos were tied to the concept of holiness (v. 2). Every family meal was a reminder of God's provision for them and their commitment to him.

What do they mean now?

For orthodox Jews, this and the next passage form the basis for elaborate dietary regulations, but for Christians they are obsolete. Jesus himself implicitly cancelled them by declaring that what enters the body cannot defile it (Mark 7:15, 18), and Mark makes this explicit: 'Thus he declared all foods clean' (7:19). Peter was told in a vision to eat food he thought unclean, in preparation for preaching the gospel to the Gentile Cornelius (Acts 10). And Paul declares food laws simply an obsolete 'shadow of what is to come' (Colossians 2:16–23).

Does this passage have any relevance today, or is it of purely historical interest? As with so much of the Old Testament, we must focus on the principle rather than its outworking. Israel's holiness was to be seen in a vital everyday activity—eating. Her commitment to God was to be expressed as much in daily meals as in weekly sabbaths and annual festivals. But even in Deuteronomy, and certainly elsewhere in the Old Testament, the moral issue behind the ritual practice is stressed. God wants holy and obedient living. That applies as much to believers today.

REFLECTION

Is my faith seen in my daily activity?

CARCASSES & KIDS

Finders keepers?

'Finders keepers, losers weepers,' chants many a child in the school playground, especially after swooping on some treasure dropped from another's pocket. And many an adult is happy to pocket a stray bank note, often without stopping to look for its owner.

But Israelites were expressly forbidden from being 'finders keepers' of dead animals. Meat was usually a luxury, only eaten at festivals or other special occasions, and a dead animal might be a welcome bonus. The problem was that its blood hadn't been drained properly, so the carcass was unclean. It might be desirable, and cooked properly it might pose no health risk, but Israel's whole existence was about far more than what was expedient. Blood represented the principle of life, and where a carcass had not been properly drained it could not be eaten (as in 12:23). To do so would be to violate an important principle of holiness.

The link between blood and life is repeatedly asserted, though never fully explained. This prohibition was certainly linked to the shedding of blood in sacrifice, and would have underlined its importance. Unknown to ancient Israel, the association was a crucial foundation for the central Christian understanding of the death of Christ. However much or little the ordinary people may have understood, though, they were still called to obey the law.

Nevertheless, others could still benefit from the dead animal, notably any local non-Israelites. It could be given to a 'resident alien', whom Israelites were obliged to help, or sold to a passing foreigner, towards whom there were no such obligations. The find need not be wasted, but the principle involved was more like 'finders givers' or 'finders sellers'!

No kidding?

In millions of observant Jewish homes today, as for many centuries, dairy and meat products are kept strictly apart. They require separate saucepans, separate cooking utensils, separate rings on the cooker, even separate cutlery and crockery. They are never served together in the same dish. And strict Orthodox Jews even wait a prescribed number of hours between meat and dairy courses in meals. Amazingly, the sole basis for this elaborate and complex procedure is the present verse. From the time of the Roman empire onwards, Jewish scribes and rabbis have reasoned that this law against boiling a kid in its mother's milk implies the complete separation of all meat and dairy foods.

The text as it stands is much more limited, however. Far from referring to all meat and dairy products, it mentions only one species, specifically a mother goat and her kid. There are a number of other stipulations regarding mothers and their newborn. Exodus 22:30 and Leviticus 22:27–28 prohibit sacrificing any calf, lamb or kid under seven days old, and sacrificing 'an animal with its young on the same day', while Deuteronomy 22:6–7 prohibits taking a mother bird along with its eggs or chicks. No explanation is given for any of these laws, and there may be different reasons behind them. Taken together, they show a concern that reaches beyond human welfare to that of the animal world as well.

The great medieval Jewish scholar Maimonides noticed that the prohibition occurs twice in Exodus at the end of sections on pilgrimage festivals (23:19; 34:26). So he guessed that it was a rite practised in Canaanite festivals, and was prohibited to Israelites for this very reason. Its repetition here fits the strong antipathy in Deuteronomy to anything deemed pagan. This is possible, though there is no independent evidence—a Ugaritic text once thought to allude to it is now interpreted quite differently.

In parts of the Middle East even today, meat boiled in milk is a delicacy, since it is tastier than meat boiled in water. This law doesn't prohibit the practice. It simply notes that it is wrong to use the milk of the very mother whose young has been taken. Animals may be killed and eaten, but some natural boundaries must be respected. This respect for the animal world is a safer basis for interpretation than either the complete separation of two types of food or the allusion to an unproven Canaanite practice.

REFLECTION

Faith sometimes requires obedience for the sake of important principles, even to personal disadvantage. Does mine?

TITHES

Tithing was common

Tithing was very much part of Israelite life. Abraham gives a tithe to Melchizedek, priest of 'God Most High', in thanks for military victory (Genesis 14:19–20), while Jacob promises a tithe if God brings him back safely (Genesis 28:22). Various laws apart from the present passage deal with tithes. During the monarchy, Amos (4:4) records that Israelites offer regular tithes, but lambasts them for neglecting larger issues of social justice. After the exile, Nehemiah (10:37; 13:10) notes the importance of tithes to maintain priests and Levites, while Malachi (3:8) sees parsimonious tithing as 'robbing God'.

Tithing was by no means unique to Israel. It was practised across the ancient fertile crescent, for example, in Egypt and Mesopotamia, and at Ugarit and Lydia (southern Asia Minor) in between them. Our evidence is patchy, however, and it is unclear whether tithing was either widespread or compulsory. The biblical texts give the fullest picture of all. This may be simply because these texts have survived better than others. But it may be more than this, especially when compared to the major civilizations for which we have many texts: in Israel the tithe had greater importance, both religiously and socially.

Tithing was varied

There is an intriguing variety in the various laws. The last paragraph of Leviticus (27:30–33) notes that agricultural and pastoral tithes are 'holy to Yahweh', which normally means that they are given to priests and/or Levites. Crops may be redeemed by paying their value plus 20 per cent; animals may not. Numbers 18:21–32 stipulates that ordinary Israelites give tithes to the Levites, who in turn give 'a tithe of the tithe' to the priests (also Nehemiah 10:38). These texts do not state explicitly that the tithe is compulsory, but this seems implicit.

Our present text talks of two different tithes. The annual tithe, or its monetary equivalent for convenience, is taken to the central sanctuary and eaten there by the offerers themselves (v. 23). While the sanctuary priests benefit, the distinct feature here is that the offerers do too, and joyfully, with wine and spirits (v. 26). As so often in

Deuteronomy, a duty becomes a pleasure! The other tithe is triennial, and this time is stored locally for the benefit of Levites and others without land (resident aliens, widows, orphans: vv. 28–29). Presumably, different families gave the triennial tithe in different years, so that there was always enough for people in need.

This variety may seem perplexing. If all the law goes back to Moses, why does it say different things in different places? However, this question misunderstands the nature of Old Testament law. Moses was the founding father of Israel's law, but Mosaic law doesn't all come from Moses, any more than Napoleonic law all comes from Napoleon. It continued to develop over the course of time, and this is reflected in different law collections now gathered together in the different biblical books. Some scholars trace chronological development between different collections; others find insufficient evidence for such an idea. More importantly, the different laws show that this was a living and vibrant tradition, with various adaptations in different times and places.

Tithing showed faith

Two reasons for tithing are given here. Israelites are to eat their annual tithe at the sanctuary 'so that you may learn to fear Yahweh your God always' (v. 23). And they should store the triennial tithe 'so that Yahweh your God may bless you in all the work that you undertake' (v. 29). As before, fearing God is a positive response of faith and trust. If they maintain an ongoing, year-in year-out commitment to God, he will honour it and bless them. We can't take this Old Testament principle as applying directly to us. The New Testament gives us both teaching and example to show that faithfulness may not bring material reward, but it certainly honours God.

Tithing and Christians?

The New Testament never tells us to tithe, but it frequently exhorts us to be generous—indeed, to follow Christ's example of generosity (2 Corinthians 8:8–15). This is less specific, but more demanding!

PRAYER

Lord, help me to develop a generous heart, and to start by giving............ to............ this week.

GIVE GENEROUSLY *to the* POOR

Which is better, capitalism or socialism? I expect many of us would immediately answer: capitalism. In the late 20th century, it decisively won the showdown between the two, both in the collapse of communism in the Soviet Union and Eastern Europe, and in the shift from left-wing to centrist and right-wing policies in the Western world. Also, most readers of this commentary will be enjoying the economic, social and medical benefits of living in the capitalist West.

At the same time, we are aware of the harsher side of capitalism, which ignores the welfare of individuals. Their jobs may be lost without recompense in the constant flux of commerce, their savings may be halved by the fall of the stock markets, and their pensions may be wiped out by financial malpractice. Hence, most Western economies have various social measures in place. Also, capitalism has a harsh effect on developing countries, with mounting debt and crippling trade arrangements. The alienation of workers from the fruits of production, of which Marx wrote so passionately, is recurring, only this time on a huge international scale. Socialism, perhaps even communism, will make a comeback.

More important than our own preferences: which is the better economic system according to the Bible? The answer, not surprisingly, is neither! Instead, the Old Testament presents an amazingly novel third way. It legislates for a rural economy of individual success and failure. Some will work hard and prosper, others will work less and flounder, and the poor will have to borrow from the rich. But over against that, it has an astonishing balancing mechanism. No family should ever become landless, condemned for ever to be 'alienated from the means of production'. Every 50th year was a 'jubilee', when all land reverted to its original family (see Leviticus 25:13–24). One generation might suffer, but the next could reclaim the land and start afresh. However, 50 years was a long time, so there were also interim arrangements.

Release from debt

An earlier law in Exodus (23:11) declared that every seventh year the land should be 'released' from ploughing. The passage here in

Deuteronomy takes up the same vocabulary and applies it to debt in the community: fellow Israelites should be released from repayment. In a primitive agricultural economy, debt would often be repaid not in cash but in kind—for example, the harvest of certain fields for a certain number of years. This law of release means that the full harvests would again revert to the land's owners, and that they would not become permanently destitute. The implied link with the land explains why foreigners are excluded (v. 3): they don't own land. It isn't xenophobia —as we have seen, Deuteronomy repeatedly urges Israel to include 'resident aliens' in its community life. Rather, it is that they would earn their living through trade, and loans to them would be commercial transactions rather than humanitarian gestures.

The idea is so startling that some interpreters think the debt would have been merely suspended for a year. This would still be significant, as the creditors forgo their repayment for at least a year. But the logic of the following argument is that the release is total. Loans are simply written off. These are your own kin, God says. Don't reduce them to ongoing poverty. Be generous in cancelling their debt. If this maxim was applied between nations today, the world economy would look very different!

Idealism and realism

There is a judicious blend of idealism and realism in this passage. On the one hand, obedience would bring such blessing that nobody should be poor. Instead, they would all be able to lend to others (vv. 4–6). On the other, there would always be poor people around (vv. 7, 11). The former raises our sights and appeals to our imagination; the latter confronts our independence and challenges our compassion. So the text encourages us as believing communities to set our sights high but also to keep our feet firmly on the ground.

It was tempting to be tight-fisted when the year of release was near (v. 9). But God had been generous to his people, and they in turn should be generous, without calculating returns. After all, this is about helping out one's neighbours in hardship, not investing capital. Their generosity would both reflect God's goodness and prompt further blessing.

REFLECTION

'The one who sows bountifully will also reap bountifully... God loves a cheerful giver' (2 Corinthians 9:6–7). Am I one?

GIVE GENEROUSLY *to* YOUR WORKERS

Slavery is an emotive subject. It conjures up images of exploitation, cruelty, abuse and neglect. It implies callous disregard for welfare, let alone happiness. Slavery has been all too prevalent in human history from ancient times, and still exists in some parts of the world. It has been responsible for horrendous human suffering. So what is it doing in the Bible?

Limited bond-service

For a start, the word 'slave' is not really appropriate here. In most situations, slaves have no rights at all. They are treated as goods or animals, and are discarded once their economic usefulness is over. But 'slaves' here are really 'bonded servants', as the original text makes clear. They may have entered into their situation voluntarily: that is, they 'sold themselves' (v. 12: so NRSV note and NIV text; the Hebrew verb can mean this). And they were 'servants' as much as 'slaves' (the Hebrew word *ebed* can mean both).

Further, these bond-servants have rights, notably the right to freedom after six years of service. Whether they enter such service voluntarily or not, they have a fixed term of labour which cannot be flouted. However, they may actually find the security of perpetual bond-service in someone else's household preferable to the insecurity of freedom in their own home. The very fact that they have the option to choose to remain a servant implies that their conditions of service are satisfactory, even pleasant. Indeed, the text says they may 'love' their employer and his family and find themselves 'well off' (v. 16). This option must be exercised by the servants themselves; they cannot be forced by their master against their will. Indeed, the end of the section (v. 18) underlines that masters should consider freedom as normal and right. This is a very far cry from slavery as commonly understood.

Leviticus 25:39–46 restricts these provisions to fellow Israelites, and gives different conditions for foreign slaves. Deuteronomy simply demands enlightened treatment, perhaps implying that this is the model for all types of slave service.

Severance package

What's more, when servants opt for freedom, they should be given a generous bonus (v. 14). Here Deuteronomy goes beyond the older law of Exodus 21:2–11 in typical fashion, and insists that the servant not only goes free but goes laden with food. This is redundancy money and a golden handshake rolled into one—some recent Jewish communities have even applied the passage in this way.

Naturally, it is impossible to compel people to be generous, especially when they have entered into an economic contract. So several reasons are given, dealing with different aspects of life. *History:* God has been generous to you—you do likewise. God's redemption of his people from slavery in Egypt forms a powerful motivation for human action. *Economics:* the servant has easily earned his reward, since hired workers would have cost far more (some versions say twice as much). This pragmatic argument supports the altruistic one. And *faith:* if you are generous, God will in turn bless you even more. You believe in a generous God—put your money where your mouth is! We live in very different times, yet these reasons for generosity apply just as forcefully to us.

Perpetual service

Exodus 21:2–11 gives a further motive for remaining in service: a man may have acquired a wife and children who are not free to leave, and he may wish to remain with them. Deuteronomy makes no reference to such a family with its divided future, and its emphasis on generosity perhaps implies that any family could leave too. Instead, the motive given here is entirely positive: servants may 'love' their master and his family and want to stay. 'Love' may be too strong a translation, since the Hebrew word also means 'like'. But there is clearly a good relationship between servant and master, such that the servant has almost become part of the family.

Those who opt for perpetual service have their ears pierced, as a permanent physical sign of a now permanent status (see Psalm 40:6). Thus they commit themselves to this state for life, presumably confident that they will continue to be treated well.

REFLECTION

Israel's economics were radical. What about ours?

The FIRST IS SPECIAL

There is often something special about a first time: first day at school, first date, first kiss, first wage, first child's birth. Of course, the first may be followed by second, third, fourth, and many more, and may be superseded by better experiences. But the first still remains special in our memory, even if we can't always explain why.

The first male offspring

In Israel, the first male offspring in homes and farms was special in the sense of being consecrated to God, or holy. (The NIV's phrase 'set apart for' doesn't adequately capture the religious aspect.) There were clear reasons for this. Historically, the male firstborn of humans and animals were all killed in that dreadful final plague in Egypt, except in Israelite homes where a lamb had been killed and its blood smeared on the doorposts (Exodus 12:1–13). God's judgment fell on the Egyptians for refusing to let Israel go free, and on their gods who were represented by various animals. So as a perpetual memorial to that critical night in Israel's history, all male firstborn were henceforth to be dedicated to God. Theologically, the consecration of firstborn to God was an ongoing acknowledgment that all life belonged to him.

This law became fundamental in Israel. It is woven into the account of the tenth plague (Exodus 13:2, 11–16), features in the early sets of laws (Exodus 22:29–30; 34:19–20), and recurs in Numbers (18:15–18) and here in Deuteronomy. This is hardly surprising, given its importance for families and farming communities. Humans were to be redeemed by a monetary payment of five shekels, but clean animals were to be killed in sacrifice, and unclean animals were to be 'redeemed' by a clean one sacrificed in their place.

Adaptation but no relaxation

Originally the law stipulated that an animal should be killed on the eighth day after birth (Exodus 22:30). This was possible in a small nomadic community in the desert, but hard to implement once the people had settled throughout Palestine, often at considerable distance from the central sanctuary. So the law was sensibly adapted to allow for sacrifice any time up to one year old. However, these were consecrated animals, so should not be worked or fleeced (v. 19; even though lambs produce the softest wool). The adaptation to new conditions allowed flexibility, but was not to be exploited.

Blemished animals were unacceptable (v. 21), and must be replaced by unblemished ones. As a result, a defective firstborn animal was not holy and could be eaten in a non-sacrificial context like any other clean animal (vv. 22–23; see 12:15–16). There would always be a temptation to use blemished animals in sacrifice, but a later verse calls this practice 'abhorrent' or 'detestable' (17:1) and it was roundly condemned much later by Malachi (1:6–9). You wouldn't do it for your political boss, he argues, so why do you think you can do it for God?

Human ingenuity will always try to find ways round requirements and restrictions, and Christians are certainly not immune from the temptation to cut corners. We may be able to fool the tax inspector and the church treasurer, but we certainly won't fool God!

Reason

In one sense, the consecration of the firstborn was simply a way of providing animals for sacrifice on the great pilgrimage festivals. The people were told to go regularly to the temple and they needed animals to sacrifice when they went there, so this law regulated for one half of the equation. Certainly the laws fit together, giving a system that works well when each part is observed faithfully. But the sacrifice of firstborn male animals is much more than an expedient to provide the necessary animals. It is a powerful reminder of that night when Israel was set free, and of God's first claim on our lives.

Similarly, our gifts to the church and other Christian work aren't simply an expedient to ensure that their ministry continues. They are a powerful reminder of our salvation, and of God's first claim on our lives.

PRAYER

Lord, help me to put you first, and to give you the best.

The FIRST GREAT FESTIVAL

Many years ago, a Belgian friend was visiting me. He spoke English fluently, and had visited Britain frequently. Then for the first time in his life he watched *The Last Night of the Proms* on TV, and was absolutely flabbergasted. He had never seen British people behave like that: clowning around at a classical concert, singing ridiculously jingoistic songs and thoroughly enjoying themselves. Here was an aspect of popular culture totally new to him, and its discovery meant a significant revision of his view of the British.

The way we celebrate social events reveals much about ourselves and our values. Similarly, the way we celebrate religious festivals reveals much about our faith.

Israel's festivals

Chapter 16 deals in turn with the three great pilgrimage festivals in Israel, held in spring, early summer and late summer. These were the occasions when everyone was expected to travel to the central sanctuary, to bring their sacrifices or offerings and to celebrate together. It's hard to know how many people actually did this, and how often. But we do know that people like Samuel's parents (1 Samuel 1:3) went at least annually, even in the troubled period of the judges. Deuteronomy 16 presents the ideal of a faithful, joyful, celebrating community, regularly expressing its thanks to Yahweh on these great occasions. And it stresses that this must occur at a central location (see ch. 12), not scattered throughout the land.

The three festivals are mentioned repeatedly in the Pentateuch (see Exodus 12—13; 23; 34; Leviticus 23; Numbers 9; 28—29). This shows their importance in national life. There are some slight variants in the details given, reflecting different emphases in each literary or historical context, but the essential features remain unaltered.

Passover

Passover was the first and greatest Israelite festival. It commemorated the critical night that led to the exodus from slavery in Egypt, and many aspects of its celebration reflected that original dramatic event. The sacrificial animal had to be entirely consumed in the one meal, since originally they departed that very night. And it had to be accompanied by unleavened bread, 'the bread of affliction' (v. 3), since originally there wasn't enough time to bake ordinary bread with yeast.

The traditional translation 'Passover' goes back to Jerome's Latin Vulgate, which speaks of Yahweh 'passing over' Israelite homes when killing all firstborn males in Egypt (Exodus 12:27). However, this remains a guess at the meaning of the enigmatic Hebrew term. Some scholars today think it refers more to God's protection of the Israelites. The meaning of the term may not be clear, but that of the festival certainly is. It celebrated God's salvation of his people, and their birth as a nation.

Unleavened Bread

The feast of Unleavened Bread involved eating this dry bread for the week immediately following Passover. During this time, people may well have returned home (the meaning of 'to your tents' in Joshua 22:4 and 1 Kings 8:66) and got on with their normal farming work. At the end of the week there was another 'solemn assembly', presumably now in their home town.

Passover and Unleavened Bread inevitably merged and are sometimes referred to by only one of the two names (for example, 16:16). For this and other reasons, some scholars argue that the festivals were pre-Israelite, for shepherds and farmers respectively. Whatever their earlier associations, they were clearly combined with fresh meaning— just as Christianity imbued the Roman winter solstice with significant new meaning as a celebration of Christ's birth.

Christ himself imbued the Passover with new meaning, inaugurating a new salvation, substituting its animal sacrifice with his own life, and replacing its memorial meal with another (see 1 Corinthians 5:8). Further, he occasionally likened yeast to a corrosive agent (Matthew 16:6), to be shunned as in the ancient festival.

PRAYER

Thank you, Lord, that we can celebrate Holy Communion both solemnly and joyfully, because of Christ's salvation.

OTHER FESTIVALS

For many of us, the traditional holiday periods of Christmas, Easter and summer give a rhythm to the year, occasions when we have certain regular family gatherings, church events, travel and rest. Israel's holidays combined all these functions, and this passage describes the other two main festivals.

Festival of Weeks

This festival marked the early wheat harvest, and so was also called 'First fruits' (Numbers 28:26) or 'Harvest' (Exodus 23:16). In later intertestamental times, when Jews increasingly spoke Greek, it became known as 'Pentecost', that is, 'fiftieth day', the seven-week period since the start of the barley or corn harvest. Unlike the other two pilgrimage festivals, this festival lasted only one day, as a longer break at the height of harvest would have been impractical. Also unlike the others, it is not linked specifically to the foundation of Israel's faith, and it is mentioned less frequently in the biblical records. But it was still very important, as one of the three key festivals, and as a celebration of God's blessing on his obedient people. That dominant theme of Deuteronomy is given clear expression at Pentecost.

Festival of Tabernacles

The festival of Tabernacles, or 'Booths', was the ultimate harvest festival, in several senses. It was the last of the agricultural year, when 'all was safely gathered in': grain, grapes, olives, and so on. It was also the last word in festivals, a joyful one-week camping holiday rather like the many Christian festivals that have sprung up in Britain in recent decades. For a whole week, Israelites were to live in temporary shacks (also called booths or tabernacles, hence the festival's name), usually made from tree branches and leaves. This may have reflected the temporary dwellings of harvesters busy in the fields from dawn to dusk. It also recalled the temporary tent dwellings of those heady months after the exodus, and the many long years in the wilderness. Even today, orthodox Jews construct some sort of hut in their gardens and live there for the festival week.

It's interesting how festivals develop. While Passover remained the most fundamental in terms of faith and ritual, Tabernacles became the one anticipated most keenly and celebrated most joyfully. When the Judean exiles returned from Babylon, the first festival they are known to have celebrated was Tabernacles (Ezra 3:4). And when Nehemiah had rebuilt Jerusalem's walls, the event was celebrated at Tabernacles. Here Ezra and colleagues read the law, as was intended every seven years (Deuteronomy 31:10–11). Passover was more profound, but Tabernacles was more popular. Similarly for Christians, while Easter is the most profound occasion for faith, Christmas often eclipses it in popular appeal.

How to celebrate

Deuteronomy stresses several key aspects of these major festivals.

- **Celebrate the past:** The foundational events of the exodus, covenant, law and new land are frequently recalled. Some of them are relived, allowing each generation to experience something of the emotion, drama and faith of those formative events.

- **Celebrate the present:** Each festival was a reminder of God's continuous provision for his people, especially the two linked to harvest. In a rural peasant economy, each harvest was vital to survival, let alone prosperity. God's eyes on the land (11:12) and the resulting successful crops were well worth celebrating.

- **Celebrate joyfully:** Other texts give more detail on the timing, the ritual and the sacrifices of each festival. Deuteronomy stresses more their spirit, especially joy, which is noted three times (vv. 11, 14, 15, though the last is translated differently in NRSV).

- **Celebrate generously:** The summary for all three festivals (vv. 16–17) notes that everyone should bring gifts with them. The celebration of God's historical salvation merits a response of gratitude. And the two harvest festivals were times of sharing God's bounty with those in need (vv. 11, 14). Israel was to be generous to its God and to all its people.

REFLECTION

Do these features mark our celebrations of faith?

LOCAL JUSTICE

How should a country be governed? Where is the overall authority? What are the checks and balances? What are the respective roles of elected representatives, the executive, the judiciary and civil servants? To what extent should decisions be devolved, and how do the different levels of authority relate to each other? All these questions are just as pertinent in the early 21st century as ever before, both for our own country and further afield. The USA and Britain, for instance, led invasions of Afghanistan and Iraq to enforce 'regime change', but then found this far more difficult than they initially thought. Another unexpected result was the exposure of some of the hidden ways their own regimes work. Meanwhile, there is continued discussion of how much responsibility for hospitals, schools and so on, should be devolved to regional and local levels. Is there any biblical advice for all this?

This passage introduces two chapters of Deuteronomy which deal successively with the roles of judge, king, priest and prophet, obviously the key roles in its governance (16:18—18:22). Here is a blueprint for the new, settled society, and together these sections give a good indication of how it should be governed. However, we notice immediately the inclusion of priest and prophet, balancing civil with religious authority. This reminds us that ancient Israel was very different from today's society, and underlines the fact that we must be careful in applying its structure to our own time. But we can still note important principles.

Local judges

In matters of justice and authority there was a strong measure of devolution to local level. This was a fundamental feature of Israelite life, which permeated its institutions and had important theological implications. It can be seen in many different ways. Here (v. 18), judges and officials were to be appointed throughout the land, not just in the one central sanctuary, or the six cities of refuge, or the dozen or so important towns. In the rest of the book (and indeed the rest of the Old Testament law), we read repeatedly of local elders and judges settling disputes and administering justice. The verses following our present passage imply that their authority extended to serious crime, including even capital offences. The three cases noted (16:21—17:4) are probably cited as examples, since all are also mentioned elsewhere: sacred poles or pillars (7:5; 12:3), blemished animals (15:21), apostasy (13:6, 13). And the way the passage then immediately discusses the number and role of witnesses in capital cases implies that local courts had power of execution.

So we see that the administration of justice was highly devolved and localized. This would have clear advantages in a peasant society. The local elders meeting regularly in the city gate (see Ruth 4:1–2) would know their people very well, and have a good idea of the rights and wrongs of each case. Justice could be administered speedily and fairly. But there were also great risks. These same elders could be inherently biased or open to bribery, or might not want to upset certain influential people. Nevertheless, God was willing to trust the people who knew the situation best to take responsibility for their own affairs. This certainly has implications for authority in both church and society today.

Justice, and only justice

How can abuse of the system be prevented? There is clearly a role for checks and balances throughout government, in whatever context and at whatever level. But the greatest protection is given by the personal integrity of the officials. So the two chief sources of corruption are 'named and shamed': partiality and bribery (v. 19). Both of these points are repeated constantly elsewhere and occasionally developed. It would be easy to show favour to the rich and powerful, the seemingly upstanding citizens. Equally, as Leviticus 19:15 notes, it would be wrong to favour the poor simply because they are poor. Bribery is easy to disavow when named directly, but it can be very pernicious. What about a tip, or a gift, or a court fee, or payment for services rendered? As the prophets repeatedly note, any money exchanged for justice is simply bribery, and unacceptable (see Isaiah 1:23; Micah 3:11; 7:3). There must be justice, pure and simple.

PRAYER

*Pray for those today who administer justice
and take decisions in government at all levels.*

PRINCIPLES *of* JUSTICE

The previous section focused on local judges. This one extends the responsibility for justice in both directions. First, those under their authority as witnesses in any local proceedings bear major responsibility and must exercise it accordingly. Secondly, those placed above them as a court of referral must be treated with the utmost respect.

The village court

Most court cases involve witnesses, and any case in Israel that might have involved the death penalty required two or more witnesses. In fact, 19:15 shows that the same principle of multiple witnesses applies across the board. Here, in the specific case of apostasy, the witnesses are presumably heard in the course of the 'thorough inquiry' (17:4) which is to be conducted. The principle of thoroughness is implicit in all justice, but perhaps stressed here since worship of other gods could be done in secret and the traces hidden. The witnesses would need to be responsible in their testimony, but they would also be responsible in instigating the sentence, as the first to raise their hands against those condemned. It was an awesome responsibility.

This paragraph illustrates several key principles of Israelite justice. It applies equally to men and women (v. 2), without favour for either. It is conducted in public, with the charge, the investigation and the court proceedings to be open knowledge. There is no place for secret vendettas. The charge must be proven, and on the basis of several witnesses (v. 6), so the defendant is presumed innocent until shown to be guilty. Courts must protect the innocent as much as convict the guilty. And those who testify must take full responsibility for the consequences of their evidence (v. 7). While our own judicial system is far more complex, like our society itself, these principles are still valid.

The court of referral

Local judges were ordinary farmers and villagers who occasionally fulfilled this extra duty as senior members of the community. They had the advantage of local knowledge, but would hardly have known all the detail of the law. For difficult cases, then, there was the back-up of a central 'court of referral' (vv. 8–9). This was a bit like a modern court of appeal, except that it was the local judges rather than the defendants who could appeal to it. The original system was set up by Moses himself, on the good advice of his father-in-law Jethro (Exodus 18:22). The examples listed here are somewhat imprecise, but show that appeal could be made for different reasons, for example, the seriousness of the case, the uncertainty of the evidence or the precise details of the law.

The court of referral was located at the central sanctuary, which in due course became Jerusalem. Here there would be Levites (v. 9), who knew the law well because they taught it, as well as the central judge and the high priest (v. 12). The exact functioning of this court is not spelt out, and the central judge is not mentioned elsewhere, perhaps because his role was taken over either by another leader (like Samuel: see 1 Samuel 7:15–17) or later by the king (like Solomon: see 1 Kings 3:16–28). The court may have evolved over time, but it was still a vital component of the justice system. Indeed, Absalom exploited the fact that it wasn't working properly to foment rebellion against his father David (2 Samuel 15:1–4). It needed to work in practice, not simply to be there in theory. A justice system is no good if it's not accessible to the people who need it.

As the highest court in the land, its judge deserved utmost respect. His verdict was to be the final word in the interpretation of God's law, since he effectively spoke on God's behalf. Contempt for the central judge, like contempt for the high priest, was as bad as contempt for God himself, an evil to be purged from their midst by death (v. 12). Interestingly, the same is not said in the next section for the king, despite his greater power. The judge who administered divine law was in principle more important than the national ruler. That's a sobering thought!

PRAYER

Pray that our justice system will become increasingly
wise, fair and accessible.

The FIRST *among* EQUALS

We live in a world where power is increasingly concentrated at the top. In national politics, we want to hear from the relevant minister, or directly from the prime minister, not from junior ministers or press officers. In any election, the party leaders generate more column inches of comment than all the other candidates put together. In international affairs, we focus almost exclusively on presidents and premiers, tending to ignore their senior colleagues. It's the one at the top that counts.

Our present passage is therefore rather disconcerting. For a start, it's not at the beginning of the section. We've already read and thought about judges and priests. If order reflects importance, as probably in this part of Deuteronomy, the judge comes before the king. Secondly, kingship seems to be an optional extra. There is a direct command to appoint judges (16:18), but merely permission to appoint a king (v. 15). Israel *can* live without a king, without a single figure at the apex of political power. Indeed, for several centuries before and after the monarchy, Israel did just that. But it cannot survive without justice. This is a salutary correction to our skewed priorities.

A king, like other nations

It's hard to go it alone, to be different from everyone else, to stick out from the crowd. Every other people known to Israel had kings, so it was almost inevitable that Israel would want one. It seemed to be how societies worked. And God was not against kingship *per se*. There were several different viable authority structures in Israel, just as there are several different models of church government that have their roots in New Testament practice. The key feature is not so much the structure as the way it operates.

Here, the crucial issue is: what kind of king? In Egypt, the king was accepted during his own lifetime as a god, whose very word was law. In Mesopotamia, kingship was seen as created by the gods, and indispensable for social well-being. In the Canaanite city-states, the king topped the feudal pyramid, with absolute authority. In Israel, however, there must be limits to his power and guidelines for his behaviour.

A king unlike other kings

Clear guidelines are given for an Israelite king. First, he should not be self-appointed, but chosen by God—that is, via a prophet (v. 15). Secondly, he should not be a foreigner, but one of the people, sharing the faith and values of those he governs (v. 15). Thirdly, he should not acquire the trappings of power: horses, wives and wealth (vv. 16–17). Horses meant prestige and power, with the added complication of having to return to Egypt to get them. Women and wealth were the common trappings of oriental courts but should not characterize Israel's. Israel could have a king like other nations had, but not a king like other kings.

Just as importantly, Israel's king did not make the law, but was to be governed by divine law. This was a crucial difference between Israel and its neighbours: there was no absolute right of kings. He should have his own copy of the law, read it frequently, and follow it diligently. This was the only way to inculcate the right attitude (not exalting himself) and the right conduct (not turning away).

A chequered history

Throughout Israel's long history, this ideal was seldom achieved. When they first asked for a king, their motives were certainly mixed (1 Samuel 8:5). David usually tried to follow divine guidance, though he did have several wives. Solomon had many more, and added horses and wealth. (Indeed, many scholars think that this section of Deuteronomy was drafted with Solomon in mind.) But the story isn't all bad. Kings were often confronted by brave prophets, and sometimes heeded their warnings. Even Ahab, one of the worst kings on record, recognized that he didn't have absolute power to take someone else's land (1 Kings 21:4). Even a bad Israelite king was different from those of other nations. The principle explained here had long-lasting effect.

PRAYER

Pray that we and our leaders may have a biblical view of political authority.

SUPPORT YOUR MINISTERS

As I write, our local church is looking for a church worker. Unfortunately our small size means that we cannot afford someone full-time, and this makes it difficult to attract a suitable person. Other small churches address the problem in various ways: part-time work, job-shares, linking parishes together. These can be innovative and creative in exploring new ways of ministry. They can also be painful in adjusting to different patterns of church life. Does the Old Testament system of ministry have any relevance?

Priests and Levites

In a context where everyone needed land to survive, the Levites were the noted exception. Alone of all the tribes, they had no allotted land (v. 1). Instead, they lived in 48 towns scattered throughout the territory (Numbers 35:1–8), with various religious duties like teaching the law and adjudicating cases of leprosy (Deuteronomy 24:8). Only one clan within the tribe, Aaron's family, had responsibility for the central sacrifices (Leviticus 7:31–36; Numbers 3:10).

The Levites' inheritance was not land but Yahweh (v. 2). As well as the spiritual connotations, this meant that they lived largely off the offerings and tithes of the people. Hence their share is carefully set out: part of the sacrifices (v. 3), and the firstfruits of crops and of wool (v. 4). This was their main source of income, though they also had some grazing land around their towns (Numbers 35:5).

Their well-being obviously depended on the faithfulness of the people. We have already read several times of the need to support the Levites. Here it is addressed directly. Faithful obedience to God involves faithful support of his ministers. They had a special place in God's service, and should have a special place in the people's hearts. In a nutshell: support your ministers.

Were all Levites priests?

These verses seem relatively straightforward, but they actually pose a number of challenges when compared to other texts. The first phrase reads literally, 'the priests the Levites all the tribe of Levi' (v. 1). Are these three expressions for the same people, or do they indicate different levels in the tribe (like Numbers 3:10)? The next phrase allots 'offerings made by fire' to them all, but elsewhere these offerings are restricted to the priests performing the sacrifices (Leviticus 7). And verse 6 seems to allow any Levite to minister at the sanctuary, but other passages restrict this ministry to Aaron's descendants.

There are two common ways to resolve these and other differences in the Mosaic laws. The traditional approach is to read them harmonistically. Thus, here the first phrase sets out different groups within the tribe of Levi, and the following phrases must be applied to whichever group is appropriate. Deuteronomy assumes the distinctions given elsewhere and does not repeat them, since its purpose is more to encourage faithful provision for the whole tribe of Levi.

By contrast, a common scholarly view is to trace historical development in the priesthood: first, an early period when any authoritative figure could offer sacrifice, as Samuel did (1 Samuel 9:13); then restriction of this ministry to the Levites, as reflected here; finally restriction to one particular family, as reflected elsewhere. These various texts are then put into a chronological order, with Deuteronomy dated to the late monarchy period, and Leviticus and Numbers dated to the exile and after. This reading sees the Mosaic law as an ancient legal code which went through various changes and adaptations in different times and places before all the traditions were recorded together.

The truth is probably somewhere between the two. The law very probably did develop over time, and later developments were written in without affecting the overall attribution to Moses. At the same time, the distinction between priests and Levites could well be very ancient. Unlike earlier scholars, we now know that elaborate sacrificial ritual and fine priestly distinctions were common in the ancient world long before Israel existed, and were not a later, evolutionary development. The various sections of Mosaic law may have been codified much later, but this doesn't disprove the authenticity of their essential features. Regardless of this discussion, however, the main point here is the support of all Levites.

REFLECTION

How best can we support our ministers?

DARK DEEDS

Do you read the stars? Do you pay any attention to those daily predictions of your work, money, friendships, and so on? If you do, and you're also reading this book, you probably don't take them seriously. 'Just a harmless piece of fun, just to see what strange coincidences they come up with,' you might say. 'We're all a bit curious, we like to know what's going to happen, and while of course we don't believe in the stars, they're still interesting…'

We're all certainly curious about the future. Fortune telling is big business, and some practitioners earn big money. It has been said that France has more full-time fortune tellers than full-time doctors. I haven't been able to verify this, or to find figures for other countries, but the assertion clearly illustrates the scale of human curiosity.

So it may come as a shock to read that fortune telling is totally abhorrent to God, lumped along with other detestable deeds like witchcraft, sorcery, spiritualism and even child sacrifice. These were defining characteristics of the peoples whom Israel was to wipe out, and by implication any Israelite practising them was also to be put to death. In God's eyes, it was not exactly harmless fun! Why so?

Dark days

Before discussing the question directly, it's worth noting instances in Israel's history when people did turn to these practices. Their first king, Saul, started out well and banished all spiritualists (1 Samuel 28:3), but later turned away from God and was shunned by Samuel. Then in desperation he consulted a medium at Endor (1 Samuel 28:7). He got his message from the dead Samuel, a message identical to those given in Samuel's lifetime, and sadly it was fulfilled the next day in Saul's own death. Centuries later, when Assyria seemed poised to sweep both Israel and Judah into oblivion (and succeeded with Israel), Isaiah castigated Judeans who 'consult the dead on behalf of the living' (Isaiah 8:19). In both these situations of pressure, people turned from the God of the living to the spirits of the dead.

There are also a few horrific examples of child sacrifice. The Moabite King Mesha sacrificed his heir to get out of a tight spot (2 Kings 3:27). It seems to have had the desired effect (though the text is not entirely clear), but at what dreadful cost! The Judean kings Ahaz and Manasseh also sacrificed their sons, presumably in order to influence the future (2 Kings 16:3; 21:6). Manasseh was the worst offender of all, introducing the whole panoply of practices forbidden here. Again, there seems a clear link for the biblical writers between child sacrifice, necromancy (or consulting the dead), and simple sooth-saying (or fortune telling). They're all part of the same phenomenon, and they're all fiercely forbidden.

Dark powers

Scripture never denies that these practices work. On the contrary, it makes it clear that they do. Saul *was* able to contact the spirit of Samuel, and to ask about the future. It didn't do him any good, but it worked. (Some traditional Jews and Christians have insisted that an evil spirit impersonated Samuel, but the text doesn't give any indication of this.) King Mesha's horrific act *did* bring military relief, as the Israelite army then withdrew. Scripture doesn't forbid these things because they don't work—rather, because they do!

The Old Testament frequently calls Israel to look to Yahweh alone for direction and guidance. All other forms of discovering or influencing the future come from spiritual powers opposed to him. To turn to them is to turn away from him. It is essentially apostasy. And the clear implication is that what starts with fortune telling progresses when under pressure to spiritualism and worse. It's a very slippery slope.

The New Testament says more about malign 'principalities and powers' (Ephesians 3:10; Colossians 2:15, RSV) and roundly condemns all forms of the occult in principle and in practice (Acts 8:9–24; 13:6–12; 16:16–18; 19:18–20). Guidance comes from the Holy Spirit, not a host of other spirits. Many today can testify that a simple curiosity about the future can lead from fortune tellers to ouija boards to spiritualists and beyond, until uncontrollable forces have taken over. Thankfully many can also testify to divine deliverance from these evil powers—for example, Doreen Irvine in her remarkable testimony, From Witchcraft to Christ (Concordia, 1973). But it is far better not to get started in the first place.

PRAYER

Pray for those caught up in the spirit world, that they may find release from evil forces and true guidance from the Holy Spirit.

The PROPHET

Many churches today have prophets. In Europe these tend to be the newer churches and networks which have proliferated as a result of the charismatic renewal. In Africa they tend to be the numerous indigenous churches with exotic names like 'Seraphim and Cherubim'. Some insist on a fixed number of recognized prophets, while others remain flexible, but they all insist that prophetic ministry is still pertinent for today. Much of the discussion about it centres on how we apply New Testament patterns of leadership. But some of it also looks to the Old Testament prophets, including this paradigm text.

The true prophet

In contrast to all the illicit sources of guidance just listed (the plethora of mediums, witches, sorcerers and diviners), God would provide one true means, a prophet. The singular form, 'prophet', indicates the model prophet, not that there would only be one prophet at a time: later, several ministered concurrently, like Micah and Isaiah. Nor does it restrict prophecy to men: several women prophets made crucial contributions, like Deborah who led a famous victory (Judges 4—5) and Huldah who encouraged a reformation (2 Kings 22:14–20).

Several key features would mark true prophets. First, God would choose them (v. 15). God had provided an intermediary, Moses, and now promised to continue to do this. Second, they would be like Moses (v. 18). The great man is here presented as an exemplar of the prophet, and what a model he was, with his constant concern and self-sacrificial intercession for the wayward Israelites. Third, they would deliver God's message, clearly and directly. God would put his words in their mouth, and they would speak with all his authority. Fourth, they should be obeyed, on pain of giving account to God himself (v. 19). When the northern kingdom of Israel was swept off into exile, never to return, the primary reason given was disobedience to 'his servants the prophets' (2 Kings 17:13–14, 23).

The phrase 'put my words in his mouth' (v. 18) must be interpreted in light of the later prophetic books. Amos thundered God's message of judgment, while a few years later Hosea pleaded with the same people. It was a very similar message, but in a very different tone. Micah and Isaiah preached to Judah at the same time, but again with different emphases. After the exile, Haggai and Zechariah both encouraged the dispirited returnees, but they had significantly different messages. God clearly worked through the personality and temperament of each prophet. His message was conveyed in words and phrases which were authentic to each individual. God worked through people, not puppets. And he still does.

The false prophet

But anybody could get up and say, 'I'm a prophet, God has sent me.' How would people know who was true and who was false? Here, one obvious test is given: incorrect prediction (vv. 20–22). If a 'prophet' predicted something that didn't happen, he was clearly false. He was usurping God's authority, which he had no right to claim, and must pay the penalty of death. This was a very serious matter. Of course, fulfilment might not be immediate. Jeremiah had ongoing tussles with various 'prophets' who claimed that their predictions of Jerusalem's safety were being fulfilled, while Jeremiah's message of gloom and doom was simply paranoia (see Jeremiah 23; 28), but Jeremiah was proved right in the end.

It's important to note that the reverse is not necessarily true. Chapter 13 warned that even if a prophet's prediction came true, if he taught something against God's law then he was a false prophet. Accurate prediction was a necessary but not a sufficient condition. Their teaching also needed to conform to God's revelation. This is what set Jeremiah apart. He refused the facile message that God would always preserve Jerusalem, no matter what, and proclaimed that he would punish his sinful people no less than other peoples. It wasn't very palatable—but it was right.

Deuteronomy cannot determine whether God still uses prophets today or not. Even the New Testament texts can be interpreted differently. Any prophet today, however, must still work within the framework of truth already revealed in scripture, and above all in Christ.

REFLECTION

Where do I turn for spiritual authority and guidance?

Without MALICE AFORETHOUGHT

How can a society function without police and prison? We are so used to both that we cannot imagine life without them. How on earth would we maintain order without the enforcement of law and the sanction of incarceration? But we live in a complex, impersonal, industrial society, and we have little or no experience of anything else. By contrast, most early peasant societies, including Israel, were simple and highly personal. They couldn't afford imprisonment, and they functioned mostly without it.

Today's passage, however, gives the one major instance in Israelite law of physical confinement. It applied to anyone who committed accidental manslaughter, which the courts gloss as 'without malice aforethought'. These people could flee to one of six cities of refuge— the three already established east of the Jordan were noted in 4:41–43. Here they would have to remain until the current high priest died, when they could return home. As elsewhere, Deuteronomy only gives a summary, and focuses on the need for three more cities. Further detail on the cities and the procedure is given in Numbers 35:9–34.

Bloodguilt and manslaughter

The fundamental principle underlying these laws is bloodguilt. Anyone who killed someone else incurred bloodguilt and deserved to die, and the deceased's next of kin had the right to execute them. This principle is stated in the aftermath of the flood (Genesis 9:6), and illustrated by Gideon (Judges 8:19) and Joab (2 Samuel 3:27). The guilty must be punished, and the blood of the innocent must be avenged.

How could this work, though, when a death was accidental? Avenging the blood of one innocent person would mean shedding the blood of another innocent person, and would only perpetuate the problem. The solution was for the killer to flee to a designated city before the avenger of blood caught up with him. These cities of refuge were scattered through the country so that one could be reached from anywhere in a matter of hours. But delay would show contempt for the victim's family and for the law, and the consequences would fall on the killer's own head, literally. He was responsible for shedding innocent blood, even if unintentionally, and had to flee.

Numbers 35:28 adds that he should remain there until the high priest dies, and concludes that atonement must be made for shed blood. This clearly implies that in his death the high priest atones for unintentional killing, just as in his life he offered sacrifices of atonement for all sin (Leviticus 16:33). This way the bloodguilt is avenged, no further blood is shed, and the killer can return home a free man. The death of the innocent has been taken seriously, but further killing avoided.

Bloodguilt and murder

The system must not be abused. Obviously the elders of the cities of refuge would only hear the stories of those who fled there. They would have no idea whether their fatal deed had been intentional or not. So in cases of dispute the elders of the killer's own village would adjudicate (v. 12). Again we note that responsibility is devolved to a level of immediate accountability. If the killer was guilty of murder (Numbers 35 spells out some ways of telling this), then he wasn't safe, even in a city of refuge, but should be put to death. Bloodguilt had to be avenged. Sadly, this system was later abused. Hosea (6:8–9) writes of two cities of refuge that Ramoth Gilead was full of culpable murderers who should not have received sanctuary, while in Shechem the priests murdered legitimate refugees. No wonder God let Assyria wipe out Israel!

This whole situation is alien to us, whatever we think about capital punishment, but it shows a clear concern that only the guilty be punished, not the innocent. It also shows that people had to take responsibility for their actions, even unintended ones. And it shows that in this case at least, one particular person's death could atone for many others. This last point is far more richly exemplified in Christ's death for sinners, the cornerstone of Christian faith. The other two should be enshrined in the legal systems reflecting a truly Christian culture. We may want to add many further points, but we mustn't forget the basics.

PRAYER

Pray for the release of those unjustly imprisoned.

HONEST LIFE, HONEST SPEECH

Land

Several lengthy chapters in Joshua (13—19) make boring reading to us, since they simply record in great detail the division of the land among the twelve tribes. But this was a vital document for ancient Israel. The tribe's land was subdivided for clans, and then in turn for families. Each family's allotted land would provide its livelihood for generation after generation—indeed, the only livelihood available. You couldn't up sticks and go off to find a job elsewhere—there were none. Everyone lived and worked on the land. This meant that the exact position of boundaries was crucial. Of course they couldn't be guarded, and unless they were really secure they could be moved surreptitiously, but this would be gross dishonesty.

Further, there is some evidence that land was worked in long, narrow strips, rather than in the squarer pattern of fields generally used in Europe. Moving a marker even a metre or two could result in a significant amount of land being gained by you and lost by your neighbour down the whole length of a strip. So moving a marker (v. 14) was serious theft. And it wasn't just a one-off, but a theft repeated year-in year-out for as long as it went unnoticed. No wonder the crime merits a formal curse (27:17), the rebuke of prophets (Hosea 5:10), and the notice of Wisdom writers (Job 24:2; Proverbs 22:28).

Similar agricultural patterns are found elsewhere in the ancient east, and hence similar insistence on boundary markers. For instance, the Egyptian *Teaching of Amenemope* says, 'Do not carry off the landmark at the boundaries of the arable land' (*ANET*, 422c). Yet Israel's law was different from its neighbours' in one significant way: people were never executed for property offences. However serious these crimes, they never merited the death penalty. Unlike Mesopotamia, Egypt, Rome or, for that matter, medieval Christendom, no one faced death for stealing. People were more important than property.

Stealing was still a crime, though. Interestingly, later Jewish law used the Hebrew phrase here for 'moving landmarks' (v. 14) to cover other forms of 'violating boundaries' in any way that might encroach on another's livelihood and rights. The application could be far-reaching.

People

The principle of multiple witnesses was stated in 17:6 in relation to apostasy and the death penalty. Here it is extended to all crime (vv. 15–21). One person's evidence was insufficient for conviction. This basic principle of justice would immediately limit people trying to settle personal scores through the courts. God's concern for justice to be done and to be seen to be done was paramount.

What if there was a suspicion of false witness, as assumed in verse 16? Two safeguards are spelt out. First, the case would go to the court of referral based at the central sanctuary ('before the Lord'), and the judges there would conduct a full enquiry (v. 17). The big guns would come down from Jerusalem, and leave no stone unturned! As the Hutton Enquiry in Britain in 2003 showed, such scrutiny can be very uncomfortable for all concerned. Second, those found guilty of false testimony would pay the exact penalty that they had hoped to inflict on someone else (v. 19). Here the law is absolutely categorical. False witness and the attempt to convict the innocent were simply 'evil', and must be purged from Israel. Further, the punishment meted out would have a clear deterrent effect (v. 20).

Even with these safeguards, the law could be abused. Jezebel organized for two 'good-for-nothings' to testify against Naboth, and he was stoned to death (1 Kings 21:13). The prophets rail against the rich who twist the legal system to their own ends (see Isaiah 1:23; Amos 2:7). All the safeguards in the world cannot stop corrupt people acting corruptly. But at least the safeguards could act as brakes, and as reference points for brave prophets to refer back to. The same principles of thorough investigation of testimony and tough penalties for perjury are fundamental to justice today. They also illustrate the importance of honesty and integrity in everyday individual lives.

REFLECTION

Honest life, honest speech—is that how others see me?

To FIGHT *or* NOT *to* FIGHT?

To fight or not to fight? Christians throughout two millennia have agonized over this. Some insist that it is wrong in all circumstances, and many have paid for this principle with their lives. Others argue that war is sometimes necessary to defeat an even greater evil. The former take their cue from Jesus' apparent pacifism, not allowing his disciples to take swords on the fateful night before his crucifixion. They note the galvanizing effect of the non-violent resistance of Mahatma Gandhi and Martin Luther King, and the bloodshed avoided by their courageous stance. Others take their cue from Paul's apparent support of force, urging submission to temporal rulers (Romans 13). They note the need for police and security forces to stem violence at home and argue that warfare can stem evil elsewhere, whereas Gandhi maintained that non-Germans and Jews should accept Nazi rule without armed resistance.

Each generation and each Christian has to wrestle with this thorny issue, and there will always be some disagreement. We cannot appeal directly to the militarism of the Old Testament, since the church is no longer ethnic or territorial, and Christian warfare is directed against superhuman rather than human powers (Ephesians 6:12). But those who acknowledge a place for war in a sinful world can draw some lessons from the present chapter, and we can all note some underlying principles.

Fighting for God

The Israelites were about to invade a land whose inhabitants often had greater numbers and superior weapons, particularly chariots, the ancient equivalent of the tank (v. 1). Israel should remember, though, that God was fighting for them. He had already destroyed the Egyptian chariots, as they frequently sang around the campfires: 'I will sing to the Lord for he has triumphed gloriously... Pharaoh's chariots and his army he cast into the sea' (Exodus 15:1, 4). He could do the same to the Canaanite chariots. Sadly, Israel showed this trust only initially, and later were unable to dislodge chariot forces (Judges 1:19). Facing equally heavy odds in their spiritual warfare, Christians are given the same exhortation, and detailed advice (Ephesians 6:10–17). This is vital for our whole life of faith, not just its initial stages.

Before battle, the high priest rallies the troops, reminding them of their divine resources. In the context of fighting for God, this makes sense. But in the Christian era, religious blessing has often been misappropriated for secular reasons. I still remember some lines from a powerful Harvey Andrews song of the 1970s, referring specifically to Northern Ireland ('Soldier', from the album *Writer of Songs*):

> *The priests they stood on both sides, the priests they stood behind.*
> *Another fight in Jesus' name, the blind against the blind.*

The slogans of warring factions continue to cite God, whether 'God save Ireland' against 'For God and Ulster', or 'God bless America' against '*Allah aqbah* (God is great)'. But today we never have the same mandate as ancient Israel for warfare, and must be very careful not to dragoon God automatically to our cause.

Only the best

After the priest come the junior officers (v. 5), whose job seems strange. Faced with greater numbers, their job is actually to reduce their own army. This underlines their dependence on God for victory. While several questions are asked, essentially two groups are dismissed. First are the young men starting out in life, just engaged and setting up home and farm (vv. 5–7). These would be among the youngest and fittest potential soldiers—but no, they are the ones to return. One reason would be to start a family, so that if they were killed their widows would have offspring to work the farm and to perpetuate the family name. Another reason was that to die before fathering children was considered a divine curse, as noted later (28:30) and in other ancient texts.

The second group are all the fearful, the doubters, the pessimists, the morose (v. 8). They are to return home before their fear poisons the others. This may have had a psychological effect in boosting courage among those who didn't want to be shown up, though plenty admitted to fear when Gideon allowed them to go home (Judges 7:3). More importantly, both measures would remind the nation that God was the true victor.

REFLECTION
We must fight God's battles, and only God's battles.

RULES *of* ENGAGEMENT

War is always dreadful, with terrible consequences for both military and civilian casualties and their families. Now, from the Vietnam War onwards, the horror of death and destruction is beamed directly into all our homes. But for many of us it only truly comes home when we're personally affected, by losing people we love.

Even the classical 'just war' theory, carefully established in Christendom over centuries, acknowledges that war should only be engaged as a last resort, and only when there's a good chance of winning. Otherwise the deaths caused would be indefensible. It also establishes the principle of proportionate force and of discrimination between combatants and non-combatants. From 1864 onwards, these and other principles have gradually become enshrined in a body of international law known as the Geneva Convention, and have become widely accepted in principle, if often broken in practice. Even when war is thought to be justified, steps are taken to limit its ravages.

Perhaps it comes as a surprise to read of certain 'humanitarian' conventions back in the Old Testament. Admittedly they cover only international warfare, not the conquest; and they protect only women and children, not men. But in a world where might was right, and where other nations (and sometimes Israel itself later on) practised whatever barbarities they could get away with, it is remarkable to read of such conventions. And they even extended to ecological concern!

Offer terms of peace

The procedure for distant towns was that Israel should offer them a vassal treaty, that is, one where the subject town or nation would supply labour, goods and taxes to the conquering nation (vv. 19–20). This was a common procedure in the ancient world, enforced by many different groups as empires ebbed and flowed. But Israel's protocol stipulated that it must first seek peace through negotiation if at all possible (vv. 10–11). If terms were accepted, then forced labour ensued, but no other brutality, abuse or violation of human rights was sanctioned. While freedom may have been lost, dignity was to be preserved.

This stipulation was only partially fulfilled in Israel's history. For instance, when David established his empire, he had to defeat in battle his more immediate neighbours, but he accepted tribute without battle from northern Hamath in acknowledgment of its vassal status (2 Samuel 8). Others were less accommodating. The Ammonites threatened Jabesh Gilead that even if it surrendered peacefully, all its men would be half-blinded before hard labour was imposed (1 Samuel 11:2). Further afield, many Assyrian reliefs boast of the cruelty inflicted on subject peoples, whether they surrendered or not, with many captives strung together by hooks in their noses.

Only if terms were rejected could Israel go to war (vv. 12–15). In this case, after victory, all males could be killed, since they were assumed to be combatants, and everyone else taken as spoil along with the livestock and goods. Even then, there were regulations on how captives were to be treated, as the next chapter shows.

Of course, these options were not on offer for the Canaanites, who were to be annihilated (vv. 16–18). The tone of the text suddenly darkens from explanation to condemnation, as if the author is shuddering at the threat to Israel's faith of allowing the Canaanites to live. We have already considered this absolute command in relation to chapter 7, where it is expounded more fully. Here we note its repetition and the reason given, but look beyond it to the other rules of warfare outlined in the passage. Thus we can see at least some silver lining to the very dark cloud of war.

Leave trees in peace

Perhaps the most interesting feature of this legislation is its environmental concern. Fruit trees, often planted near towns, should be left alone. Only non-fruit trees could be used for siegeworks. The justification is phrased almost comically: 'Are they human, that you should attack them?' Beyond the question, however, is a clear principle of respect for God's creation.

Our age is at last rediscovering the importance of environmental concern. Here in Deuteronomy, several millennia before the environmental destruction of trench warfare, carpet bombing and napalm, or the rise of Greenpeace and other pressure groups, God shows his concern for his world. Even war must take second place.

PRAYER

Pray for those who today are trying to prevent war
or to limit its ravages.

UNRESOLVED MURDER

At first sight, this is one of the strangest laws in the book of
Deuteronomy. And not just at first sight—scholars too puzzle over
the meaning of some aspects. Why should the heifer be taken to a
wadi-valley, that is, a valley with a stream? Why should the wadi be
uncultivated? What was the purpose of killing the animal? Which
priests came and why were they there, when they had no stated role?
And does this passage have anything to say to our times?

Solemn procedure

A corpse is found out in the open, not close to any particular town,
and presumably there is no way of determining who committed the
crime. So officials from the several possible towns work together to
determine which town must assume responsibility for the body.
These officials are first called 'elders and judges' (v. 2), then just
'elders' (vv. 3, 4, 6), which suggests again that elders were very often
judges.

Priests then come to observe that all is done correctly. They could
be those with sacrificial duties at the central sanctuary, since they
'minister' and decide disputes (see 17:9). However, this ministry is
unspecified, and the role of deciding disputes may have been partly
devolved to local Levites. In practice, it would take several days to
send word to Shiloh or Jerusalem and get a delegation from there. But
whether they are central priests or local Levites, their presence gives
a solemnity to the proceedings.

Elders and priests then go together to an uncultivated valley.
English versions mostly describe the valley as having running water,
though in the dry season this would mean travelling a considerable
distance. However, the word translated 'flowing/running water' (v. 4)
could also mean 'rugged', which would explain why the valley was
uncultivated, and means that most towns would have a suitable location reasonably near them. The lack of cultivation ensured that the
land was not associated with any one family, which might have given
the impression that they were implicated.

Purging bloodguilt

An unworked heifer is taken there and its neck broken. The elders wash their hands over the animal, swear their innocence and pray that Yahweh would absolve Israel of the bloodguilt. This is clearly the crucial issue. The dead person's blood has been shed, and it must be absolved or atoned for. Clearly the animal takes the place of the culprit, and its death therefore purges the land of bloodguilt. Strictly speaking, the animal is not sacrificed. There is no altar and the priests do not participate. Its throat is not cut but its neck is broken, as for firstborn animals which cannot be sacrificed (Exodus 13:13). Nevertheless, the apparent substitution of animal for culprit and the prayer for atonement (the same word is used of sacrifices in Leviticus) imply that it has a similar function.

Many scholars suggest that this is a 'rite of elimination', where the guilt is transferred away from the human environment and washed away in water. Such rites were common in the ancient world and also occurred in Israel: for cleansing from leprosy, one bird was sacrificed and another released (Leviticus 14:1–7); on the Day of Atonement one goat was sacrificed and another sent off into the wilderness (Leviticus 16:20–22). Here the guilt is symbolically removed in the hand-washing (vv. 6–7).

While this rite may have puzzling aspects and different connotations, its central feature is clear. God had redeemed his people (v. 8) and given them a land (v. 1), but it had become tainted through bloodshed. The elders of the nearest town now prayed that God would absolve them of guilt. The rite did not effect the forgiveness; God in his covenant love provided it.

A single death

Perhaps the most interesting feature is that this whole elaborate and costly procedure is brought into play following a single unaccounted death. Sadly, our world has become inured to violence. Murder is so common that it only makes national news when there is some particularly nasty aspect of it. In ancient Israel, every life was important, and every death had to be atoned. We would do well to recover this perspective.

PRAYER

Pray for those bereaved through murder, for those who support them, and for those who work to bring the culprits to justice.

65 DEUTERONOMY 21:10–14

A CAPTIVE WIFE?

Here's another passage that raises all our hackles! Israelite soldiers who have slaughtered all the men of a captured town are then allowed to take their pick of the women and bring them home as their wives. These chosen women are carted off to the conquerors' country, to a strange people with a different religion, and to forced marriages. And all this is sanctioned by God!

As always, we need to remind ourselves that the Bible deals with the reality of life. It acknowledges human barbarity and yet still sets out godly ideals. In the New Testament, Christ and his apostles worked within the social conventions of the day, yet laid foundations that led eventually, if tortuously, to the freedom of slaves and the equality of women. In the Old Testament, the fact of war is accepted, but certain limits and safeguards are established. It would be wonderful to live in a world without war and its ravages, but reality is much harder and messier, and scripture recognizes this.

Also, we need to set this passage against the ancient background where might was right. The conquerers could do what they liked with captured women, and usually did (see Judges 5:30). Rape and pillage have been a terrible consequence of war from time immemorial, right down to the present. It probably happened in Israel too. But it shouldn't, and this passage places some remarkable limitations on it.

A captive wife

First, the woman concerned was probably unmarried, since verse 13 mentions mourning her parents but not mourning her husband. She would be a teenage girl, an unmarried virgin, not a widow forced into immediate remarriage after her husband was killed. At least that trauma was avoided.

Secondly, verse 13 clearly implies that no sexual intercourse should occur for a full month, until the period of mourning is over. Far from allowing male lust and battlefield adrenalin to have unfettered rein, this law insisted that any relationship should be long-term, and regulates for it. It also inherently gave a month for reconsideration.

Thirdly, the young woman was given a month to mourn her parents, either their death or her permanent separation from them. A

30-day period of mourning (Numbers 20:29; Deuteronomy 34:8) is still recognized in modern Judaism, which formalizes mourning custom into periods of a week, a month and a year. This month gave time for adaptation and readjustment. Shaving her head, cutting her nails and changing her clothes all symbolized leaving her old life and adopting a new one.

A free wife

Fourthly, and most remarkably of all, the act of marriage freed the young captive. She was a wife, not a slave. She may not be the man's first wife, since polygamy certainly occurred (v. 15). But she now had equal rights to any Israelite wife. If the marriage failed, she was free to leave as a citizen, not a slave. She could not be sold as unwanted 'damaged goods'. By contrast, an old Assyrian marriage contract allows a man to take a slave-wife and then, after she has borne his child, to 'dispose of her by sale wheresoever he pleases' (*ANET*, 543b).

The more we think through the passage, the more striking it appears. The power of the military victor is accepted but clearly circumscribed. The primal urge of sex, heightened in war, is acknowledged but channelled into long-term commitment. And the girl at the mercy of the conqueror is given protection and status. What at first seems barbarous actually emerges as counter-cultural.

This gives an interesting model for legislation in a fallen world. Christians often want to exert an influence in politics, but their insistence on absolutes is often politically naïve and counter-productive. Everett Koop, Surgeon General of the USA in the 1980s, was a staunch Presbyterian with strong conservative convictions on issues of sexuality and human life. Yet he argued that if American evangelicals had been prepared to dialogue with others in the 1960s, legal abortion may have been limited to so-called hard cases (mother's health, malformed foetus, rape and incest) rather than being permitted for all pregnancies. Legislation cannot force people to attain an ideal, but it can set markers and protect the powerless.

REFLECTION

How can we protect the powerless?

66 DEUTERONOMY 21:15-17

FATHERLY RESPONSIBILITIES

Families and How to Survive Them (Methuen, 1983) was the title of a book by Robin Skynner and John Cleese. It neatly summarizes how we've all felt at one time or another, especially when someone in our family is being awkward to us, and we become awkward to them in return. Sadly, one way that many people today 'survive' difficult families is to clear out as soon as possible and set up home elsewhere. This may solve an immediate dilemma, but it doesn't really address the problem. Family life is seldom easy.

This passage and the next present two family laws that balance each other: the responsibilities of a man towards his wives and children, and the responsibilities of a son towards his parents. Both come from an alien culture and seem rather strange to us, and they cannot be adopted directly. As always, however, there are important underlying principles to note.

Family favouritism?

Polygamy was known in Israel, as elsewhere in the ancient world. It occurred in pre-Mosaic times among patriarchs like Jacob, and later among kings like David and Solomon. However, it is very hard to know how widespread it was among ordinary Israelites: Samuel's father Elkanah had two wives (1 Samuel 1:2), but this is the only significant example in the Old Testament.

The biggest problem of polygamy or bigamy (the case cited here) was favouritism. Almost inevitably, one wife would be preferred to the other(s), and this in turn provoked rivalry, jealousy and family strife. The dynamic is amply illustrated in the story of Jacob, with his wives reduced to bartering for his sexual services (Genesis 30:14–16), and his older sons ganging up on the late-born favourite Joseph (Genesis 37:3–4). Indeed, this specific law may have been framed precisely with that unhappy family history in mind.

Rights of inheritance varied in the ancient world, with some cultures allowing the father absolute discretion and others insisting on strict procedures. In Israel it was the latter: the firstborn or oldest son would have a 'double portion' (v. 17), that is, twice as much as each of the other sons. The reason for this is never given directly, but the result would have been that the eldest maintained the core of the family estate, giving greater social stability over the centuries.

However, in a polygamous household, the term 'firstborn' might be ambiguous, with each wife having a firstborn son. This law makes it clear that it is the father's firstborn who inherits the double portion. It doesn't matter whether this son is born to his favourite wife or a less favoured one. The status of the firstborn is protected. The most likely scenario of polygamy would be when a man grew tired of his wife and took a younger, more attractive girl, who then became his favourite and bore him further children. The law at least prevents him bypassing his first family in favour of his second.

We note in passing that the term for 'disliked' or 'unloved' can also mean 'hated'. This illustrates a typical Semitic idiom of speaking in absolute terms. We see the same in Jesus' comment about 'hating' one's own family (Luke 14:26). There, as well as here, the thought translates better into our more nuanced modes of expression as 'not preferring', or 'putting second'. Sometimes a so-called 'literal' translation can mislead more than clarify. Accurate translation requires a knowledge of culture as well as language.

Family fairness

Today, bigamy is illegal in many countries, so the situation envisaged doesn't arise. However, the basic principle of fairness is still relevant, expecially in contexts of divorce and remarriage. A father was to treat his sons fairly in accordance with accepted social conventions, whatever his feelings towards them or their mother. If there is an application, it is that of fairness in dealing with our own families. Wills are still contentious matters today, especially where they exhibit favouritism and unfairness. Some biased wills make the headlines. Many more pass unnoticed by the wider world, yet wreak bitter family quarrels and division which continues on to subsequent generations. Wills have great potential for harm as well as good. They need to be clear, and above all fair.

REFLECTION

Are we treating our children fairly?

FILIAL RESPONSIBILITIES

Here's a law that seems incredibly harsh, and confirms all our worst impressions of the Old Testament. A son who rebels against his parents can be executed. In other words, parents had absolute control of their children; fathers ruled the roost, and any son who stepped out of line would be put to death. What barbarous times! Thank God we live under grace, and in a more enlightened era!

There is some truth in this initial assessment. The rebellious son certainly could face execution, and pay for his stubbornness with his life. But only some truth, as we shall see. The situation and its remedy were more complex than they initially appear. As always, understanding the context is crucial.

Integrated society

In any peasant society, ancient or modern, the family is absolutely central. Parents provide for children as they grow up. Children in turn provide for parents as they grow old. There is an interdependence that changes through time, but remains vital and links families inexorably together. Hence the importance of each person recognizing their place and fulfilling their role. Hence also the importance of each person acting fairly towards others. Fathers should deal with inheritance fairly, without favouritism, and sons should learn to respect their parents and care for them as they become old and frail.

In this context, a rebellious son threatens not just the family's harmony but its very survival. His profligacy threatens not just his parents' peace of mind but also their future existence. The son's attitude noted here is clearly well-formed and habitual, as shown by the several different descriptions: stubborn, rebellious, disobedient, glutton and drunkard (vv. 18, 20). He has been repeatedly disciplined in the home, but with no effect. Peasant society needs stability above all, and this son threatens seriously to disrupt it.

At this point, the parents may bring their son to the elders. Both parents must be involved, and must act together. Bringing the matter into the open would be a significant admission of family failure and a painful opening of their lives to official scrutiny, something only undertaken as a last resort. No one likes to be exposed to public gaze and potential shame. Given the role of elders in village life, they would probably already know the family situation well enough. Although unmentioned in the text, they would need to approve the parents' verdict before participating in the execution. Parents could not act alone; they needed the consent of the whole community as expressed through the elders. So this is neither a vengeful father acting on his own, nor even the parents together wielding total authority. The whole community shares the responsibility.

Covenantal law

There is another fundamental issue underlying this provision. The obligation to honour one's parents was enshrined as the fifth commandment in covenantal law. It was part of the basic treaty between God and his people, part of what made them distinctive. So rebellion against parents was disobedience to God himself—in other words, apostasy. It was as bad as going after other gods, or making images, or murder. God's law didn't just concern religious observance, as many today might think. It went to the very heart of daily life, and required obedience at this most basic level. A rebellious son not only dishonoured his parents and threatened their future, he disobeyed God.

Execution of the rebel would have two results (v. 21). In the short term, it would 'purge the evil' of hardened rebellion against God and his values. It would also have an explicit deterrent effect: the whole nation would 'hear and fear'. Interestingly, there is no record that this punishment ever occurred in Israel, and it may be that the severity of the warning was sufficient to prevent it from happening.

We live in a very different world, and thankfully do not face the immediacy of punishment like this. But we do well to heed the reminder to demonstrate faith in family life, in obedience to New Testament instructions and with the help of the Holy Spirit.

PRAYER

Pray for all parents and children, especially where there is disobedience and conflict, that love and forgiveness may prevail.

The CURSE *of* DEATH

In some ways this law is clear. It states simply that the body of an executed criminal could be exposed from a tree, but it must be removed and buried before nightfall. Not to remove the body would defile the land. In many other ways, however, the law is less clear. Whose bodies were exposed like this, and why? Were they killed first, or in the act of hanging? And if the former, is the New Testament wrong to apply this law to Christ? Was the criminal's death by hanging or impaling? Was God's curse a result of their crime or of their hanging, and why does it apply in this situation rather than others? Why would the land be defiled?

The law itself

The first few questions are straightforward. Someone guilty of a capital offence was first put to death, and then their corpse was hung from a tree (v. 22). The grammar makes it clear that death preceded exposure. The verb clearly implies hanging: the NJPS translation as 'impaling' is unduly influenced by the Assyrian practice of impaling victims, and perhaps by a desire to dissociate this practice from crucifixion.

There is no law which stipulates that a criminal must be exposed in this way, so the procedure was probably reserved for heinous offences, or where the deterrent value was crucial. There are a few biblical examples of the exposure being carried out. The imprisoned Joseph predicted that the Egyptian Pharaoh would do it to his cup-bearer (Genesis 40:19), and the victorious Joshua did it to several defeated Canaanite kings (Joshua 8:29; 10:26). However, neither instance concerned Israelite criminals. Later, David hung the bodies of two opportunists who treacherously assassinated Saul's son Ish-bosheth (Ishbaal), adding further indignities (2 Samuel 4:12).

The questions about God's curse are also reasonably straight-forward. The divine curse applied specifically to the exposed body (v. 23), which supports the idea that exposure was reserved for serious criminals. We have just seen that an unresolved crime pollutes the land (21:8). Also, death in general brings pollution (Numbers 19:11). So it is a logical extension of these concepts that an exposed criminal's body would defile the land. The accounts of Joshua burying the exposed bodies of the conquered kings before sunset suggest that even in warfare he recognized this law. Immediate burial would also have spared the criminal's family from yet further humiliation.

2 Samuel 21 doubly illustrates this defilement of the land. The source of a famine in David's reign was traced to unrequited blood-guilt caused by Saul. To atone, David brutally ordered that some of Saul's surviving sons be killed and exposed, and one of their mothers then assumed guard over the bodies. It was only after the bodies were recovered and buried, along with those of Saul and Jonathan, that God 'heeded supplications for the land' (21:14) and the famine ended.

Later developments

Death by hanging was a punishment used in the Persian empire. The powerful Haman built gallows for the Jew Mordecai, although it was Haman himself who was hanged on it (Esther 7:10). Hanging was taken over by the Greeks and Romans in turn, and developed into the dreadful punishment of crucifixion.

Long before Christ, texts from the Qumran community show that Jews extended this law in Deuteronomy to apply to death by hanging. Thus the famous Qumran Temple Scroll reads: 'If a man is guilty... you shall hang him also on the tree, and he shall die... he who is hanged on the tree is accursed of God and men' (11QT 64:12). The extension is logical. If exposure after death merits divine curse, then exposure while dying as well as after death is equally accursed. So Paul's application of the law to Christ (Galatians 3:13) is completely in line with contemporary Jewish interpretation.

This law reminds Christians yet again of the deadly seriousness of sin and its consequences. Bloodguilt led to death, death to separation from God, and unburied corpses to pollution of the land. It also reminds us of the extent of Christ's sacrifice, becoming accursed by God the Father in our place. We cannot begin to understand, let alone fathom this unholy disruption of the holy Trinity, but we can respond in love, faith and commitment.

REFLECTION

'Christ redeemed us from the curse of the law... "Cursed is every-one who hangs on a tree"... so that we might receive the promise of the Spirit through faith' (Galatians 3:13–14).

DO *to* OTHERS...

Recently a young teenage boy found £9000 in a plastic bag at a bus stop in South Wales, and handed it in to the police. At the time, he was saving up a few pounds to buy a new fishing rod. But when the chance came of a windfall that would have made him unbelievably rich, he had the honesty and decency to return it to its rightful owner. The family of the confused elderly owner, who would have lost his life-savings, was certainly grateful. The press was full of admiration, though also incredulous that anyone could be so honest in this day and age. And the nation was warmed by one person's act of decency.

Respect for people's animals

'Do to others as you would have them do to you' (Matthew 7:12). For centuries, this saying of Jesus has been called the Golden Rule. As he goes on to explain, it sums up 'the law and the prophets', that is, the whole Old Testament. Here in Deuteronomy this golden rule is spelt out in very practical ways.

Ancient Israel's territory was not subdivided into a patchwork of fields by neat hedgerows and stone walls. It was almost entirely open, with nothing but boundary markers indicating different agricultural plots. Animals could roam far and wide, and often did. Thus Saul had to travel a considerable distance in search of his father's donkeys (1 Samuel 9:4–5). It was so common for animals to stray that several prophets used this as a metaphor of wayward people, most famously in Isaiah 53:6: 'All we like sheep have gone astray'. The basic rule here is: look after stray animals, at your own cost, and make sure they are returned safely to their owner (vv. 1–3).

Do similarly for anything else belonging to your neighbour, particularly that all-important coat which often doubled as a blanket. Do similarly too for any animal which had fallen down and couldn't get up because of its heavy load. The owner would probably be walking alongside the animal, but it needed two people, one on either side, to lift the load and let the animal get up. So, the law says, help the owner out (v. 4). A small inconvenience for you would be a vital help to him.

Respect for people

A similar principle of responsibility is enshrined in verse 8: do all in your power to prevent accidents. The flat roofs of ancient houses were used for all sorts of things: drying agricultural produce (as used to hide the spies in Joshua 2:6), social events (like mourning: Jeremiah 48:38), sleeping (so Saul: 1 Samuel 9:25). So it was imperative to prevent accidents by building a balcony. Not to do so was 'culpable negligence'. The same principle has rightly become enshrined in most Western law, though it is not always vigorously maintained.

The first four verses repeatedly mention 'your neighbour', literally 'your brother' (six times in the Hebrew text). Deuteronomy continually stresses the communal aspect of God's people. They are all in it together. Every other Israelite is your neighbour, your brother or sister. Jesus was once asked, 'And who is my neighbour?' and extended the category to anyone we meet, including those of different race or religion. And that well-known parable ends with the searching command, 'Go and do likewise' (Luke 10:37).

Respect for creation

Within this section, verses 6–7 probably present another form of respect. It has similarities to the law about mothers and offspring, considered earlier (14:21; see also Leviticus 22:27). As noted already, the intent of these laws is not immediately obvious, and some scholars see them as restricting ruthless cruelty or forbidding a local religious practice. However, there may be a better explanation. This law doesn't prohibit killing and eating animals, nor does it seek to reduce the mother bird's distress. The clue to its meaning perhaps comes at the end of the verse: 'that you may live long'.

To take a mother and offspring together would be to reduce the species' population, and therefore to reduce your own food supply. By contrast, to let the mother live would provide further food for the future. Respect for creation would have obvious benefits. Here the long term takes precedence over the short term. Whether as individuals or as a society, we often find it hard to accept this principle.

REFLECTION

'No man is an island...' (John Donne)

DON'T CONFUSE CATEGORIES

We sometimes wish for 'the good old days', when everything was so much simpler: men were strong and went out to work; women were gentle and looked after the home; children were obedient and respected parents; right and wrong were clear-cut, ethical decisions easier, and so on. But of course, this won't do. For one thing, scripture warns us not to live in the past: 'Do not say, "Why were the former days better than these?"' (Ecclesiastes 7:10). For another, the past wasn't nearly as simple or as ideal as it seems. The old stereotypes were often inaccurate, and caused as much hurt and resentment as the present abundance of choice. Also, we cannot enjoy the current benefits of scientific and medical advances without facing up to the moral issues they raise. Each generation has its own advantages and difficulties, its own joys and sorrows. We need to make the best of our own generation.

The current passage seems at first glance to promote simple, well-defined categories. Verse 5 forbids cross-dressing, and verses 9–11 forbid mixed planting, mixed ploughing and mixed weaving. Keep it simple: one kind only, and each to its kind. What's the thinking behind these laws?

One kind only

These verses repeat instructions given in Leviticus (19:19), a book which has much more to say about categories. Humans could be 'holy', 'clean' or 'unclean', with pollution effecting changes in the direction away from holiness, and cleansing/purification making changes in the other direction. Only 'clean' animals could be sacrificed, and only 'clean' animals, birds and fish could be eaten. Certain sexual relations were allowed; others were forbidden. The obvious intent in Leviticus is to highlight the difference between God and humans. He is holy, and we need to be made holy to approach him—hence the stress on different categories and the importance of not confusing them. Arguably, this principle extends to all the categorization, including sacrifices, food, agriculture and clothing. There may have been other advantages, like hygiene connected to the food laws, but the primary purpose was to teach people a vital lesson.

Anthropologists of 'primitive' cultures around the world, past and present, have observed that such cultures often maintain clear distinctions like this, without necessarily linking them to religion. So it may be a universal trend in such societies. (It's important to remember that 'primitive' is a short-hand description, without value judgment. These societies could also be very complex in other ways.) Some scholars explain it in terms of social evolution, with the Old Testament retaining and codifying fundamental human concepts which were not unique to Israel. On this view, the theology was added later. Others see the universality of distinctions as a worldwide echo of God's original intent in creation, marred by the fall but still visible. On this view, the theology was original and was revealed to Israel but unknown to other peoples. Whatever the explanation, such categorization had a significant place in Israel's view of the world.

Each to its kind

The Mosaic law repeatedly stresses that God's difference from humans must be mirrored by Israel's difference from other nations, particularly the Canaanites. And this applies particularly to the case of cross-dressing (v. 5), which has the strong condemnation of being 'abhorrent' or 'detestable' to Yahweh. There is some evidence that transvestism in the ancient world was strongly associated with religion and the occult. Ishtar in Mesopotamia and Anat in Syria were worshipped as bisexual goddesses, and a Hittite magic ritual for curing childlessness involved cross-dressing for the would-be parents. Thus transvestism evoked pagan religion and rites, and was thoroughly condemned. It was far removed from the innocence of pantomime or the dubious taste of drag artists today.

Nevertheless, there remain differences inherent in the created order. Men and women are different. The understandable emphasis on social equality in the 20th century has evolved into a renewed interest in psychological complementarity in the 21st. We may not need to guard against occultic cross-dressing, but we do need to promote the God-given differences between and complementarity of the sexes.

REFLECTION

How can we move on from the simplistic 'battles of the sexes'?

SUSPECTED UNCHASTITY

Recently a Nigerian woman was condemned to death by stoning under Muslim *sharia* law. Some time after her husband had divorced her, she had given birth to a child. She had obviously had sex outside marriage, so she was sentenced to death. After an international outcry, the sentence was commuted and her life spared.

Many Christians in the West applauded this reprieve as a victory for mercy and for civilized behaviour. But when we turn to our present passage, we find exactly the same punishment for sex before marriage. What's more, the only way to disprove such an allegation is what seems to be an intrusive and degrading spectacle. The wedding night sheets are presented to the village elders to determine whether they have the appropriate blood stains. (Alternatively, it may have been proof of pre-marriage menstruation that was presented, to show that the girl was not pregnant then.) Even if the young woman is entirely innocent and has been wrongly accused by a suspicious husband, her intimate affairs are broadcast to the whole village. This offends our sense of decency and fairness. Does the law have any good points worth salvaging?

Baseless charge

Surprising as it may seem to us, the primary intent of this law is actually to protect women! This can be seen both in its social setting and its presentation. Marriage was more of a social and economic contract between two families than a romantic attraction between two individuals. It still is in some cultures today. The bride's family parted with a young girl who would have been a useful worker, while the groom's family parted with the dowry, normally 50 shekels (see 22:29). This law, then, protects a young wife whose husband dislikes her for an unspecified reason and accuses her of premarital unchastity.

The law begins by assuming that the man is guilty of false accusation, not the woman of immorality. Rather than simply divorcing her, as he could do, he wants to vilify her so that he can reclaim the dowry on the basis that she was not a virgin when he married her. At this point, the wife's parents produce the evidence. The fact that they kept it, not she, again underlines the social contract of marriage. The man is then duly convicted of lying. He is punished, presumably by beating, and fined double the amount he attempted to reclaim: 100 shekels was a very large sum. (Similarly, a convicted thief had to pay back double what he stole: Exodus 22:7.) He.is also forbidden ever to divorce his wife. While this might leave an unhappy marriage, it gave the woman security and the prospect of children, while divorce could result in permanent singleness.

The severity of the punishment, and the fact that the wife's family kept the evidence to disprove a false accusation, meant that this procedure would hardly ever be invoked. So this first section should be entitled 'false accusations': the law actually protected women from being used and discarded.

Valid charge

However, there might be a situation where the accusation was true. The marriage had taken place on the assumption that the woman was a virgin, whereas in fact she wasn't. Here there was duplicity as well as immorality, and she must pay the penalty of death (v. 21).

Even when we maintain (I think rightly) that sex should be confined to marriage, we find it hard to understand the death penalty here. But as with inheritance law and parental respect in the previous chapter, we must remember the social context. Chastity outside marriage maintained family integrity and protected the all-important issue of lineage. Changing social values and contraception have significantly altered our perspective, but we have lost as well as gained.

PRAYER

Lord, please comfort those who are falsely accused and imprisoned.
Help them and those working for them to gain their speedy
acquittal and release.

SEXUAL SIN

Sex again! We quickly tire of sex thrust at us so frequently today. Some of us are single, whether by choice or by circumstances, and struggle with our desire to have sex. Others of us are married, and fluctuate between the joys of sexual fulfilment and the pain of uneasy relationships. For all of us, today's widespread flaunting and exploitation of sex make it harder to put sex in its proper place as the wonderful and precious centre of a committed, lifelong relationship.

So we may wince when we come to yet another passage dealing with sexual intercourse, especially one dealing with a very different social culture and a now obsolete theological era. But of course the sexual drive has always been a great power for both good and ill. This text seeks to rein it in, to regulate the contexts for it, and to put in place sanctions against its misuse.

Sex and marriage

The basic concept is well-known. Sex is only for marriage, only for that lifelong personal commitment and that stable framework within which to bring up children. This principle is enshrined in the seventh commandment (5:18), and is fundamental to Israelite and indeed Christian sexual ethics.

The penalty for breaking the commandment was death for both parties (v. 22). The law is absolutely even-handed, unlike those who brought to Jesus only the woman caught in adultery (John 8:2–11). Adultery disregards God's pattern for humanity, disrupts society and brings untold personal misery. It may no longer attract any sanction, let alone the death penalty, but it remains as corrosive as ever.

Sex outside marriage

Engagement or betrothal in Israelite society was as binding as marriage is in ours. It marked the formal commitment of the two families to the marriage, and the start of the lifelong relationship between the two partners, though not of their living and sleeping together. For the girl, the engagement also provided a transition period, usually fairly short, between living in her own home and moving to her husband's.

Sexual intercourse with an engaged girl was the same as adultery.

She was already another man's wife. And the penalty for both parties was the same as for adultery (vv. 23–24). This section assumes that unmarried girls were normally virgins, which implies that the sexual ethic was more closely adhered to than we might think possible.

The only exception was where the intercourse occurred out in the countryside. Here the woman is given the benefit of any doubt. She could well have cried for help without anyone hearing (impossible in an ancient town), so is not to be punished. This contrast is reinforced by the verbs used. In the town scenario, the man simply 'lies' with the woman (v. 23), whereas in the country he 'seizes and lies' with her (v. 25; NIV translates this as rape). As in the previous passage, the law seems to assume the woman's innocence unless there is proof to the contrary. And as with manslaughter (v. 26; see 19:4–13), care is taken to distinguish different cases.

A further scenario is the rape of a girl who is not engaged. Here there is no adultery, so no death penalty. However, the culprit must pay the girl's father the full dowry and marry her, without the possibility of divorce (vv. 28–29). As with the falsely accused wife (22:19), this law protected the girl, giving her the opportunity of a home and family where otherwise she might well have been shunned for life.

Marrying your father's wife

Though alien to us, it was quite plausible for a man to marry his father's wife (v. 30). In his later years, a man could take another wife who was as young as his children, either following the death of their mother (and death in childbirth was not infrequent) or as an additional wife. A son could obviously not marry this new wife while his father was alive, but was not to marry her after the father's death either, as this would violate the previous relationship. The rationale is not given, but the law was clearly designed to prevent sexual licence within the extended family.

These laws cover certain key issues of sex and marriage. As in other areas of law, local elders would presumably extrapolate from this basic framework for various situations not mentioned explicitly. The laws given are programmatic rather than comprehensive.

PRAYER

Lord, help me to be true to the biblical ideals of chastity outside marriage and faithfulness within it.

WHO CAN VOTE?

Who can vote? Who can enter a country? Who has full citizenship? These are live issues for us as much as for ancient Israel. The collapse of the Iron Curtain in the late 1980s led many Eastern Europeans to seek new life in Western Europe. The continued poverty of developing countries propels millions to the developed world. And political and religious persecution prompt many others to flee and request asylum elsewhere. Western countries are faced with huge numbers of refugees, and have to work out policies for acceptance and rejection. It's a political hot potato, and those of us who criticize politicians often have little idea of its complexity.

These next two chapters give various regulations for the community, so they begin by discussing the true extent of the 'assembly of the Lord'. It was the nearest thing to nationality that ancient Israel had, and it inevitably had a religious flavour. Israel wasn't just an ethnic group, still less a secular state, but 'Yahweh's assembly'. Here, as throughout Israel's life, their relationship with God was pre-eminent.

Insiders excluded

First, two groups of 'insiders' are excluded from the assembly (vv. 1–2). The first group are those emasculated by removal of testicles or penis, probably intentionally rather than through a birth defect. There is some evidence from ancient Syria of emasculation for religious rites, and more widespread evidence of eunuchs holding high political office there. This rule in Deuteronomy may well be a rejection of such mutilation as part of pagan practices abhorrent in Israel. It may also reflect the same concern for wholeness shown in the ban against priests with physical defects from ministering, or against animals with defects from being sacrificed (Leviticus 21:17–20; 22:24).

The second group is unclear, since the Hebrew term *mamzer*, translated 'illicit union' (NRSV) or 'forbidden marriage' (NIV), is rare. Older versions took it to mean 'out of wedlock', but scholars now think it refers rather to marriages that break the prohibited degrees of relationship (Leviticus 18:6–20) or marriages with proscribed foreigners (as in the following verses). Their offspring are excluded from the assembly 'even to the tenth generation', that is, in perpetuity. While the exact reference is unclear to us, it must have been clear to Israel, as was the reason behind the law: God's insistence on certain standards could not be broken with impunity.

Outsiders excluded or included

Again there are two groups of 'outsiders' mentioned, but they are treated very differently, for clear reasons. First, the Ammonites and Moabites are excluded (vv. 3–4). They were distant cousins of Israel (see Genesis 19:30–38). However, when Israel had asked them for food and water, they not only refused help, they tried hard to hinder by hiring Balaam to curse Israel directly. And when that didn't work, they tried to subvert them indirectly (v. 4; Numbers 22—24; cf. 31:16). For such contemptuous disregard of kinship ties and repeated attempts to destroy Israel, these people are to remain perpetual outsiders.

By contrast, Edomites and Egyptians are treated very differently (vv. 7–8). The Edomites weren't particularly hospitable to the Israelites either, but at least they didn't actively oppose them—and they were much closer cousins (Genesis 36:1). Most remarkable, though, is the treatment of the Egyptians. Here, Israel is to look back beyond their slavery under recent pharaohs to an earlier welcome. As so often in this book, their own experience as aliens should remind them to be hospitable. For both Edomites and Egyptians, third-generation children may be admitted to the assembly. Even in our own experience of emigration and immigration, we can see that the first generation often looks back to the home country, the second generation looks two ways, while the third feels much more integrated into the host country.

The great historical watershed of the exile led, much later, to a reconsideration of the nature of Israel. After then, God promised that foreigners and eunuchs (perhaps Jews in imperial service in Babylon) who kept his laws could be part of his people (Isaiah 56:3–5). This widening of God's people was a powerful influence on the fledgling Christian church. Perhaps not surprisingly, one of its earliest converts was a foreign eunuch (Acts 8:26–40). There are now no ethnic barriers to faith—only unbelief.

REFLECTION

'There is no longer Jew or Greek… slave or free… male and female;
for all of you are one in Christ Jesus' (Galatians 3:28).
Give thanks, and live it out!

CAMP LATRINES & RUNAWAY SLAVES

The rest of chapter 23 and the following two chapters deal with a variety of issues, all extremely relevant to Israel and containing important principles from which we can learn, but not necessarily linked to each other or to one general theme.

Holiness and health

The first section (vv. 9–14) deals with propriety in the army camp. It begins with a general admonition against 'everything impure' (NIV), and then gives two specific cases. As often elsewhere, these are probably illustrative examples rather than the complete list of possibilities. The first example is nocturnal emission of semen, which presumably could be from an involuntary 'wet dream' or masturbation (about which the Bible says nothing directly). Whatever the cause, the man in question is quarantined for a day. This shows that it is a matter of ritual, not moral, impurity, since the latter would require sacrifice. Sexual intercourse had the same result (Leviticus 15:18), though of course the military camp was male only, and soldiers on duty were supposed to refrain from sex, as illustrated by David's men (1 Samuel 21:5) and Uriah (2 Samuel 11:11).

The second example is defecation, which should be done outside the camp into a makeshift hole, with the faeces then covered. This would of course keep the camp healthier, not to mention better-smelling. Unburied excrement allows insect-borne diseases to spread rapidly, as is sadly the case still today in many parts of the world. But the motivation given here is religious: this procedure would keep the camp holy and allow God's continued presence there (v. 14). Here, cleanliness really was next to godliness. Bodily emissions of all sorts caused defilement in Israel, including skin eruptions, menstruation, and even childbirth (Leviticus 12—15). This is never explained, but probably has to do with the essential elements of life (semen, blood) being lost, and with bodily wholeness being diminished.

Here, as in the food laws, we see that attention to holiness led to better hygiene and health. God's laws, presented in concepts familiar at that time, had beneficial effects which have been understood only in recent centuries. A confidence that God really does know best should help us, in our day, to stick to biblical principles, even when we may not see valid reasons.

Hospitality to escaped slaves

The second section (vv. 15–16) deals with runaway slaves, and is one of the most surprising pieces of legislation in the whole book. Wherever slavery has been practised, from the ancient world to classical Rome, to American plantations, to modern Africa, two factors have co-existed. Slaves have tried to run away, and authorities have imposed severe penalties, often death, on the runaways and on their protectors. In ancient Mesopotamia, law codes and international treaties stressed the importance of returning runaways, on pain of death (*ANET*, 167a) or of a hefty fine and having one's hands cut off (*ANET*, 531c). Most countries kept on good terms with each other by returning runaways, as a Philistine king once did to Israel (1 Kings 2:39).

However, this remarkable law insists that runaways should *not* be returned. Instead they should be treated well and allowed to settle wherever they want. Most scholars deduce that these are foreign runaways because of the phrasing of verse 16 ('reside with you... in any one of your towns') and the lack of reference to Hebrew kin, in contrast to the Israelite slave laws (Deuteronomy 15:12—see comments on p. 118). This law would, then, extend the common principle of temporary asylum in a temple to permanent refuge in the whole of Israelite territory: all the land is God's temple.

We are not told why Israel should risk alienating all its neighbours by harbouring their runaway slaves. We can only extrapolate from what is said elsewhere: when in need, the nation's ancestors were welcomed into Egypt; and they are repeatedly urged to care for the disadvantaged. This divine principle of compassion overruled all others. We don't know whether it was ever enacted—but we can see here a wonderful example of the New Testament motto that mercy triumphs over judgment (James 2:13).

PRAYER

Pray for areas of the world still oppressed by slavery and poor health facilities.

PROSTITUTION *by another* NAME?

Prostitution is often called 'the oldest profession' and is assumed to be inevitable in human society, ancient or modern, primitive or advanced. This may well be true. Sex is a hugely powerful human drive, and even those who accept monogamous relationships in principle often fail to stick to them in practice. But prostitution can take different forms, and this leads to different interpretations of this passage.

'Holy sex'?

The standard view is that this law forbids a practice which our English translations call temple prostitution and which scholars call sacred or cultic prostitution. The Hebrew terms translated 'temple prostitute' in verse 17 are literally 'holy-girl' (*qedeshah*) and 'holy-boy' (*qadesh*), very similar to the word translated 'holy' (*qadosh*) in 23:14. These prostitutes were 'holy' in that they worked at local shrines. Worshippers had intercourse with them in the hope that they would encourage the local fertility god to make their own fields and family fertile. The appeal of sex and the aim of fertility were an irresistible combination! However, this form of prostitution was completely forbidden for Israelites. They must not follow the local gods and so shouldn't go to their shrines: Deuteronomy repeatedly and forcefully forbids it. Instead they must worship only Yahweh, and occasionally go to his one centralized shrine or temple (ch. 12). True worship was certainly to be joyful, but not because of some extra sex.

Sadly, this law was not followed, and Hosea later condemns Israelite women for prostitution and their men for sacrificing with 'holy-girls' (Hosea 4:14). Indeed, sexual unfaithfulness is the central image of Hosea's book: the prophet himself experiences heartbreak over an unfaithful partner, and through this he understands more of God's heartbreak over an unfaithful people.

However, although this standard view is found in most Bible dictionaries and commentaries, the evidence for such practice in the ancient world remains uncertain. Indeed, Tigay comments forcefully (p. 481), 'There is probably no subject in the field of ancient Near Eastern religion on which more has been written, with so much confidence, on the basis of so little explicit evidence, than "cultic prostitution".'

Temple sex

Earlier, in Mesopotamia in the third millennium BC, there was a tradition of a sacred marriage ceremony, symbolizing the union of the deities Inanna and Dumuzi. Some scholars surmise that the ceremony was enacted by the king with a priestess or 'holy-girl', and that it may have led more widely to 'sacred prostitution' in imitation of the divine marriage. But this remains hypothetical—there is no textual evidence of such enactment by the king, let alone others.

Later, in the Mediterranean world of the late first millennium BC, various Greek and Latin sources record that prostitutes (called *hierodules*) earned money for some temples, notably that of Aphrodite in Corinth. In some places, girls even had to spend time doing this before marriage (according to Herodotus and Lucian). But the motivation for their clients was simply sex, not imitating the gods or inducing fertility.

Throughout the ancient world, religious shrines were places of celebration and of diversion from the hard graft of subsistence farming. These 'holy places' were an obvious place for prostitutes to work, and this led to their nickname of 'holy-girls'. Some scholars now think that the name implied their location rather than any religious motives for them or their clients. The references in Hosea and other prophets could also fit this interpretation. In this case, the present text forbids all forms of prostitution for Israelites.

It's hard on present evidence to judge between these two interpretations. On the one hand, the concept of 'sacred sex' has probably been exaggerated in the past. On the other, there is a clear association between prostitution and shrines, here and in other texts. In fact, both explanations may be partly true, since all sorts of reasons may have been given to justify this prostitution. But it was totally unacceptable to God, and hence forbidden to Israelites.

PRAYER

Pray for prostitutes, for those who use them and for those who seek to help them.

INTEREST, VOWS & SNACKS

Charging interest

What are the main barriers to economic progress in developing countries? We probably think immediately of the major international issues of national debt, IMF policies and world trade agreements. These are certainly important, and need to be addressed. But the biggest barrier of all, which existed long before these others emerged and still exists today in many rural contexts, is the exorbitant interest rate charged by the local money lender. In the West we have become used to single-figure loan repayments, but many subsistence farmers must repay loans at 20 per cent, 30 per cent or even more. And sometimes these rates apply to a few months, not even a year. No wonder many poor farmers have to pledge part of their crop in repayment, and are never able to break out of the cycle of poverty. No wonder, too, that many development agencies on the ground focus on forming co-operatives with low-interest credit facilities.

The law in verses 19–20 addresses the issue in typical Deuteronomic style. Interest must not be charged to fellow Israelites. In subsistence agriculture, as proved time and time again, interest charges on a poor farmer lead to further poverty. So, as a matter of kinship solidarity, interest must not be charged in Israel. The principle is then extended to all loans, to close all possible loopholes. Those in difficulty needed help, not extra burdens. This became a key feature of Israelite economic ethics, stated several times in law (see also Exodus 22:25; Leviticus 25:36). And those approaching the temple should be people 'who do not lend money at interest' (Psalm 15:5).

By contrast, foreigners could be charged interest. This may be partly because the Israelites' primary obligation was to their own kith and kin, even if they are urged elsewhere to be generous to resident foreigners (10:19; 14:29; 16:11 and so on). Similarly, Paul instructs Christians, 'Let us work for the good of all, and especially for those of the family of faith' (Galatians 6:10). More probably, though, it is because the foreigners would not be impoverished landowners. Foreigners sometimes settled temporarily in Israelite towns for trading purposes, in which case money was part of their trade and charging interest was therefore legitimate. There is an economic as well as ethnic reason for the different provision.

The Jewish and subsequent Christian ban on interest was largely maintained until the 16th century, when economic conditions, as well as the arguments of the Protestant Reformers, led gradually to change. Our economy is very different, but the principle of protecting the vulnerable, especially those who share the faith, remains valid.

Fulfilling vows

The only vow most of us take today is that of marriage, but vows were much more common in the ancient world. People often vowed to make an offering to their god if they were granted their request—for example, pregnancy, safe childbirth, victory in battle or recovery from illness. Vows were entirely voluntary, but they were always serious. The crucial point here (vv. 21–23) is that, if undertaken, they must be fulfilled. Better not to vow than to make a vow and not fulfil it.

The best-known Old Testament vow was that made by Hannah, to give back to Yahweh the son she longed for (1 Samuel 1:11). She fulfilled it, despite the personal cost, and God blessed her with five further children (1 Samuel 2:21).

Taking snacks

The law in verses 24–25 is typical of Deuteronomy in so many ways. The hungry must eat, even if it means taking produce from other people's land. Travellers may take a few grapes and some grain for a snack as they walk by. However, they mustn't abuse this allowance by carrying the produce away—no baskets or sickles allowed!

This law reminds Israel of two things: first, people are more important than property; and second, the land is God's gift to all, with the individual farmer simply as God's tenant. At the same time, the law is given in principle only, and it would take neighbourly trust and co-operation to ensure that it really worked in practice.

REFLECTION

Money, promises, trust—what can I do to foster integrity in my community?

DIVORCE & REMARRIAGE

Britain has the highest divorce rate of Western Europe, and many readers of this book may have experienced divorce themselves or in their families. Whatever our personal experience, we need to be cautious with generalizations about such a complex phenomenon. Divorce has many different causes and many different results, including relief and new opportunities as well as agony and hardship. It formally acknowledges human failure by one or more parties, and draws a line under a marriage relationship.

The present passage is not about divorce *per se* but about a specific consequent situation, the remarriage of a twice-divorced woman to her first husband. Nevertheless, it includes important information on the practice of divorce in Israel.

Divorce

The basis of divorce is that the husband finds something 'objectionable' (NRSV) or 'indecent' (NIV) (v. 1). The Hebrew phrase, 'the nakedness of a thing', is difficult to interpret precisely, and no more details are given here. We can only assume that in Israel the specific grounds were widely known or left to local elders to determine.

Inevitably this led to much debate in later Jewish circles. The more conservative school of Shammai took the phrase to mean sexual indecency, perhaps including adultery, although the death penalty was already given for this. The more liberal school of Hillel took it as any matter that displeased the husband. The latter view led to divorce occurring for what we would consider trivial reasons. When Pharisees asked Jesus, 'Is it lawful for a man to divorce his wife for any cause?' (Matthew 19:3), they were asking his opinion on this debate, not on whether divorce was permitted at all. Jesus' reply against divorce (Mark 10:2-10) and the exception for 'sexual immorality' (Matthew 19:9) takes the more conservative view.

The divorce had to be formally ratified by a 'certificate of divorce'. This certificate gave some protection to the woman, since it acknowledged that she was now legally unmarried and free to marry someone else. Men could not leave women in legal limbo—either they remained married and part of the reciprocal responsibilities within the home, or they were free and entitled to go elsewhere. We note in passing that the concept of divorce here includes by definition the possibility of remarriage. To argue that divorce is acceptable but not remarriage, as some Christians do, is to misunderstand this basic point. (An excellent, succinct and inexpensive guide on this complex issue is D. Instone-Brewer, *Divorce and Remarriage in the 1st and 21st Century*, Grove Book B19, 2001; see www.grovebooks.co.uk.)

Remarriage to a former partner

As noted, the law here envisages one specific situation, and prohibits remarriage to a former husband after marriage to someone else. (Presumably it could happen if there was no interim marriage.) No reasoning is given, but the law clearly protected a vulnerable woman from being swapped back and forth between various men. The woman is 'defiled' or ritually unclean as far as the first man is concerned—that is, she is off-limits to him. The term is used here in a legal sense, without moral connotations (v. 4).

David either ignored or was ignorant of this law when he insisted on the return of his first wife Michal, whom Saul had remarried to someone else when David fled. Tragically, political machinations marked the whole of this unhappy story (1 Samuel 18:27; 25:44; 2 Samuel 3:13–16; 6:16–23).

The law was well known to the prophets, though: Jeremiah (3:1–5; 4:1–4) wrestles with whether unfaithful Israel can return to her first husband Yahweh, while Isaiah (50:1) seems to respond that it is possible because there was no formal divorce. More poignantly, Hosea is commanded to buy his wife back from her pimp, after she had returned to prostitution (Hosea 3:1). Here one prophet learns, through personal tragedy, the true extent of God's grace to a wayward people. And that same God remains gracious today.

PRAYER

Lord, show your grace to those suffering in unhappy marriage or from painful divorce.

A MISCELLANY

The next few passages have more short, unconnected laws. This makes them somewhat disjointed to read and discuss, but it also gives more chance that one particular law—probably different ones for different readers—will capture our interest and spur us on to imaginative reflection and engaged prayer.

Long honeymoon

Here's a little jewel (v. 5). A newly wed husband is exempt from military duty for a year, so that he can bring happiness to his wife (so NIV). No doubt this would make him happy too (so NRSV), but the Hebrew text emphasizes the effect on the young wife. Of course there are factors not mentioned here, notably the opportunity for them to conceive a child, who would bring comfort and support to the wife in the case of her husband's death. But Deuteronomy delights in the young couple's happiness, and leaves it at that.

Most of us don't face obligatory military service, and our society doesn't depend as much on offspring to provide for widows. Nevertheless, in a very different world and for different reasons, church and society would still benefit from allowing newlyweds the time to 'give each other happiness' at the start of their married lives.

No kidnapping

The slave trade has led to untold human misery. It still blights the world in whatever form it takes, whether open slavery or ruthless exploitation of illegal immigrants. Amos vociferously condemns some neighbouring states for their involvement (Amos 1:6, 9). Deuteronomy (like Exodus 21:16) stipulates the death penalty for this 'evil' in Israel (v. 7). It is the only case where theft is punishable by death. But then the Hebrew expression for 'kidnapping' is 'stealing the life', which shows how serious it is.

Watch for leprosy

'Leprosy' (v. 8) is the traditional translation of a Hebrew term covering a variety of surface conditions affecting people, clothing and buildings. Regarding people, the term covered serious and often infectious skin conditions, but probably not what we now call leprosy (Hansen's Disease), which, as far as we know, didn't reach the Middle East till much later. Leviticus 13—14 gives the detailed measures for dealing with these 'leprous' conditions. Here the text simply refers lay people to the priestly legislation, and urges both compliance and vigilance. Nobody was immune, not even Moses' sister Miriam (v. 9; see Numbers 12). Everyone needed to be on their guard.

Treat the poor with dignity

As we have seen, the law encouraged generosity in both giving and lending, especially to fellow Israelites. Sadly, though, human nature often means that the lender can become arrogant and callous of the feelings of the importune. Various laws sought to temper this tendency by going back to basic human values: everyone has rights and should be treated with dignity, however poor they are.

Verse 6 forbids a millstone to be taken. Each family would have its own millstones, with a large fixed base and a lighter grinding stone. To take the latter would disable the mill and prevent the family from making its daily bread. The 'pledge' mentioned here (unlike in vv. 10–13) is a term for property impounded when debtors have already defaulted on a loan. It's what the bailiffs take! So not even when the debtors default should a millstone be taken. Even the impoverished must be allowed to eat.

Verses 10–13 apply to more common pledges. A poor man had little more than his cloak. If that was his pledge, he needed it for a blanket, and it should be returned by nightfall. In practice, this meant that the pledge was effectively nominal, but no matter. His needs were more important than the lender's rights. Similarly, his house, however much a hovel, was still his home, and the lender had no right to enter (v. 10): the poor should be treated with dignity. And finally, verses 14–15 insist that wages should be paid daily. This shows how poor many people were, and how much they needed their pay immediately to prevent their family from going hungry. Their need again is primary. Treat them well!

REFLECTION

Reflect on whichever of these laws has caught your interest, and develop it imaginatively in prayer.

Another Miscellany

Individual responsibility

A basic principle of the Israelite law-courts was that everyone was answerable for their own actions, not those of their parents or children. This is an entirely laudable principle, and the bedrock of many modern legal codes, but 24:16 raises several important issues.

Firstly, within Deuteronomy itself there are situations where whole families are punished together, notably Canaanites in the conquest (ch. 7), or Israelites in apostate towns (ch. 13). And the second commandment talks of punishing children 'to the third and fourth generation' (5:9). However, these texts all concern offences against God, his fundamental laws and his *herem* judgment. By contrast, the present verse deals with ongoing day-to-day local justice. This law was explicitly cited later when a king's assassins were executed, but not their children (2 Kings 14:6).

Secondly, this exclusion of children was uncommon in the ancient world. Punishment for the crimes of parents was well-known: for example, Hammurabi's famous Law Code decrees the death of an innocent son or daughter for their father's offence (*ANET*, 170d, 175c, 176a). Israel was to be markedly different.

Justice for all

Care for widows, orphans and resident aliens has been stressed repeatedly in Deuteronomy. They were to receive the triennial tithe (14:29) and be welcomed at annual festivals (16:11). Here (24:17–18) they have equal standing before the law, and must receive justice as well as generosity. So the prohibition against keeping garments taken in pledge applied as much to an impoverished widow as to anyone else. Israelites—or at least their forebears—knew what it was like to be destitute, and must never forget this in dealing with others.

Harvest bounty

One very practical provision for the poor was at harvest time, when Israelite farmers were to leave something for them (24:19–21).

Anything not gathered from fields or trees first time round was to be left for others to glean. Further details in Leviticus (19:9–10) include leaving field edges purposely unharvested. The phrase 'it shall be left for' could even be translated 'it belongs to'. The poor had a right to the leavings, and to a share in the blessings of the land in general, even if they didn't own any in particular. This means that they were not totally dependent on handouts from others, but had the opportunity to work for themselves. It may have been hard, back-breaking work, but it was *their* work. This law is beautifully brought to life in the story of the widow Ruth, who trusted in Naomi's God, gleaning in Boaz's fields, and found love and security in a new home.

Proportional punishment

Justice must be done and be seen to be done, so disputes must come to the proper courts, not be settled by personal vendettas (25:1–3). In ancient society, corporal punishment was often the only option available, and judges were left to determine how it should be administered. But there were two very important principles. First, punishment must be proportional to the offence, not left to the demand of the wronged party or the whim of the judge. Second, it was limited, so that the person receiving it would not be 'degraded' or humiliated. Even in punishment, human dignity must be respected. No other ancient law code limits punishment like this.

In later times Jews reduced the maximum penalty to 39 lashes, so that even if they miscounted they still wouldn't transgress the law. Paul received this punishment five times for the sake of the gospel (2 Corinthians 11:24).

Fairness to animals

The principle of letting everyone share in the fruit of the harvest is extended even to animals (25:4). The ox who drags the heavy sledge over the grain to separate wheat from stalk must be allowed to benefit from his work. This principle is later applied by Paul to Christian workers: if God wants animals to benefit from their work, how much more Christian evangelists and preachers (1 Corinthians 9:8–12).

PRAYER

*Again, pray imaginatively about one of these sections
and its possible implications today.*

LEVIRATE MARRIAGE

'Am I my brother's keeper?' Cain famously asked God when feigning ignorance of Abel's fate (Genesis 4:9). 'Yes' was the implied response. The present passage deals with one situation where an Israelite should very definitely be his brother's keeper. If a married man died without children, his brother was to marry his widow, and their first son would then be counted legally as the son of the deceased brother. This is called Levirate marriage (from *levir*, Latin for 'brother-in-law').

There are several Old Testament illustrations of this custom (Genesis 38; Ruth 1; 4). It was a common practice in the ancient world, and still exists in some places. For instance, after hearing a sermon on Ruth, a Nigerian visitor to our church confirmed that similar customs existed until recently among his ancestral people.

Moral duty

The brothers are residing together (v. 5), so they are still part of the extended household under their parents. This implies that the reason for the custom was to preserve the dead man's name and share of the family inheritance, as well as to provide for the widow, presumably still a young woman. Whether the surviving brother would be already married is unstated, although the more detailed accounts in other ancient law codes generally imply that he was younger and still unmarried. These codes illustrate the practice among Assyrians (*ANET*, 182d §30; 184a §43), Hittites (*ANET*, 196c §193) and others, all with slight variations on the same basic custom.

Neither the surviving brother nor the widow may have chosen each other, but then marriage was seldom a matter of choice anyway. As noted previously, it was much more an economic exchange between two families, and this provided social stability over many centuries. Here a brother is required to fulfil a family obligation.

Social disgrace

However, the Israelite man could apparently refuse (v. 7), unlike men in the other ancient cultures cited above. No cause is given here, and many could be suggested: the brother wanted to inherit the property himself, or didn't want to marry the widow, or didn't want a rival to his first wife, or couldn't afford to support another family, or the widow was thought to bring bad luck.

If this happened, the woman could approach the village elders to plead her cause. They would try to persuade the man, but, if unsuccessful, they would summon him for naming and shaming. The widow was entitled to spit in his face and remove his sandal, and from then on he was dubbed 'Unsandalled' (vv. 9–10). Spitting in the face is a universal sign of contempt, but sandal-removing is foreign to us, and the nickname seems amusing rather than shocking. However, it was obviously a severe form of rebuke for dereliction of duty in Israel and elsewhere: a Hittite text orders that a guard who deserts his post should have his shoe removed in punishment.

Developing practice

This custom has both sad and happy illustrations. Genesis 38 recounts that Judah's daughter-in-law Tamar survived his two older sons without children, but was then kept from the third. So she took matters into her own hands and bore Judah's children directly. In Ruth 1, Naomi tells her childless daughters-in-law that she has no sons left for them, and they shouldn't wait for her to have more. However, the story has a happy ending in chapter 4 when Boaz steps in, redeems the mortgaged property and marries Ruth. This story is complicated by dealing with land redemption as well, and has the intriguing feature that the father of Ruth's son Obed is recorded as Boaz, not her first husband Mahlon, whose name was not, then, preserved. But these accounts show that the custom was well established in early Israel, and that it developed and varied in different times and places.

Our social and economic situation is very different, and most of us are less concerned with continuity of family name or preservation of family inheritance. Nevertheless, we should still care for our relatives. As Paul reminds us forcefully, 'whoever does not provide for relatives, and especially for family members, has denied the faith and is worse than an unbeliever' (1 Timothy 5:8).

REFLECTION

Whose keeper am I?

A THIRD MISCELLANY

Immodest brawls

Verses 11–12 present another strange and rather unappealing law! Apart from its sordid picture of brawling men and an immodest woman, it is the only Old Testament law to prescribe mutilation. This alone suggests that the crime was very serious, but quite why remains unsaid. Perhaps it was the effrontery of a woman grasping a man's genitals in public. More probably it was because of damage to his testicles, leaving him unable to bear children. This would explain the severity of the punishment, given all that we know about the importance of children in the ancient world and particularly in Israel.

An Assyrian law has exactly this rationale: 'If a woman has crushed a seignior's testicle in a brawl, they shall cut off one finger of hers, and if the other testicle has become affected along with it by catching the infection... or she has crushed the other testicle in the brawl, they shall tear out both her [eyes]' (*ANET*, 181a—the final word is a guess). This law prescribes hand mutilation for partial injury, but more severe punishment for full injury. Other laws in the same collection prescribe various other stomach-turning forms of mutilation for assorted offences (*ANET*, 181), and other law codes from Mesopotamia are similar. While we may shudder at the law in Deuteronomy, we can at least note how rare the punishment of mutilation was in Israel.

Weights and measures

Ancient Israel, like most rural, peasant societies, had as much a barter economy as a cash one. Goods were commonly exchanged, so the weighing and measuring of farm produce was a daily activity. Archaeological work has uncovered many hundreds of weight-stones from different places, which have now been carefully studied. Indeed, whole books have been written on them. One interesting feature is that no two weight-stones are exactly identical—such standardization was too difficult in ancient times.

What was crucial, however, was that each farmer or trader used the same weights for buying and selling. Weight-stones were kept in a bag, and it would have been possible to have a secret pouch inside the bag.

Thus a dishonest trader could pull out the heavy one when buying, to get more, but the light one when selling, to give less (vv. 13–15). Similarly, different sized measures could be used for large quantities to gain an unfair advantage.

For Yahweh, such practice was 'abhorrent' (v. 16): exactly the same strong word is used of Canaanite idols in 7:25. It is far from being a minor misdemeanour, a little cooking of the books. In God's eyes, it is as bad as idolatry. No wonder the prophets often thundered against it (see Amos 8:5; Micah 6:11).

This is the last law in Deuteronomy dealing with day-to-day life. Fittingly, it encapsulates two key themes of the book: fairness to all, especially the vulnerable, and God's blessing on obedience and faithfulness. This is one very effective way to 'choose life' (see 30:19).

Treacherous Amalek

Exodus 17 recounts the first attack of the nomadic Amalekites on the Israelites just after they left Egypt. Verses 17–19 suggest that there were other attacks, when the Amalekites dogged Israel's route and attacked the stragglers. Those lagging behind were inevitably the elderly and the young, the sick and the pregnant, and no mercy was shown to these poor vulnerable people. So the Amalekites were not just anti-Israel, they were anti-human. As in Amos 1—2, a foreign people outside God's covenant is nevertheless held accountable for 'crimes against humanity', and placed under perpetual judgment. The Amalekites periodically attacked Israel after the conquest (see Judges 3:13; 1 Samuel 30:1), but were finally wiped out in the time of Hezekiah, some two centuries later (1 Chronicles 4:43).

Sadly, it is not hard to find many instances of crimes against humanity in our own day, especially those against the weak and vulnerable. Physical extermination of the guilty parties is not a Christian option, but God calls us to equally forceful resistance, by doing all in our power to publicize, protest, lobby, educate and confront, both to bring the perpetrators to justice and to avert such crimes in the future.

PRAYER

Pray for the persecuted, and do something today to help them.
For instance, you could write a letter, or consult the website of
Christian Solidarity Worldwide, Amnesty International,
or any other group with whom you have links.

A NATIONAL ANTHEM?

We hear it on state occasions, at the Olympic Games, and at count-less other humbler occasions. It opens meetings, closes proceedings, accompanies flag-raising and medal-giving, and adorns many other-wise straightforward events. *It*, of course, is the national anthem.

For many people, the anthem goes to the core of who we are, and affects us profoundly. For some, the words are crucial; for others, it's the words, tune and concept together that transform the song. The tune may be unexciting or difficult, the words may reflect a distant past, but it still remains *our* national anthem—and we prize it.

The Israelites had no national anthem. But they did have one dec-laration which everyone should know by heart and recite year after year. Like most anthems, it gave a brief summary of their past. Like many, it attributed the past to God's goodness. And like some national ceremonies, it accompanied a pledge of continued allegiance.

National testimony

The declaration in verses 5–10 has been called an Israelite creed. It certainly affirms their faith, though not in the style of later Christian creeds. It mentions Abraham (the Aramean), his later family's descent to Egypt, their growth, Egyptian oppression, God's mighty deliver-ance, and their entrance into the land. It then fleshes out this bare outline with threefold description. Abraham's family was small, but became 'great, mighty and populous' (v. 5). The Egyptians 'treated us harshly and afflicted us, by imposing hard labour on us' (v. 6). We cried to the Lord, who saw 'our affliction, our toil, and our oppres-sion' (v. 7). The brief story then comes to a climax with a longer description of God's deliverance: 'with a mighty hand and an out-stretched arm, with great terror and with miraculous signs and wonders' (v. 8, NIV). Finally there is the double reference to their new situation: 'he brought us into this place and gave us this land' (v. 9). This piling up of synonyms suggests a ritual text which has become honed over the years by regular recitation.

Just as important as the form is the content. Israel's creed was a theology of thanksgiving. God had delivered and provided for them; they now gave something back to him. He had given them a fertile land; they acknowledged this in offering the harvest's firstfruits. So every year their harvest festival was a national testimony. Everyone recited the same words, identifying with the national story and affirming it as true for themselves (vv. 1–2). God had blessed them, and they were honouring him with their offering.

Individual ceremony

Interestingly, while the ritual was the same for everyone, the timing could well have been different. Everyone was to go to the national sanctuary in turn, presumably at different times and on different days. The declaration was the same, but each person proclaimed it individually as they presented their offering (vv. 3–4). Perhaps churches that require all members to re-affirm their allegiance individually and annually (for example, in the Methodist covenant renewal service at new year) have preserved something precious from this ancient procedure. God has been good to us all, and we each need to assert it personally.

Communal harmony

After the ceremony, there is to be a great feast, to 'celebrate with all the bounty that Yahweh your God has given to you' (v. 11). This is a time of feasting and rejoicing. And, as so often in Israel, it is to be welcoming, openhearted and inclusive. Therefore, Levites, who don't have their own fields, and resident aliens, who probably don't either, are invited to the celebrations. By now we expect mention of the former, but the latter is more surprising. Foreigners who have settled in Israel and made it their home are to be included.

We tend to think of the Old Testament as erecting a huge barrier between Israelites and others. Certainly Deuteronomy stresses the religious difference. But for those who choose to settle in Israel and presumably accept her ways, there is to be open acceptance and an invitation to join the feast. This is already a step on the way to the removal of all ethnic distinction in the gospel of Christ.

REFLECTION

Is there an appropriate church context for us to reaffirm annually our individual faith, and how would this benefit our Christian life and witness?

GENEROSITY *with* INTEGRITY

As well as a national anthem, many countries have an oath of allegiance. This is intoned solemnly before the national flag, or a picture of the head of state, or sometimes both. It may happen when gaining citizenship, or when joining the armed forces, or as a regular feature of life. In many an American school, there is the daily pledge of allegiance to the flag as symbol of the country.

Ancient Israel didn't have an oath of allegiance as such, but it did have a declaration of integrity and obedience. Every head of a household was expected to make this declaration every three years (v. 12), when presenting his tithe. This may seem to us to be an obscure context: why not a national ceremony with trumpets and fanfare? Yet its very practical nature illustrated something crucial to Israel's life: that acting faithfully towards God involved acting generously towards others.

Tithe for the needy

Regulations for the tithes have already been given in 14:22–29. For two consecutive years a family would take their tithe to the central sanctuary for a joyful feast, but every third year they would store their tithe locally for distribution to those in need. The text now provides a new dimension to the third year: the declaration of integrity.

The third year was obviously special, so much so that it was named 'the year of the tithe' (v. 12). This name wasn't strictly accurate, since a tithe was of course given every year. This tithe was different, though, since the givers didn't eat any of it themselves, and it was very obviously 'the year of the tithe' for those who received it. The texts don't say whether all families gave this tithe in the same year, or whether a third of the country gave it each year, though the latter would make more sense.

The third year's tithe is specifically called 'sacred' or 'holy' (v. 13). Perhaps this is to emphasize that, although it isn't taken to the sanctuary like in the other years, it is just as much consecrated to God. Sacredness is not limited to the tabernacle or temple. It applies to anything given over to God for his use. Giving to the poor is just as sacred as giving to the priests. Israel had a more developed sense of the holy than we do, with a spectrum of holiness (very holy, holy, clean, unclean, very unclean) which applied to many different aspects of life: time, places, food and people. The book of Leviticus has much to say about that. But the extension of holiness to all tithes, regardless of where they were presented, teaches us a valuable lesson about God's values.

Declaration of integrity

In presenting his tithe, probably in front of local elders and Levites, each householder makes a solemn declaration, incorporating several elements. All is given, not just some. It is given to those in need. It is not defiled in any way. This shows obedience to God's commands, both positive and negative. And the giver then prays for blessing. Several elements of this ceremony merit further thought.

Since the tithe is deemed holy, it cannot come into contact with anything unclean—hence the triple negative declaration that covers 'anything unclean' as well as death and mourning. Death and the dead render the living unclean, so the tithe must not be used in any way relating to them (v. 14). In ancient times, the living often provided the dead with some food to speed them on their way; and in some cultures, like Egypt, they continued to present them with food regularly. There is some evidence in Israel for the former gift, though nothing conclusive for the latter. The text here does not ban this practice, which implies that it was rather innocuous, perhaps like our placing flowers on a grave. However, it disallows any association with the tithe, since this is deemed holy.

The declaration concludes with a prayer for blessing. The earlier regulation promised that God would bless those who honoured him in this way (14:29), but here the giver specifically prays for the blessing—and not just for his own family, but for the whole nation. God's gift had prompted its appropriate human response, and now he was asked to bless the nation. The cycle was to be renewed.

A GIVER'S PRAYER

As I present these holy gifts to you, Lord, use them to help those in need. Look down from your holy place and bless your church with faith, and your world with peace.

CARPE DIEM!

Carpe diem—'seize the day'. Many of us will remember this phrase from the 1989 film *Dead Poets Society*. Robin Williams played a progressive English teacher in a traditional boarding school, who encouraged his pupils to think creatively, outside the box. As a result they set up a clandestine Dead Poets Society with its Latin tagline, *Carpe diem*.

Carpe diem could also be the tagline for this passage. Three times the text says 'this day' or 'today' (vv. 16, 17, 18). This is the concluding paragraph to the long section of laws given in general in chapters 4—11 and then in detail in chapters 12—26. These sections have covered all sorts of interesting issues and important details, some obvious and some more arcane. It now comes to a conclusion with a resounding flourish and an immediate challenge, in similar terms to those with which each section started (see 5:1 and 12:1). This is not just theoretical. This is for real. This is for now, today. And it demands a response.

Israel's response

The response itself is just as heavily emphasized as is the immediacy of the challenge. Quite simply, Israel must obey. Notice how this emphasis is conveyed. See the many different verbs, for example, in NRSV: observe (twice, v. 16), walk, keep, obey (v. 17), keep (v. 18); the strong qualifiers: diligently, with all your heart and with all your soul (v. 16); and the multi-faceted object: statutes and ordinances (v. 16), ways, statutes, commandments and ordinances (v. 17), commandments (v. 18). This is the ancient equivalent of large font, bold and underlined. The message could hardly be clearer.

The text reads as if it is first proclaimed on the day the covenant was renewed, since it refers to the declaration or agreement affirmed 'today' (v. 17a, though the NRSV phrases this rather awkwardly). An elaborate and colourful covenant ceremony is described in the next few chapters, so perhaps the current section anticipates the following narrative account by giving the legislative contents of the covenant, which is then affirmed. To set up or confirm a covenant was a solemn undertaking, as seen in Exodus 24, and as we shall see again in the next chapters of Deuteronomy. Yet in the midst of all the ceremony and celebration, at its heart is a simple but profound commitment of the two parties to each other. When all is said and done, Israel's response boils down to a very simple concept: obey.

God's response

If Israel's part of the deal is obedience, God's part is to make them his 'treasured possession' (v. 18, NIV), the Hebrew term *segullah*. Any ancient monarch had access to all the riches of the kingdom, but the *segullah* was their particular personal possession. Often it indicated the best and most prized part, something like the crown jewels. Any king could amass this treasure (Ecclesiastes 2:8), while David devoted all his *segullah* to pay for the temple (1 Chronicles 29:3). The *segullah* was a king's personal property—and God declares that Israel is his *segullah*, his crown jewel.

The term is used in another memorable covenantal passage, Exodus 19. Immediately after leaving Egypt, as the people arrive at Sinai and are about to receive the Ten Commandments and the law, God declares that he has brought them out on eagles' wings and they are now his 'treasured possession' (Exodus 19:4–6). Deuteronomy has been at pains to show that this was not due to Israel's being bigger or better than other nations. On the contrary, they were numerically fewer (7:7), and God was punishing others rather than praising Israel (9:4–6). But he chose them for his own purposes.

The result

That purpose is given here (v. 19): that they would be a shining example to everyone else, lifted high for all to see. They were to be an example of holy and obedient living, and of the result of this in God's blessing, a blessing shown in the ways which were meaningful in that ancient context. Implicitly, this means that they would point others to the unique God; they would be the 'blessing to the nations' of the patriarchal promise (Genesis 12:3), the 'light to the nations' of the prophetic oracle (Isaiah 60:3). Such was the challenge, such the glorious opportunity. All they had to do was *carpe diem*, and obey!

PRAYER

Thank you, Lord, that you treasure us. Help me to 'seize the day' in obedience and faith.

FIRST THINGS FIRST

What is the first thing that conquering troops do when they overcome the enemy? They tear down the flag of the overthrown regime and hoist their own. Whether it's the Allies landing on the Normandy beaches, or the Soviets capturing the Berlin Reichstag, or invasions in later wars, the hoisted flag of the victor proclaims a new regime.

However, Israel's entry into Canaan would be significantly different. It wasn't just that ancient peoples did not have flags—at least there is no archaeological or textual evidence of them. It's rather that Israel's symbol of conquest was to be a sign of subservience, not of power. Their first act when they had secured a foothold in the country would be to set up a monument proclaiming God's law, and an altar for sacrifices to him.

The setting

Camped in the rift valley just east of the Jordan, Israel looked across to a forbidding range of hills that blocked the view into the promised land. But they knew from their spies and others that the central part of the country was dominated by two mountains, Ebal and Gerizim. This was to be their first destination, their first pause to pay tribute to God and to pledge their loyalty to him.

Joshua 8:30–35 recounts how they fulfilled this aim. After capturing the first towns of Jericho in the valley and Ai up in the hills, they travelled to Ebal and Gerizim for the spectacular ceremony described here. These mountain peaks were only two miles apart, yet they towered some 300 metres above the intervening valley. Deuteronomy 27:2 states literally that 'on the day' they cross the Jordan they are to set up their monument, whereas of course it would have taken several weeks. The phrase implies that building the monument must follow crossing the Jordan, not that it must happen on the same day.

The law

Many ancient cultures preserved their law codes and other royal decrees on stone. One of the best-known ancient monuments, pictured in many Bible handbooks and reference works, is that of Hammurabi, who ruled the central Euphrates area, around 1750BC.

This 2.5-metre-high monument, now in the Louvre Museum in Paris, pictures the great king paying homage to the sun god, then gives the full text of his law code chiselled out in cuneiform.

Israel was to follow the Egyptian practice of writing on plaster. Plastered writing like this has now been found in the Jordan valley, referring to Balaam son of Beor (see 23:5–6 and commentary, p. 165). They were to build a basic structure of stones, cover it in plaster, and then inscribe the laws. If it was a very large monument, it could contain all of the laws in chapters 12—26. More probably, it was a summary or a selection, perhaps the Ten Commandments, as found today in synagogues around the world, or a smaller sample, as in Exodus 21—23 or Exodus 33:17–26. Whatever the text, it would be a huge, visible reminder of where their allegiance lay.

Many an old church in England has panels displaying the Ten Commandments and the eight Beatitudes of Jesus, a visual reminder of the old and new covenants. Whether or not we see them regularly at the front of church or on a bookmark in our Bible or anywhere else, it is vital to be reminded regularly of where our allegiance lies and of God's pattern for our lives.

The altar

Alongside the written law, Israel would build an altar and immediately offer sacrifices. A large stone structure has now been discovered at the foot of Mount Ebal. If this was the altar described here, it would confirm the account in Joshua that the ceremony actually took place.

The full version of sacrifices is given in Leviticus, but the two mentioned here, which were probably the most important and most frequent, are burnt offerings (v. 6), entirely offered to God in worship; and fellowship or 'well-being' sacrifices (v. 7), mostly consumed by the worshippers in fellowship with God and each other. Law and worship, principles and practice are combined in affirming allegiance to God in the covenant he has established.

REFLECTION

Christians also have a powerful symbol of humble service—the cross.

SECRET SINS

Say it out, say it loud, say it clear! Whether the raucous songs on the football terraces, or the rhythmic chants of soldiers on exercise, or the swell of a Spring Harvest crowd raising the roof, there is something very primal in singing along with many others. It reinforces our commitment to the cause, and strengthens our resolve to see it through. From its earliest days the church has acknowledged the power of collective response, and many Christians today can still recite from memory large sections of their church's liturgy. Israel was to enact a great liturgy when they first entered the land, and possibly at regular intervals from then onwards.

Ancient covenants always ended with a 'bottom line'. Simply put, if you obey the great king, you'll prosper; if you don't, you won't. Their way of expressing this was with a series of blessings and curses. The standard textbooks give many such examples (see *ANET*, 199–206). Another parallel with our present text is an oath from the ancient Hittites (central Turkey), where soldiers declared their loyalty to the king by taking various objects symbolic of disaster and declaring with each, 'So be it!'—that is, 'So may it happen to me if I break this oath' (*ANET*, 353d). The curses the Israelites proclaimed were like the treaty curses, and the 'Amen' after each implied, 'So be it'.

The spectacle

The valley between Mount Ebal and Mount Gerizim was a spectacular setting for this ceremony. At its eastern end near Shechem, it is barely 500 metres across, so that large groups assembled on the rising slopes on each side could easily be heard by each other. Further west it is nearly a mile wide, but large bays opposite each other form natural amphitheatres which would magnify and project sound across the valley. In either place, the 'Amen' would have resounded from one side to the other and echoed back memorably.

The tribes are split into two groups of six for each side (vv. 12–13). The division was probably geographical: those on the northerly Mount Ebal were those that settled in the north and east; those on the southerly Mount Gerizim settled in the centre and south. It could also have been genealogical: the tribes proclaiming blessing came from Jacob's two wives, Rachel (two tribes) and Leah (four); those proclaiming the curses came from Jacob's two concubines, Bilhah (two) and Zilpah (two), plus two others from Leah (Zebulun, the youngest; and Reuben, the oldest, who lost his birthright after his incest with Bilhah). However, the Old Testament never implies that these tribes were less favoured because of their ancestry or because they pronounced the curses. All the tribes were equal before God, except the Levites, and that was for other reasons.

The curses

As so often elsewhere, the list of curses here is illustrative rather than exhaustive. Nevertheless, it covers a wide spectrum of Israel's law, and illustrates its important features. The first three curses (vv. 15–17) refer to God, parents and neighbours, in line with the second, fifth, eighth and tenth commandments, and effectively covering all of them. To make an image was to reject all that the Mosaic law taught about God; to move a boundary stone was to steal land from a neighbour. The next two (vv. 18–19) reflect concern for the vulnerable, a fundamental issue for God and hence for his people. The following four (vv. 20–23) deal with family and sexuality, particularly incest, which might be more of a problem in large family groups and threatened the morality and stability of society. Another two (vv. 24–25) return to social issues, condemning murder and corruption, again matters that touch core values. And the final one (v. 26) is a general curse on all law-breaking.

Another feature of these curses is that they highlight what is often clandestine activity. This is explicit in verses 15 and 24, which mention acts committed in secret. But all these activities by their very nature are done in secret or in the confines of the home: images of God, insults to parents, exploitation, corruption, sexual sins. Often the risk of being found out keeps us from breaking the law—here that support is lacking. The people needed to be extra vigilant. And on similar issues, so do we.

REFLECTION

'Who shall ascend the hill of the Lord? And who shall stand in his holy place? Those who have clean hands and pure hearts...'
(Psalm 24:3–4).

IF YOU OBEY...

Recently at home our family has been sorting through cellar and roof-space, cupboards, cases and boxes, in preparation for moving house. Naturally we've rediscovered a lot of memorabilia that has lain undisturbed for many years. We've relived the memories and enjoyed the experience, but then thrown most of the stuff into the recycling box or rubbish bin.

Last night my wife and I came to all our engagement and wedding cards. What odd tastes everyone seems to have had two decades ago! Rereading these cards, I was struck by the large number that included a verse, and the fact that it was nearly always a verse of promise or blessing. Numbers 6:24–26 ('The Lord bless you and keep you...') and Proverbs 3:4–5 ('Trust in the Lord with all your heart...') were apparently the favourites, and appropriately so. We all like a promise, especially a promise of blessing.

Literary form

The previous section began with six tribes lined up on Mount Gerizim 'for the blessing' and six on Mount Ebal 'for the curse' (27:12–13). Then came a series of twelve curses proclaimed by the Levites, after each of which the whole people solemnly declared 'Amen' (27:15–26). Curiously, there is no set of twelve blessings, with similar proclamation and assent. What happened to them? The memorable pageant would have been rather lopsided with half the people actively involved and the other half passively silent, and the message would have been dauntingly severe as all stick and no carrot.

Instead of such responsorial blessings, we now have a chapter in which blessings and curses are presented differently from the way outlined above, but in a similar way to each other. Each set has a brief introduction (28:1–2, 15), six short, punchy declarations (28:3–6, 16–19), and an expansive discourse of illustration and application (28:7–14, 20–68). The only significant difference is that the discourse on the curses is a lot longer than that on the blessings. Sadly, we often respond better to the stick than the carrot!

Obviously we have material of two different styles here, and it is quite logical to look for an explanation. The spoken curses in chapter

27 certainly reflect a public ceremony, and may contain the actual words used on the original occasion, perhaps as remembered (and developed?) in periodic re-enactments. The six pithy blessings and curses in chapter 28 may reflect another, shorter tradition, or an easily memorized summary. However, they are now embedded in a discursive literary setting, which may well contain the gist of the original proclamation, but is unlikely to be the form used by the Levites on any such occasion. When, where and by whom this chapter was written in its present form is as elusive as the whole origin of Deuteronomy, but at least these sections are testimony to a literary history. The building of an altar on Mount Ebal (rather than in Jerusalem) and the spoken form of the first curses suggest that some of the material is genuinely early. The more reflective nature of the following blessings and curses suggest that some is a later theological distillation. More than that, it is hard to say.

Theological content

There is nothing new here: the urgency of obedience and the promise of blessing have been leitmotifs throughout the book. But these punchy blessings (vv. 3–6) have a lovely lyricism, like many an ancient prayer or Celtic blessing. 'Blessed' comes six times (twice in v. 3 and in v. 6), and in each case except verse 4 it is followed by just two words in Hebrew. Together they express the totality of life (town and country, coming and going), fertility (human, animal and agricultural) and food (gathered and grown). It is simple and profound, unadorned and evocative.

The discourse (vv. 7–13) expands on this, repeating it in a different order and adding national security, international renown and divine favour. And of course the passage begins and then concludes with the condition: 'if you obey… if you do not turn aside…' (vv. 1, 14). God wants to bless, but he also wants our obedience. We like the promises, but do we accept the condition?

REFLECTION

Through the Holy Spirit, we can know far more security and blessing than the Israelites. But do we accept the different vision of blessing that Jesus presented (Mark 10:29–30)?

IF YOU DON'T OBEY...

What a litany! The word 'litany' of course comes from the long penitential prayer still used in some church liturgies. In the Book of Common Prayer, the Litany has 41 sentences or paragraphs said by the minister, after each of which the congregation responds with 'Good Lord, deliver us' or something similar. The latest Church of England form, in *Common Worship*, still has 34 sentences and responses. These litanies move on from prayer for deliverance to intercession for the world and confidence in God, but the dominant tone remains sombre. No wonder the word 'litany' is now used to mean any long list of unpleasant events.

This is the longest section in Deuteronomy covered in one comment section, and you may feel you've already done quite enough by simply reading the passage, let alone these notes! No wonder it remains one of the least favourite passages for reading in synagogues. However, taking the whole section in one sitting has the advantage of seeing it all together, as well as getting through it all in one go. The alternative would be to spend days ploughing through it in great detail, and perhaps ending up thoroughly depressed!

In detail

After an opening sentence, there are six formulaic curses (vv. 16–19), which mirror almost word-for-word the previous pithy blessings (28:3–6), covering the totality of places and activities, and the essentials of fertility and food. Again, this sums it up: disobedience leads to divine curse on everything. Nothing escapes. No one can run away and hide in the corner, hoping to escape judgment.

These curses are then spelt out in repetitive and unrelenting detail. The first section (vv. 20–24) promises disease and drought; the following one (vv. 25–29) military defeat and attendant illnesses; the next (vv. 30–37) the tragedy of wrecked families, oppressive rule and shameful exile; then (vv. 38–44) agricultural disaster and financial ruin; then (vv. 45–57), in greater and horrific detail, the conditions of invasion and siege. Finally a long summary (vv. 58–68) contrasts the peace and prosperity of blessing with the dread and horror of punishment. It is all graphically encapsulated in the despair of verse 67: 'In the morning you shall say, "If only it were evening!" and at evening you shall say, "If only it were morning!"' An apt epitaph for this calamitous state of affairs could come from David's famous lament over Saul and Jonathan: 'How the mighty have fallen' (2 Samuel 1:19, 25, 27). How high were the possibilities following obedience; how low the consequences of disobedience.

In general

Standing back from the detail, Wright helpfully notes several general points. First, these disasters were not imaginary, but part of the real world, then as now. The old Anglican Litany prays for deliverance 'from lightning and tempest; from plague, pestilence and famine; from battle and murder, and from sudden death'. Sadly, Israel's unfolding history illustrates that all these catastrophes occurred, and blames them on the people's unbelief.

Second, as well as mirroring the blessings on offer, these disasters reverse the great promises to the patriarchs of a numerous people, secure in their land, in communion with God and mediating his blessing to others (Genesis 12:2–3; 17:4–8 and so on). Each of these momentous possibilities will be completely negated.

Third, the claims that the local Baals were a better bet for fertility than Israel's God Yahweh would be shown up as cruelly false. Instead of the anticipated blessing, there would be unmitigated disaster: people would be barren, cattle sterile and land arid. Israel would end up in a foreign land, worshipping these idols to which they had sold out (v. 64), but by then their impotence would be apparent to all.

Fourth and hearteningly, all this is conditional. Disaster is not inevitable. The chapter gives a warning to be heeded, not a prediction to be fulfilled. This is one alternative: catastrophe and death. Over against it is the other: obedience and life. You choose!

PRAYER

From all evil and mischief; from pride, vanity and hypocrisy;
from envy, hatred and malice; and from all evil intent,
good Lord, deliver us.

The opening section of The Litany, *Common Worship*

IT'S *the* COVENANT, STUPID!

Some things are absolutely foundational. At election time, certain issues may loom large: education, health care, immigration, terrorism, war, and so on. But the one that looms largest and dwarfs them all is neatly expressed in that catchphrase of 1990s American presidential elections: 'It's the economy, stupid!' What matters most, to most people, most of the time, is their own job. This of course has many aspects—salary package, work conditions, job security, promotion prospects—but all relate to the economy in general. So the central electoral issue is the economy. And if you don't understand that, you're stupid!

Similarly in Israel, there was one fundamental issue that dwarfed all others. Not that they ever had elections; nor that they themselves understood it this way, as the historical accounts sadly show. But in God's perspective, one issue dominated: the covenant. This is what set them apart from other nations and made them distinctive. This was the basis both for their uniquely monotheistic and aniconic faith, and for their egalitarian social structure and humanitarian concern. They alone had a special contractual relationship with the one Creator God. And if they didn't understand that, they were being wilfully stupid and everything else would unravel.

This is why, in these closing chapters, the book returns relentlessly to the theme of covenant. Chapters 27—28 have given a covenant reaffirmation ceremony to be conducted as soon as they enter the promised land, with blessings and curses spelled out in delightful and forbidding detail respectively—but that ceremony still lies ahead. Chapters 29—30 present a covenant renewal ceremony for Israel here and now, one to be entered into in faith, trusting that God would indeed lead them into Canaan to stand on the slopes of Mounts Ebal and Gerizim. The whole book has led up to this. The information has all been given. Now is crunch time; now they must sign on the dotted line.

Review of the past

These two chapters have all the essential elements of an ancient covenant. They begin in verse 2 (since verse 1 concludes the long second speech of Moses that started in 5:1), with a brief historical review: the signs and wonders in Egypt that preceded and enabled the exodus (vv. 2–4), the miraculous provision of food and clothing during 40 years in a barren wilderness (vv. 5–6), the recent defeat of two kings to the east of the Jordan (v. 7), and the apportionment of their land already to some Israelites (v. 8). This is a brief summary of chapters 1—3, and of the longer accounts in Exodus and Numbers. Here it is a vital reminder of God's work in deliverance and provision.

Nestled in the midst of this heart-warming summary is a salutary warning. They, or rather their parents, had seen all these things literally (vv. 2–3), but they hadn't seen them theologically (v. 4). They hadn't understood their significance, or taken them to heart. The warning of 'seeing but not seeing' echoes ominously through scripture, notably in the ministry given to Isaiah (Isaiah 6:9), the citation of it by Jesus (Matthew 13:14) and the paraphrase by Paul (Romans 11:8). We too can easily see God at work, but not understand the significance of it or act in accordance with it.

Renewal in the present

The covenant was based on the past, with the promise to the patriarchs and the momentous events of the previous 40 years. It extended to the future, explicitly including those not yet present (v. 15). Essentially, though, it was about the present. Hence, the current Israelite community must assemble and commit itself to all the terms outlined in chapters 5—26. They must all come, every last one (vv. 10–11): leaders and populace, men and women, adults and children, Israelites and foreign servants. Ancient Israel was certainly not democratic in the modern sense, but when it came to affirming the covenant, everyone's assent mattered. After all, it was for their own good, so that they might 'succeed in everything' (v. 9). That's what the original promise to Abraham was all about. That's what the covenant with Israel is all about. And, albeit with a different understanding of what it means to prosper, that's what the Christian gospel is all about.

REFLECTION

An old hymn, which became the unofficial anthem of one missionary society (OMF), puts it succinctly: 'We'll praise him for all that is past, and trust him for all that's to come.'

ROOTS *of* POISON

We all like to be individuals, to stamp our own personality on life. Walk down any high street, and see the variety of clothes and styles. Stroll along any suburban avenue, and see the different ways houses have been altered and extended. Go into any teenager's or student's room and see their likes and dislikes displayed on all the walls. We all like to express ourselves.

In many ways this is a good thing. God made us different, and gives us ample opportunity to develop differently. In one area, however, it is fatal. When it comes to how we represent God and respond to him, we cannot do as we wish. Home-variety religion is not a valid option. What's more, home-variety masquerading as biblical faith is disastrous.

Flawed religion

Almost all ancient religions had images of their deities. The Israelites' forebears had seen and practised this image-making in Egypt, and the current generation had seen it among the east-Jordan peoples whom they had recently passed (v. 16). The temptation to make an image of God was, we might say, very natural. And the act of making such an image was, we might think, no great deal. But we would be profoundly mistaken.

The vocabulary of verse 17 is far stronger than we realize. The two terms used for these human fabrications occur only here in the book, and are highly derogatory. The first, 'detestable', is traditionally translated 'abomination', an English term which is now nearly obsolete but captures well the intent here. The second, 'idols', comes from a stem meaning 'to roll', and is very similar to the word for excrement. Indeed, the Authorized Version has a marginal note to its translation here, 'Hebrew: dungy gods'. An image might seem a harmless little talisman, but here it is described as 'abominable dung'. Depending on whether the image is of Yahweh or another god, it breaks the first or second commandment, and must never, never, never be tolerated.

Fatal results

The worst aspect of this idolatry is that the practitioners see nothing wrong. They think they can invoke the blessing by swearing allegiance to Yahweh, by standing on Ebal or Gerizim and solemnly intoning 'Amen' along with everyone else, and yet still do their own thing, make their own idol, stamp their own individuality on religious practice (v. 19).

God's verdict is very different. Many a root or plant looks innocent enough, but is actually full of poison. Similarly, an image of Yahweh may seem innocent enough, but is actually a religious poison, a denial of who God is, an attempt to bring him down to our size (see discussion of the second commandment, 5:8–10, pp. 56–57). And just as poison spreads rapidly through a human body and destroys it, so this denial of the true God would spread rapidly through the body of Israel and destroy it.

As a result, the curses will fall in all their hideous effect: agricultural disaster (v. 19), personal destruction (vv. 20–21), national calamity (v. 22), and complete devastation like that of the infamous sinful cities (v. 23). The international bewilderment (v. 24) and the divine response (vv. 25–28) speak of God's 'furious anger' and his 'anger, fury and great wrath'. The people would reject God as he had revealed himself, so he would reject them.

Faithful response

This terrible warning concludes in a somewhat unusual way. Instead of a ringing challenge or a climactic flourish, as at the end of the next chapter, there is more of an enigmatic proverb (v. 29). What are these 'secret things'? Several suggestions have been made. A Jewish tradition sees them as secret sins, which God knows and will punish. In this case, the 'revealed things' are publicly known sins, and the people must address these themselves. By contrast, many commentators today think that the 'secret things' are the future. It is known only to God, but meanwhile we must act in the light of what we do know.

The 'secret things' may be debatable, but the 'revealed things' clearly refer to God's law or the transgressing of it. And however we interpret the former, the latter is spelt out as 'to observe all the words of this law'. The challenge is as direct to us three millennia later as it was to the Israelites lined up on the plains of Moab.

REFLECTION

'If we deny him, he will also deny us' (2 Timothy 2:12).

WHEN THINGS GO WRONG

What should parents say to their children, when they think they are making wrong choices? Should it be stern rebuke: 'You'll never be allowed back home now that you take drugs'? Or should it be open welcome: 'You'll always have a room here no matter who you sleep with'? Or should there be some condition: 'You're welcome to come back as long as you go straight/quit the gang/keep out of trouble'? For many parents, perhaps some readers, this is no theoretical question but a real and pressing dilemma.

Some might go for firm rejection, others for unquestioning acceptance. Most of us would probably want to set some conditions, and we would agonize over exactly what those conditions should be. In particular, we would want to make clear our love for our children despite their wrong and destructive choices. Would the former undermine the latter? Will a promise to love them 'no matter what' make them think we don't really mind what they do, even if we say otherwise?

Today's passage at least gives us some guidance, although it deals with a nation. It envisages their rebellion, assumes their punishment, and promises their restoration. The parallel with human children is certainly not exact, but the ways of the divine father have much to teach us.

When you...

The opening word, 'when/if', covers all the statements of verses 1–2. The Hebrew word (*ki*) is ambiguous, and can mean either 'when' (event definite but time uncertain) or 'if' (event itself uncertain). This means that the future is open-ended. These things may indeed happen—but they may just as well not happen. In any case, the opening phrase mentions both blessings and curses, which may both come, though of course not simultaneously.

The passage clearly envisages disobedience, disaster and dispersal among the nations—in a word, exile. All the horrendous curses of the previous chapter have fallen, and a distraught and devastated people are led off into captivity. However, it then immediately looks beyond this disaster to restoration. When the exiles return to Yahweh in faith and obedience, he will turn to them and 'return' them to their previous state. The play on words is deliberate: the same Hebrew stem (*shub*) occurs repeatedly, translated variously as 'call to mind/take to heart' (v. 1), 'return' (v. 2) 'restore fortunes', 'gather' (v. 3), and 'turn' (v. 10). When Israel turns back to God, he will turn back to them.

Does this mean that the threat of punishment is undermined? Will it make them say, 'Oh, it doesn't really matter, we can always repent and be restored'? Hardly! The historical books paint a gloomy picture of both northern Israel and southern Judah: apostasy and decline, invasion and conquest, death and exile. Those who lived through those tragic years would definitely not have said, 'It doesn't matter'. And those who survived into exile ended up dispirited and depressed (see Ezekiel 18:2). The punishment was real and painful.

Then God...

Verses 6–10 focus more on restoration. When the people turn back to God, he will turn back to them, turn their fortunes around, and make them return. Further, he will then give them all the blessings and prosperity promised in the first place, and experienced in the early years (v. 9). And, as always, God will be emotionally involved: it stems from his compassion (v. 3), and results in his delight (v. 9).

It will also lead to 'circumcision of the heart' (v. 6). For those used to physical circumcision, this is a rich metaphor of personal commitment and heartfelt obedience, in internal attitude as well as external form. Earlier, God commanded it (10:16); now he promises that he himself will effect it.

This passage shows God's knowledge of humanity, his foresight of events, and his provision for restoration. The warning is real: no wonder this is the synagogue reading for the Jewish equivalent of Lent, the ten days of repentance between New Year (*Rosh Hashanah*) and the Day of Atonement (*Yom Kippur*). But so is the promise: the 'even if' of verse 4 shows that no situation is irretrievable if there is a change of heart. This doesn't instantly resolve the painful issues raised at the start, but it does give us a pointer for reflection.

PRAYER

Pray for parents who think their children are making wrong choices, and for children who find it hard to relate to their parents.

The BOTTOM LINE: CHOOSE LIFE!

It looked so good in the catalogue or shop. A great addition to the house—just the right furniture to finish off the redecorated room. So you made the purchase, you enjoyed imagining how it would look, and you were delighted to see it arrive. Now, though, when it's unpacked and in pieces on your floor, things aren't so rosy. It *should* all fit together, if only you knew how! But the instructions are in poor English, the text doesn't fit the diagrams, the pieces are hard to identify, and you sit there scratching your head and end up making another cup of coffee instead. Self-assembled products are often far from simple.

It's simple

By contrast, God's commandment is straightforward. When all is said and done, when all the previous chapters have been read, all the general law (chs. 5—11) and all the detailed instructions (chs. 12—26) absorbed, it can all be summed up as 'this commandment' in the singular (v. 11). And it boils down to a simple choice which everyone faces and which everyone must make. At the end of the day, as in Psalm 1, there is a clear bottom line, a stark decision that we all face.

We tend to complicate things, or assume the need for experts. We call in the scholars and ministers. We defer to those who have risen to great heights of understanding and wisdom, or have travelled great distances in experience and maturity. Reaching the heavens and crossing the seas (vv. 12–13) were proverbial idioms in the ancient world for esoteric knowledge and difficult enterprise (see Proverbs 30:4; *ANET*, 48c, 79d, 91b, 92d, 438d). Yet God challenges this view in verses 11–14. No, he says. You don't need abstruse knowledge. You don't need further, wider experience. You know enough already. It's all set out for you. You simply have to make a choice.

It's life or death

The choice may be simple, but it's certainly not insignificant. On the contrary, it couldn't be more important—a matter literally of life or death. The previous chapters have spelt this out in graphic detail. Life means more than just remaining alive; it means security, prosperity, fertility, health and blessing (v. 15). Death means more than being killed; it also means invasion, poverty, sterility, illness and curse.

Nor is it simplistic. Obviously, if presented with this straight choice, we would all immediately opt for life. But life here entails obeying Yahweh, living in accordance with his laws, and worshipping him exclusively. As so often in Deuteronomy, and indeed in all of scripture, it comes back to heart, mind and will. Do we worship God alone and follow his path, or do we go our own way? The latter for Israel meant other gods, which inevitably, for God, meant punishment and death. The choice must be made before those two supreme witnesses, heaven and earth (already cited right at the start, 4:26). What will it be?

Choose life

And so the main central section of Deuteronomy comes to a climactic conclusion. In doing so, it echoes many phrases from the other great seams of the book: the opening (see 1:8, 'See, I set before you…'), the climax of the introduction (see 4:26–40) and the conclusion to the general law (see 11:26–28). It has all been said before. It now has to be enacted.

Israel is not being asked to accept the covenant in principle. That has already been done. Rather, Israel in general and Israelites in particular (the chapter keeps to 'you' singular) must choose to obey it. The covenant promises are there for the taking, and the curses are equally there for the fulfilling.

And God urges them to 'choose life'. There is something very winsome and very compelling in this phrase—so much so that a friend who wrote a doctoral thesis on the ethics of Deuteronomy used it as the title of his subsequent book (Gary Millar, *Now Choose Life*, IVP, 1997). The phrase is simple, direct, urgent. It is both an invitation and a command. It is spelt out as love and obedience—two leitmotifs of the book—and holding fast, a phrase that implies perseverance and is echoed by Paul ('having done everything, to stand firm', Ephesians 6:13). And it is bursting with promise. So what will it be?

PRAYER

Lord, I choose life. I choose you. Help me to love you,
obey you and hold fast to you. Amen.

CHANGE & CONTINUITY

Leadership change is often tricky, and sometimes messy. In the political world, the media watch every move of the person at the top, and pounce on every weakness. As soon as they scent blood and start to bay for resignation, they're full of feverish speculation over who will succeed to the hot seat.

Elsewhere there may be less media attention, but the handover of responsibility can be just as unsettling. In any organization, everyone waits anxiously to see the policies of the new CEO, MD, principal or whatever. Changing church leadership brings a different set of issues, but ones that are no less important. Will the new minister share the perspectives and values of the congregation, and how disturbing will his or her new priorities be? These issues are all pertinent to me at present, living in a country constantly speculating over the Prime Minister's future, working in a college which will soon have a new principal, and attending a church looking for a new leader.

Here Moses prepares for his succession. He now seems to have accepted his exclusion from the promised land, and the emphasis of our passage lies elsewhere. He is already 120, and beginning to feel his age (v. 2), despite the fulsome tribute in the book's conclusion (34:7). The time has come for change, and he accepts it.

First, though, there is the reassurance of continuity. The human leader may change, with all the potential for anxiety that the change can produce. But God remains the leader. He has just given them some amazing victories (v. 4). He promises to do so again: all they need to do is to trust him, be 'strong and bold' and forge ahead. After all, it is 'Yahweh your God who goes with you; he will not fail you or forsake you' (v. 6). In other words, the human leader is of lesser importance. Changes of leadership in churches and Christian organizations should be less difficult than elsewhere. Sadly, this is not always the case.

A leader to take over

Like all of us, perhaps, Joshua shows a real mixture of attitudes. On the one hand, he displayed great courageous leadership in defeating the Amalekites straight after the exodus (Exodus 17:8–13) and successful leadership in the conquest itself (see Joshua 11:23). On the other hand, he seemed to need plenty of reassurance. He is repeatedly told to be strong and courageous, not to fear or be dismayed. We see that here (vv. 7, 8, 23) and again in the parallel account of his commission (Joshua 1:6, 7, 9, 18).

Since that early victory (Exodus 17) and his courageous minority spies' report with Caleb (Numbers 14:6, 30), Joshua had been marked out as a future leader (see Deuteronomy 1:38; 3:28). Now he is duly and ceremoniously commissioned in front of the whole assembly—a fuller account of this is given in Numbers 27:18–23. Here the attention focuses on Moses' charge to this capable, if fearful, leader.

Some of us perhaps feel like Moses, able in God's strength to take on whatever comes. More of us probably feel like Joshua, knowing that God has given us gifts but somewhat fearful of stepping out into leadership. Verse 8 is as relevant to us today as to Joshua over three millennia ago.

A law to be read

Alongside the new guide is to be an accessible guidebook. The law contained in the previous chapters is to be read and heard regularly, in fact every seven years. This may seem rather infrequent to us in our highly literate culture. But in an ancient, largely oral culture, where little was read and much was recited from memory, this would be enough to refresh memories and ensure that the law remained known.

Further, it was to be read at a highly significant occasion—in the year of debt remission, that powerful reminder of God's deliverance from Egypt (15:15), and at the feast of Tabernacles, that joyous celebration of God's provision of harvest (16:15). So the context of the law's reading was one of gratitude for God's grace in redemption and in sustenance. The law was part of his blessing, not a burden, and should shape their joyful obedience—similar to what Paul calls 'the law of Christ' (Galatians 6:2).

REFLECTION

'It is the Lord who goes before you' (v. 8).

LISTEN *to the* BEAT!

Music is all around us. We wake up to it and go to sleep to it. Many of us work to it. We shop, cook, clean, iron and wash up to it. We all follow our different musical tastes, unwinding at home, going out to concerts or dancing at discos. But it's all music.

Music and life

Music has a powerful way of expressing our emotions in ways that words cannot. On a visit to the USA in the 1920s, the Russian composer Igor Stravinsky was asked by a rather naïve reporter what he was trying to convey in his ground-breaking work *The Rite of Spring*. 'If I could have put it in words,' he is said to have replied, 'I would not have written the music!' Whether classical or contemporary, spirituals, blues, folk, soul, rock, punk or pop (or any other of the numerous labels), music captures our moods and feelings. It can comfort yet confront, express our feelings yet challenge our perceptions. Music is the currency of our culture.

Songs in particular have a way of lodging in our memory and returning in times of crisis. Many a song learnt in childhood is remembered for the rest of one's life. The film *Blind Flight* portrays Brian Keenan, an Irish hostage in Beirut in the 1980s, repeatedly singing or humming the haunting folksong 'Danny Boy', and teaching the words to his English cellmate John McCarthy. This powerfully illustrates the deep human instinct to use songs from the past to express emotions in the present.

Music and faith

Much the same holds true in the life of faith. It has been rightly said that many Christians learn their theology through their hymns. During the 18th-century revival in Britain, John Wesley in particular was very concerned that new converts have good Christian hymns, written with close attention to 'singability' as well as theology. He wrote detailed guidelines about this, and his brother Charles was one of many who worked hard to give us a rich heritage of English hymnody. Whether we continue to use those hymns, or instead use songs that reflect today's musical idioms, we know the power of music to express, stir and challenge faith.

The Israelites were aware of it too. The book of Psalms is the main repository of their religious songs, and the best-loved part of the Old Testament today. But elsewhere there are more songs than we often realize (see Judges 5; 1 Samuel 2; 2 Samuel 1; Isaiah 12 and 38; Jonah 2; Habakkuk 3). And it is noteworthy that the accounts of Israel's journey from Egypt to Palestine begin and end with songs: the song of Moses and Miriam after the miraculous passage through the Sea of Reeds (Exodus 15:1–21), and now the swansong of the aged leader (Deuteronomy 32). These songs memorably encapsulated their faith, with God's mighty deliverance and his ongoing challenge.

Music as witness

Ancient religion was full of witnesses—all the many gods and goddesses who swelled the various ranks of the pantheon. Israel obviously didn't have such witnesses, but it had many other witnesses to God's covenant, often visible or tangible, such as heaven and earth (32:1), and the east-Jordan memorial altar (Joshua 22:27; note memorials in Genesis 31:48–50; Isaiah 19:19–20). Now this song is to be a witness.

Here at the high point of Joshua's commissioning ceremony, as he and Moses are engulfed in the awesome cloud of God's presence, they are given a sustained and repeated warning of future apostasy (vv. 16–18, 20–21, 27, 29). But through it all, this song will be a witness to Israel, 'because it will not be lost from the mouths of their descendants' (v. 21).

This song certainly was remembered: like poetry in most languages, it contains archaic linguistic features, elements that have passed out of everyday speech or written prose. This suggests that it was preserved faithfully in its early form, in contrast to the rest of the book, which was adapted and updated as appropriate. Thus the song would indeed have been a witness against the people—if only they had taken note! May it serve as a warning to us.

REFLECTION

What music do I choose to listen to?
Does it reflect my perspective of faith?

GOD *the* ROCK

'God is the ground of our being,' say many recent theologians. 'God is a Rock,' says this ancient song, with typical Hebrew bluntness. And the ancient metaphor speaks more directly to our 21st-century age than the modern rewording, since once again we value visual image more than verbal description.

A rock immediately conjures up images of strength, permanence and unchangeability, like the proverbial Rock of Gibraltar. We imagine a great rocky crag towering over a valley, or a stark cliff-face seemingly impervious to wind and rain. We may think of a particular rock in our best-loved landscape, or a boulder where we pause on our favourite walk, or a slab that provides our ideal fishing spot. Wherever it is, the rock draws us back.

The great artist Paul Cezanne was fascinated by Mont Sainte-Victoire in Provence (southern France), and painted it repeatedly over many years. The angle, distance, weather and light changed from one painting to another. The mountain was variously peaceful, welcoming, menacing, even angry, but always dominating the scene, high and imperious. It was his rock. Similarly, through all the changing scenes of life, God was, or should have been, Israel's rock.

A profusion of images

The image of God the Rock is the leitmotif of this song, appearing in verses 4, 15, 18, 30–31, and even extending to other so-called gods in verses 31 and 37. At the first mention in verse 4, three defining characteristics of God are given: he is perfect and complete; just and upright; faithful and dependable. What more could one want for the foundation of faith? No wonder these verses have been taken up in the popular Christian chorus 'Ascribe greatness to our God, the Rock'.

But God is far too complex for one image of him to suffice, so others are immediately added in a kaleidoscope of bounty. God is his children's father (vv. 5–6) and their creator (v. 6). He gives the nations their territory and governs their borders (v. 8). He sustains them, shields them, nurses them, feeds them. He is an eagle carrying its young aloft. He is the farmer with a cornucopia of the best honey, milk, meat, grain and wine (vv. 10–14).

A proliferation of gods?

In the midst of all this comes an intriguing comment in verse 8. God set boundaries for all the nations. The 'number' is clearly 70, since there were 70 nations (Genesis 10), 70 sons of Israel (Exodus 1:1, 5) and 70 sons of one deity in a local epic tradition (see *ANET*, 134c). However, the rationale for their number varies in different traditions. According to the standard Hebrew text, it followed 'the number of the sons of Israel' (NIV; see NRSV note). According to several other pre-Christian texts (one Dead Sea Scroll Hebrew text, the Greek translation and the Aramaic version), it followed 'the number of the gods' (NRSV; see NIV note). These ancient sources all predate the standardization of the Hebrew text. Which reading is preferable?

The former reading ('sons of Israel') may seem theologically safer, but has the problems that the nations were established before Israel existed, and the traditions of the book of Exodus are otherwise unmentioned in this song. The latter reading is more likely, since it gives a context for the following verse: each nation had its god, but Yahweh kept Israel specially for himself (v. 9). And the ancient idea of a council of gods occurs elsewhere in the Old Testament (see Job 1—2; Psalm 82:1). It may seem to challenge the monotheism expounded elsewhere, particularly in Deuteronomy, but the difficulty is more apparent than real. Yahweh is so much greater than all the other gods that they might as well not exist.

A prosecution of Israel

This poem reads like a 'case for the prosecution', hence the opening summons of heaven and earth as witnesses. But it is also a song to be sung and remembered. It is impossible to know how much came from Moses himself, with divine insight into Israel's future apostasy, and how much was added in the light of unfolding events. But the lesson was there to be sung, loud and clear. God was a rock of salvation for his people, but they had scoffed at him (v. 15). How would it all end?

PRAYER

Lord, be my Rock, today and always!

DESPAIR & HOPE

What did it feel like to be rejected? When the first great love of your life decided against you, when your application for that coveted job was dismissed, when your teenage child verbally abused you, or when your partner said it was no longer for life? All of us have experienced rejection in one form or another—and along with it the cauldron of emotions: anger, hurt, bewilderment, resentment, weariness, despair, and many more, in unpredictable and uncontrollable disorder.

Passion

Not surprisingly, God reacts in some of these ways to Israel's rejection of him. There is clearly anger, underlying the whole response and acknowledged openly (v. 22). There is pain, causing him to hide his face and withdraw (v. 20). There is jealousy (v. 21), not so much of the rival deities, but for the sake of his own name and reputation. There is sarcasm over the 'no god' who has replaced him (v. 21). And there is sorrow at the people's stupidity (v. 29), compassion in their calamity (v. 16), and hope for their revival (v. 39).

For many centuries, Christian theology emphasized the 'impassibility' of God. In contrast to the many Greek and Roman gods who seemed to be constantly squabbling and displaying all the worst human attributes, the Christian God was supreme, noble, unchanged and unchanging, and hence unmoved by passions and emotions. In the classical world of the emerging church, this image was certainly attractive, and an important corrective to the prevailing all-too-human view of deity.

Eventually, however, it became too much of a doctrine in its own right, detached from the biblical portrayal of God. In medieval theology, God became distant, remote, inaccessible, and many intermediaries were needed—hence the growing role in popular piety of Mary and the saints. God was primarily an angry deity to be placated, rather than a loving father to be worshipped. One aspect of the biblical portrayal was elevated at the expense of another—and the loss was immense. This chapter reminds us that God is passionate about his world and his people. We lose that perspective at our peril.

Judgment

Right at the start of the song, God's provision is contrasted with his people's perversity: divine perfection (32:4) and human corruption (32:5). We like to celebrate the one; we prefer to forget the other. Later, Israel is called Jacob, a reminder of the nation's ancestry, and Jeshurun, an affectionate name like 'John Bull' or 'Uncle Sam' (32:15). But Israel would kick God in the teeth, and prefer counterfeit gods on offer (32:16–18).

As a result, all the curses of the previous chapters will be unleashed: hunger, plague, prowling animals, conquering armies, defeat and exile (vv. 24–26). It will be like the worst of uncontrollable forest fires, reaching even to the deepest parts of distant Sheol (v. 22). God himself will plan and orchestrate this devastation, with flashing sword and bloody arrows (vv. 23, 41–42). The future looks grim.

Hope

And yet, despite everything, there is an undercurrent of hope. Those who make Yahweh jealous through a 'no god' would themselves be made jealous through a 'no people' (v. 21). Historically, this must be a reference to exile in Babylon, which finally jolted the remnant of Judah into abandoning idolatry and worshipping Yahweh alone. And this experience does seem to have had an effect. The post-exilic community re-established in Jerusalem and Judah had its faults, as the books of Ezra, Nehemiah and Malachi recount. But both biblical text and archaeological study portray a people who no longer worship idols.

The apostle Paul reworks this theme on an even grander scale. Quoting verse 21, he argues that the conversion of Gentiles to faith in Jesus would make his own people, the Jews, jealous, and in due course provoke them to faith (Romans 10:19; 11:11). This hope fuelled much Christian mission to Jews in Europe in the 19th century, and to Jews worldwide in the 20th. And it remains the prayer, hope and goal of many Christians witnessing today.

God cared passionately for his people. Because they knew this about God, both Moses (v. 43) and Paul (Romans 11:33–36) were able to conclude in praise. May our knowledge of God enable us to bring hope to others.

REFLECTION

Where there is despair, let me bring hope.

A Fond Farewell

Have you ever seen an old friend in a new light? You'd known him for years, you'd talked through everything with her, and you really felt you knew them well. You were perhaps aware of their particular interest or hobby, but didn't share it and didn't take much notice. Then suddenly you're confronted with it—a meticulous collection, a stunning recital, a great work—and you discover something new and wonderful about your old friend.

By this stage we may feel we've got to know Moses pretty well. We've discovered an elder statesman still excited about God and passionate for his law, but also deeply concerned about the future and Israel's likely apostasy. Yet suddenly, after the melancholic foreboding of the previous chapters, with their dire warnings of disasters and catastrophes, he completely surprises us in this final blessing, as he ends his life on a note of praise and optimism. In these final words, God appears in great majesty (33:1–5), the tribes are blessed one by one (33:6–25), and Israel lives securely, prosperously and happily in its land (33:26–29). After all the pleading and warning, the great man ends on a note of unqualified hope. What faith! What example!

Moses' departure

Before that, though, Moses is himself given a final command, to climb Mount Nebo and view the promised land. The order here (32:49) and its fulfilment in chapter 34 neatly frame the grand final blessing. Moses perhaps suspected that the journey would be one-way only (v. 50). But the later narrator obviously knew the outcome, and separates instruction from fulfilment, thus building up our anticipation while framing Moses' 'last will and testament'.

All his lifetime had been geared towards entry into Canaan, from his early identification with his people, to his role in leading Israel out of Egypt, to his guidance of them through the desert. And yet one crucial act of disobedience led to his exclusion from the land: that fateful occasion when he went beyond orders and acted in anger (Numbers 20:1–13). As we have seen, Moses preferred not to mention this, usually noting the people's role in the same incident.

But God reminds him of his sin and its punishment (32:51). From those to whom much is given, much is indeed demanded.

And yet, when Moses is painfully reminded of his earlier failure and its far-reaching consequence, he rises above bitterness and vindictiveness, and turns to bless those whose previous grumbling led to his 'curse'. In this he powerfully illustrates Christ's later teaching (Luke 6:28). It is a measure of the true greatness of the man.

Yahweh's appearance

Like the patriarchs of old (see Genesis 27:2–4; 49:1–28), Moses issues a 'deathbed' blessing on those who have been like his own children. Unlike the patriarchs, though, he is called 'the man of God', which became a common epithet for him and later prophets (as in 1 Samuel 9:6). Moses is founding father and pro-phetic guide, the model for all future prophets (Deuteronomy 18:15).

Also unlike the patriarchs, Moses opens and closes his poem with a majestic hymn of praise to God. Further, these two parts balance each other, with the names Yahweh, Jacob and Jeshurun of the introduction (33:2, 4, 5) reappearing in reverse order in the conclusion (33:26, 28, 29). Whether the hymn predated the blessings or was composed along with them, it provides a fitting envelope.

Right at the outset (33:2), Yahweh is portrayed blazing forth from the Sinai peninsula (Seir is the north-eastern part, and the western edge of Edom; Mount Paran is in the east-central area), a grandiose imagery which occurs in several other great Old Testament poems (Judges 5:4–5; Psalm 68:8; Habakkuk 3:3). Here he strides forth with his myriad holy beings, all in step and ready for instruction (33:3). The giving of the law through Moses was truly cosmic as well as historical.

Further, Yahweh himself is king of the people. Like much ancient poetry, the poem has several ambiguous words and phrases, but in context verse 5 means 'He was king' (so NIV) rather than 'There arose a king' (so NRSV). Yahweh is proclaimed king three times in the Pentateuch, and all in epic poems: he defeats the enemies (Exodus 15:18), he gives security (Numbers 23:21–23), and he gives the law (here in v. 5). These are great attributes of a great king.

REFLECTION

Am I magnanimous like Moses?

The TRIBAL BLESSINGS (I)

Large families are increasingly uncommon in prosperous countries. Instead, the children can nearly always be counted on the fingers of one hand, for all sorts of reasons. The desire and need of many mothers for paid employment, the cost of providing for children, the size of houses, even the size of cars—all point to small families. So most of us find it hard to imagine a family of twelve sons. And our instinctive question would be: how do you treat them all as individuals?

My father was one of eleven children, including one set of twins and one of triplets. I never met them all, since only eight survived into adulthood. But all the stories about their childhood years on a small family farm suggested that each was seen as special, and all were loved and cared for. Each was an individual with his or her own characteristics, and all were encouraged to develop their interests and gifts.

One immediately striking feature of these blessings on the twelve tribes of Israel is the distinctive nature of each. There is something specific for each tribe, often with a wordplay on its name. The order of blessings mainly follows the order of birth of the tribes' founders, as narrated in Genesis 29—30. The main exception is that Rachel's sons were born latest of all, but their tribes are blessed after Leah's first group. The other significant feature is that Simeon has dropped out. Nobody knows why, as there is no obvious reason. Perhaps it was a scribal mistake at a very early stage. There are also interesting comparisons with the blessings that Jacob himself gave to his twelve sons (Genesis 49).

Leah's older sons

Reuben was Jacob's firstborn son, but lost this status following an affair with his father's concubine (Genesis 35:22; see 49:4). As for the tribe, they were strongly implicated in Korah's wilderness rebellion and decimated in punishment (Numbers 16:1, 31–35). They settled east of the Jordan, and were later criticized for not helping their western compatriots (Judges 5:15–16). Perhaps these events illustrate an inherent weakness, which would lead to decline. Knowing this, Moses longed that they might survive (v. 6).

Judah was the fourth son, but he seems to have received the firstborn's privileges since his father predicted that the national ruler would come from him (Genesis 49:10). This was probably because Jacob disapproved of the actions of the next two eldest, Simeon and Levi (Genesis 34:25, 30). Here Moses perhaps foresees the division that later emerged between Judah and the rest of Israel, and prays to avert it (v. 7).

Levi receives the first of two extended blessings (vv. 8–11). Moses himself was a Levite (Exodus 2:1, 10), but more importantly the tribe had stood up to be counted several times in recent years. After the golden calf apostasy (Exodus 32:26), and again decades later in the Moabite plains (Numbers 25:7), it was the Levites who were prepared to defend the true faith, even at the cost of executing their own kin. They are not explicitly identified with the events at Massah ('Test') and Meribah ('Contention'; see Exodus 17:7; Numbers 20:13), but must have been faithful there also in guarding the covenant (v. 9). The Levites, and the priests among them, would teach the law and administer the sacrifices, but would have no specific territory. Moses prays warmly for their blessing and protection.

Rachel's sons

Benjamin was the last and beloved son of his father (Genesis 42:36–38). Here he is beautifully described as 'beloved of Yahweh' too (v. 12). The brief blessing exudes peace, security and well-being.

Joseph receives the other extended blessing (vv. 13–17). It is the most lyrical and the most lavish of all, wishing the tribe the richest produce of heaven, earth and sea. Joseph was the son whom God used to save the family, back in Genesis. He was actually the forebear of two tribes, named after his sons, which became central in the growth of the nation. Manasseh had the largest territory of all, and Ephraim, appointed firstborn by his grandfather Jacob (Genesis 48:14), became the most important northern tribe: later books often use the name Ephraim to mean all northern Israel. These were majestic tribes with great potential (v. 17). If only they had lived up to it!

PRAYER

Lord, thank you for the potential you have given me.
Help me to develop it for your glory.

The TRIBAL BLESSINGS (II)

One of the major developments of recent decades is the exponential growth in travel. Road, rail, air—the growth seems relentless and the demand for more facilities unremitting. Most of us like to travel. We live in a mobile world. We travel for business, or for conferences. We travel to see family and friends. We travel on holiday. We love the chance to go somewhere different. So we warm to the blessing for Zebulun: 'Rejoice in your going out' (v. 18)!

Leah's younger sons

Zebulun and Issachar were Leah's later sons, born after a sordid barter for sex which revealed bitter polygamous rivalry (Genesis 30:9, 14–19). They were allotted territory in the north of Canaan—Zebulun in southern Galilee, and Issachar south and east of this in the Jezreel valley. Originally Zebulun's land could have reached the Mediterranean Sea, since both Moses' blessing here (vv. 18–19) and Jacob's blessing earlier (Genesis 49:13) refer to the sea. However, the territory later allotted was entirely inland, and the coastal area was given to Asher (Joshua 19:10–16, 24–31). This may reflect later development, or a lack of enterprise on Zebulun's part.

These tribes played only a minor role in later history. Yet Moses envisages them living in harmony with God and abundantly blessed by him. Those not in the spotlight can still, in the words of the Westminster Confession, 'worship God and enjoy him forever'.

Bilhah's sons

The founders of the next four tribes were born to the servant girls Bilhah and Zilpah. They became pawns in a power struggle between Jacob's wives (Genesis 30:4–12), although this gave them children whom they might not otherwise have had, and some security for later life. This was some good, at least, from the sorry tale of an unhappy home.

Dan was a tribe that moved. It first settled in the south-west of Palestine, to the west of Jerusalem (Joshua 19:40–43). Later, when the Philistines expanded and squeezed Israelite territory, the Danites looked for a new home, found it in the far north, and migrated there, capturing a Levite *en route*. This incident illustrates the growing anarchy of the Judges period (Judges 17—18).

The brief description of Dan here (v. 22) reflects this history, since the tribe is pictured as a lion cub springing out of Bashan, in north Transjordan. This could be prescience on Moses' part, but is more likely to reflect the later origin or adaptation of this poem. There is perhaps a hint of disapproval in that nothing is expressly wished for Dan.

Naphtali was given the fertile upper Galilee to the north and east of Zebulun. Unlike Dan, its brief mention is highly positive, and full of divine blessing (v. 23). It was another tribe with great potential, which sadly faded from the scene.

Zilpah's sons

Gad was one of the tribes that settled on 'the best land' east of the Jordan (3:12). Hence it could expand eastward, but needed the tenacity of a wild beast (v. 20) to keep the neighbouring Ammonites at bay. Like their fellow easterners, the Gadites promised to march into Canaan with their compatriots, thus fulfilling God's command (v. 21). From this obedient solidarity would come blessing.

Asher was given land from the western slopes of Galilee down to the Mediterranean. The hills were famous for abundant olive oil—enough to wade in, to paraphrase the metaphor (v. 24). Asher's territory also guarded the route along the coast used by many a marching army throughout the centuries, so the prayer for this border tribe includes strength for fortifications and people (v. 25). In the wording of the traditional Authorized Version, 'as thy days, so shall thy strength be'.

God's blessing

And so the wonderful song ends in a climax of praise, echoing the opening section. God is majestic and all-conquering (vv. 26–27). He offers security and prosperity (v. 28). And above all, he affirms his commitment to Israel, whom he has saved and will continue to protect. This affirmation is wonderfully captured in the memorable wording of verse 27a (NIV), highlighted for reflection below. (See a detailed commentary for the different NRSV wording.)

REFLECTION

A promise for today, and for always: 'The eternal God is your refuge, and underneath are the everlasting arms.'

MOSES' DEATH

Strange as it may sound, I like funerals. Or rather, more accurately, I find occasional funerals helpful. Death is a fact of life. We often push it away and don't think about it, but a funeral reminds us of its reality and forces us to reconsider our own lives. Don't get me wrong. I have no morbid fascination with death, and certainly take no pleasure from it. Death is an enemy of life, tearing at its very heart. I grieve at the loss of love and friendship. I know the heartbreak of separation. I experience the feeling of being personally diminished. Some time ago we had six church funerals in quick succession, and we reeled at their impact. And yet, despite all this, I find funerals helpful.

But there's one aspect of funerals that is often unhelpful: the eulogy. Here the positives are given, sometimes even inflated; and the negatives are downplayed, often completely omitted. A false picture is given of someone we have known and perhaps loved. The speaker may mean well, but actually does a disservice to the dead and demeans the occasion. Far better to acknowledge the deceased's weaknesses as well as strengths, and to thank God for his power to forgive and transform.

That's what happens in this final chapter of Deuteronomy. Moses' greatness is powerfully and eloquently proclaimed. But it stands out all the more clearly alongside his failure and mortality.

Vision of the land

First, Moses must climb the mountain and view the land. He cannot enter it, but is allowed to see it in its length and breadth (vv. 1–4). God was on the verge of fulfilling his promise to the patriarchs, and Moses, who had played such a crucial role, was given a preview. So, still physically strong at the incredible age of 120 (v. 7), Moses climbs up into the mountains towering above the Jordan plains to the highest peak, called both Nebo and Pisgah, for this stupendous spectacle.

There, facing westwards, he scans the whole horizon from right to left (the direction of Hebrew writing). Immediately north and still in Transjordan is Gilead, the land already given to the two and a half tribes who will settle there. To the far north-west is what later became

Dan (see Judges 17—18). To the nearer north-west lie the central hills to be occupied by Manasseh and Ephraim. Immediately west were the Judean hills that descend westwards to the Mediterranean, south-westwards to the Negev desert, and steeply down to Jericho in the rift valley just ahead. Normally it is not possible to see all this land—the distances are too far, and the hills just across the Jordan too high. Either Yahweh showed him it all in some form of vision, just as Satan later showed Jesus 'all the kingdoms of the world' (Matthew 4:8), or Moses saw the prominent features of all the land, as far as the eye could see.

Whichever way it was, Moses had a great panoramic view of the promised land. He would not enter, but could enjoy it from a distance, secure in the knowledge that God would fulfil his promise to the patriarchs (v. 4).

Death and epitaph

And there the great man dies, alone and attended only by God himself. The location of his unmarked grave was to remain for ever unknown, to discourage any memorial or shrine on the site (vv. 5–6). Israel was never encouraged to revere the physical remains of its great men, and there is no record of them doing so. Their graves were not to be venerated; instead, their example was to be followed.

Not surprisingly, the nation gave him full honours, if not in a funeral, at least in mourning (v. 8). The normal seven-day period was extended to 30 for national leaders (such as Aaron: Numbers 20:29), and none was greater than Moses. However, the text pointedly moves on. After the 30 days, the mourning stopped, and Joshua took over (v. 9). The land viewed now had to be entered. Life must move on.

The final word (vv. 10–12) goes to an epitaph of this great man, Moses, unequalled in Israel's history in his relationship with God and the mighty deeds he performed for God. The two clearly go together. Here was a man of great stature, let down by one display of petulance, yet towering over his contemporaries and his successors in prayer, courage and leadership. We would do well to follow his example.

REFLECTION

What will be your epitaph?

NOTES

Guidelines is a unique Bible reading resource that offers four months of in-depth study written by leading scholars. Contributors are drawn from around the world, as well as the UK, and represent a stimulating and thought-provoking breadth of Christian tradition.

Instead of the usual dated daily readings, *Guidelines* provides weekly units, broken into at least six sections, plus an introduction giving context for the passage, and a final section of points for thought and prayer. On any day you can read as many or as few sections as you wish, to fit in with work or home routine. As well as a copy of *Guidelines*, you will need a Bible. Each contributor also suggests books for further study.

Guidelines is edited by Dr Katharine Dell, Senior Lecturer in the Faculty of Divinity at Cambridge University and Director of Studies in Theology at St Catharine's College, and Dr Jeremy Duff, Director of Lifelong Learning in Liverpool Diocese and Canon at Liverpool Cathedral.

GUIDELINES SUBSCRIPTIONS

❏ I would like to give a gift subscription
(please complete both name and address sections below)
❏ I would like to take out a subscription myself
(complete name and address details only once)

This completed coupon should be sent with appropriate payment to BRF. Alternatively, please write to us quoting your name, address, the subscription you would like for either yourself or a friend (with their name and address), the start date and credit card number, expiry date and signature if paying by credit card.

Gift subscription name _____

Gift subscription address _____

_____ Postcode _____

Please send to the above, beginning with the next January/May/September* issue.
(* *delete as applicable*)

(please tick box)

	UK	SURFACE	AIR MAIL
GUIDELINES	❏ £11.70	❏ £13.05	❏ £15.30
GUIDELINES 3-year sub	❏ £29.25		

Please complete the payment details below and send your coupon, with appropriate payment to: **BRF, First Floor, Elsfield Hall, 15–17 Elsfield Way, Oxford OX2 8FG**

Your name _____

Your address _____

_____ Postcode _____

Total enclosed £ _____ (cheques should be made payable to 'BRF')

Payment by cheque ❏ postal order ❏ Visa ❏ Mastercard ❏ Switch ❏

Card number: ☐☐☐☐ ☐☐☐☐ ☐☐☐☐ ☐☐☐☐

Expiry date of card: ☐☐☐☐ Issue number (Switch): ☐☐☐

Signature (essential if paying by credit/Switch card) _____

NB: BRF notes are also available from your local Christian bookshop. **BRF is a Registered Charity**

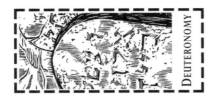

THE PEOPLE'S
BIBLE COMMENTARY

VOUCHER SCHEME

The People's Bible Commentary (PBC) provides a range of readable, accessible commentaries that will grow into a library covering the whole Bible.

To help you build your PBC library, we have a voucher scheme that works as follows: a voucher is printed on this page of each People's Bible Commentary volume (as above). These vouchers count towards free copies of other books in the series.

For every four purchases of PBC volumes you are entitled to a further volume FREE.

Please find the coupon for the PBC voucher scheme opposite.

All you need do:

- Cut out the vouchers from the PBCs you have purchased and attach them to the coupon.

- Complete your name and address details, and indicate your choice of free book from the list on page 224.

- Take the coupon to your local Christian bookshop who will exchange it for your free PBC book; or send the coupon straight to BRF who will send you your free book direct. Please allow 28 days for delivery.

Please note that PBC volumes provided under the voucher scheme are subject to availability. If your first choice is not available, you may be sent your second choice of book.